Her Father's Daughter

Anna Freud on a stroll with her father, Sigmund, 1913.

HER FATHER'S DAUGHTER

The Work of ANNA FREUD

Raymond Dyer, Ph.D.

New York   JASON ARONSON   London

Library of Congress Cataloging in Publication Data

Dyer, Raymond.
  Her father's daughter.

  "A chronological handlist of the publications of
Anna Freud, 1922–1982": p. 269
  Includes bibliographical references and index.
  1. Freud, Anna, 1895–1982 2. Psychoanalysts—
Great Britain—Biography. 3. Child analysis.
4. Child psychology. 5. Psychoanalysis. I. Title.
RC339.52.F73D93 1982   618.92'89'0924   82-11334
ISBN 0-87668-627-7

To insight and rational sense
for illuminating our inner darkness—

Anna Freud
1895–1982

CONTENTS

PREFACE

There was no satisfactory biography of Anna Freud at the time I wrote this book, and it is extremely doubtful whether an adequate account could ever be produced outside her immediate family and professional circle. Many of her close associates testify to her generally retiring nature—"She does not like to push herself forward," as one knowledgeable Hampstead senior analyst (Hellman 1977), confided—and Anna Freud herself, in her first letter to me, stated that she had "never thought anyone would think it worthwhile to establish something like an archive" for her (A. Freud 1976).

There are excellent reasons why such a lacuna in the literature of psychoanalysis can no longer be permitted. Sigmund Freud long ago argued that psychoanalysis shared the *Weltanschauung* of science, and that includes ownership of and accountability to humankind. We may each study psychoanalysis, and the near obligatory publication of the results of such serious study is all but dictated by the nature of Science itself (see Dyer 1980).

Many good reasons exist for studying Anna Freud's work. Beginning over 60 years ago as a subspecialization of orthodox psychoanalysis, Anna Freud's contribution soon came to have a powerful relevance for both child psychology and normal development, and for child psychiatry and abnormal development. Further disciplines and fields of application, including education, teaching, children's literature, and pediatrics, also have benefited from Anna Freud and child analysis. Today there is virtually no social science that has not been enriched by her work, though the caring and mental health professions inevitably owe the greater debt. Even the legal profession has not been disregarded, as witness Anna Freud's involvement with the issue of children's rights in cases of adoption and fostering (e.g., A. Freud 1971h, 1971i, 1973e).

Although this book is the first major publication written in English that thoroughly treats the work of Anna Freud, there have been two lengthy recent studies in German (see Besser 1976, Peters 1979). This recognition of Anna Freud in continental Europe is equaled by her eminent standing among child analysts and others in the United States, though her academic recognition in Britain is in some danger of being eclipsed. One is reminded here of an old lament by Sigmund Freud, that his work was more accepted outside Vienna than it was in that city.

The particular value and quality of Anna Freud's contribution to child psychoanalysis, psychotherapy, and developmental child psychology lies in her rigorous grounding in both theory and practice. She is no ivory-towered theoretician divorced from clinical realities, nor is her sound practical guidance left unrelated to current theory and model making. In Anna Freud we come to expect a recognition of the various checks and balances of the scientific process, and we are rarely disappointed.

Despite her international reputation and voluminous writings spanning over half a century, there have been relatively few comprehensive or systematic treatments of Anna Freud as an outstanding psychoanalytical and child development contributor. Some of the early, brief treatments (Kris 1948, Munroe 1957, Wyss 1961, Brown 1961, Guntrip 1961) overemphasized her prewar technical work and her now classic *The Ego and the Mechanisms of Defence*. One of the first relatively lengthy discussions of Anna Freud (Alexander et al. 1966) found our subject having to share space with her pupil Erik H. Erikson. Other studies (Kanzer and Blum 1967) limited themselves primarily to just two publications, *The Ego and the Mechanisms of Defence* and *Normality and Pathology in Childhood*, as being Anna Freud's most important works. Other serious students have concentrated on a single aspect of her applied work; for example, education (Ekstein and Motto 1969). Somewhat different, though educational in tone, was Edith Buxbaum's essay (Ekstein and Motto 1969), in which she compared Anna Freud with two other prominent psychoanalytic educators, Siegfried Bernfeld and August Aichhorn. Buxbaum noted that whereas Bernfeld impressed with his "brilliant intellect" and Aichhorn with his "compelling personality," Anna Freud was remarkable for "her clarity of thinking and lucid simplicity" (Ekstein and Motto 1969, p. 33).

The external events in Anna Freud's lifetime have led us to investigate the possibility of relationships between such worldly twists of fate and the developments apparent in her clinical leanings and theoretical writings. Any such inferred interactions between the "internal" and "external" events of life and work must, of course, remain tentative and open to refutation, though Anna Freud herself has, on occasion, drawn our attention to these interactions. An example is the successive arrival of wartime emergency conditions, the involvement with children's relief work, and the consequent focus on the issue of deprivations (A. Freud 1955a). However, this should not surprise us, since, as a psychoanalyst par excellence, Anna Freud's professional vocation—if not her personal inclination—constantly places her attention at the "filter thresholds" between the human psyche's opposing, though complementary, worlds of inner reality and outer reality.

Many other such interactional areas of interest are touched upon in the following pages, including the great personal watersheds of life—the close family ties, especially with her own father-analyst, and the succession of powerful supporting friendships with individuals such as Lou Andreas-Salomé, Dorothy Burlingham, Jeanne Lampl-de Groot, Marianne and Ernst Kris, Kate Friedlander, and others. Also worthy of note are events such as the exodus and emigration from Hitler's Europe, and Miss Freud's later international recognition and acclaim. More personal events, however, such as the tragic and premature deaths of a sister and nephew and the protracted serious illnesses of other close family members, cannot possibly be assessed by any distant academic scrutiny, though they are mentioned at the appropriate time.

The question of the public-versus-private aspects of a subject's life and work is of particular importance to psychoanalysts, many of whom have been guarded, if not secretive, about the identity of their personal training analysts. It is my view that the training analyst should be identified. The training analyst is, after all, a real figure in a real world of complex clinical and theoretical issues, and any such associated knowledge of this person may well be crucial to understanding and evaluating the subsequent path of the analysand. What must remain private and beyond even our passing curiosity is the entire content and course of the analysis per se—what one might refer to as the identity of the internal (fantasized) training analyst or object. This issue was recently debated in an article (Strawson 1981) published when the eminent French psychoanalyst Jacques Lacan died. Lacan, it seems, pried into the details of the training analyses of the members of his school.

We shall assume here that the training analysis is undertaken for didactic reasons and that there accrues to the analysand the required personal insight and development necessary for a practicing analyst-therapist.

Other writers have also examined some of the interactional issues in the life and work of Anna Freud. Seymour Lustman (1967), in outlining the epistomology of Anna Freud's fundamentally empirical scientific orientation, noted that her dislike and mistrust of the widespread division between theory and practice stemmed from those more fortunate personal and professional circumstances that had enabled her "from the very beginning . . . to move back and forth between theory and practice" (pp. 814–815). Once again, the real insight came from Anna Freud herself, while speaking of herself during a conference the previous year.

Donald Kaplan (1968) concentrated on Anna Freud's early Vienna phase and touched on the question of her emergence from her illustrious father's shadow. In recent decades, Kaplan asserted, Miss Freud's ascendancy was clear, and he referred to her as "the Princess Royal" of the world of classical psychoanalysis. Those more appreciative of Anna Freud's character and style will know that she herself could never acknowledge or accept such a spurious title. A later article by Louise Kaplan (1971) is both more comprehensive and more intuitively accurate, outlining most of the major shaping influences in Anna Freud's long life—her early career as a schoolteacher, membership in the Vienna Psycho-analytic Society, emigration, war work, direction of the postwar Hampstead Clinic, and so on.

Two major works that have become available only in the past decade require a more lengthy critique of their treatments of Anna

Freud. Paul Roazen (1975), writing as a sociologist and historian outside the psychoanalytic community, has gained a great deal of exposure and not a little notoriety for his views of Freud and his circle. Roazen devoted three sections of his book to Anna Freud. The first two are appropriately captioned "Child Analysis" and "Ego Psychology." But in his third section, entitled "Ladies in Waiting," Roazen is at least ambiguous and even derogatory. Nonetheless, Roazen does attempt to treat, in more detail than has any previous writer, Anna Freud's life from her birth onward, her close personal and family ties, and her professional work and emergence as a leading psychoanalyst. Methodologically, Roazen has the merit of having interviewed over 70 surviving members of Freud's circle who the interviewer was able to locate after an interval of 30 or 40 years. Additional information was supplied by another 40 persons who, though not actually having met Freud themselves, had nevertheless come to play important and active roles in the wider development and expansion of psychoanalysis. With this great store of raw data from important eyewitnesses, together with an undeniably sound academic awareness of existing published sources, Roazen attained an authority that was previously quite impossible outside psychoanalytic circles. It is, therefore, all the more to be regretted that he failed to consolidate his initial methodological gains and, because of often rash and speculative interpretations of his material, succeeded in antagonizing many members and associates of the Freud family.

Roland Besser (1976), writing in German, gave us the first work of any substantial length that concentrates exclusively on the life and work of Anna Freud. Though correctly identifying several of the greatest influences of Sigmund Freud on his daughter Anna, Besser believed that these influences largely involved the daughter in "following in father's footsteps"—*Der Weg an der Seite des Vaters* (1976, Pt. I). In contrast, my study notes the important influences on Anna Freud exerted by a number of other persons as well;[1] it accepts as significant the early development and promul-

---

[1]For example, Siegfried Bernfeld, Paul Schilder, August Aichhorn, Wilhelm Reich before about 1934; Ernst Kris, Heinz Hartmann, D. W. Winnicott.

gation by Anna Freud of an independent child analysis technique and theory; and it cites Freud himself as recognizing and applauding his daughter's originality and soundness.

I now believe that both my own and Besser's arguments present important aspects of this issue. Anna Freud was clearly indebted to the originator of psychoanalysis for much of her own fundamental grounding in thought, language, and metapsychology. But equally correct is the contention that from her earliest years as a practicing analyst, she chose to establish herself in a subspeciality in which Sigmund Freud had made little progress, and her work, both before and after her father ceased to play any active part, is marked by a steadily rising curve of originality and sureness in the application and further development of psychoanalysis.

Rather more contentious is Besser's view that the European emigration phase of 1938–1939 marked in Anna Freud's work a turning to a path specifically her own. Such an assertion would appear to be doubly erroneous, since on the one hand Miss Freud's own initiatives can be seen clearly to have had their origins in her Vienna period.[2] On the other hand, even after 1939 she continued to champion whatever her judgment found to be most valuable and well corroborated in orthodox psychoanalysis. With the viewpoint of a continental, Besser is also overly concerned to demonstrate that Anna Freud's later work has been undertaken *im englischen exil*, and the second half of his study has only two broad divisions, *Im Wien* and *Im Exil*. This book, however, prefers to emphasize the postwar emergence of Anna Freud as a truly international figure whose standing in the worldwide psychoanalytical community has been without equal for several decades now.

Anna Freud's own view of her standing in the wider scientific community was characteristically nowhere made explicit, though it may be gleaned from her published writings (1935b, 1967d). It was her view that she should restrict herself to commenting only on the field of investigation that she felt most competent to discuss, namely, psychoanalytic child psychology (developmental child psy-

[2]A point that Anna Freud herself was keen to make after her return visit to Vienna in 1977 (1977a).

choanalysis). In this field, Anna Freud was one of three principal figures, the others being Berta Bornstein of Berlin and New York and Melanie Klein of Budapest and London. Part of the *raison d'être* of the present book is the belief and considered judgment that Anna Freud's work is the most comprehensive, psychologically elegant, and scientifically enduring of the three.

Even so, there may be a still more compelling view of the value and place of Anna Freud's contribution to child development. The future may well place alongside Anna Freud's name the conclusion that she sought to assert no independent and transitory theory or system under her own aegis, but strove instead to broaden and enrich the framework, findings, and applications of the existing science of psychoanalysis.

ACKNOWLEDGMENTS

Grateful thanks are expressed to all those individuals, some now deceased, who contributed personal, biographical, and related information to this study. Anna Freud herself consented to answer many questions, thereby adding to the already immense daily workload of correspondence that a lifetime's recognition had brought. Other prominent analyst-correspondents included Anny Katan, Marianne Kris, Anna Maenchen, Erik Homburger Erikson, Jeanne Lampl-de Groot, Josephine Stross, Eva Rosenfeld, Dorothy Burlingham, Ilse Hellman, Liselotte Frankl, Ruth Thomas, and Alice Goldberger.

More immediate is my debt to Professor Harry Armytage of the University of Sheffield (England), who guided and encouraged my work in all its long stages. Professor Ben Morris formally examined my original material, and his insightful comments were subsequently incorporated into the revised manuscript.

A rather special debt is tendered to the late Professor Erwin Stengel of Vienna and Sheffield, for it was he who brought psychoanalysis to Sheffield many years ago. Thus was the groundwork prepared for that university's acceptance of my work.

Cambridge, England

Her Father's
Daughter

CHAPTER ONE

Early Influences

Born in Vienna on December 3, 1895, Anna Freud was the third and final daughter and the sixth and last child of a non-practicing Jewish professional family. The name Anna seems to have been chosen as a "revenant" of the daughter of her father's old schoolteacher and was thus remarkably prescient. Anna Freud's father, a neurologist turned psychologist, was only a short step away from revealing epochal scientific discoveries and spent many long hours in private practice and university work. We have it on the good authority of the oldest brother Martin Freud (1957) that except for midday meals, Sundays, and the long summer holidays, the Freud children saw rather little of their father.

The family residence throughout Anna Freud's early life in Austria was at 19 Berggasse in Vienna's ninth district. A floor plan of the Freud's apartment is available (Roazen 1975), and the covers of the first issues of the *Sigmund Freud House Bulletin* show a cutaway diagram of the entire building. Knowledgeable authorities have discussed the general cultural background of Vienna and Freud's circle at that time (E. A. and G. R. Ticho 1972), especially the predicament of the more creative Viennese, who had splendid opportunities as well as "the most stubborn resistance to their realisation" (p. 301). A splendid collection of photographs and memorabilia, edited and published by the Freud family (E. L. Freud et al. 1978), is available.

Probably in 1892 a maternal aunt, Minna Bernays, joined the family in their apartment and left Vienna with them half a century later (E. L. Freud et al. 1978, n. 17, p. 539). The complete list of the family members sharing the house for the first 13 or so years of Anna Freud's life would then be as follows: Sigmund Freud (b. 1856), Martha Freud née Bernays (b. 1861), Minna Bernays (b. 1865), Mathilde Freud (b. 1887), Martin Freud (b. 1889), Oliver

Freud (b. 1891), Ernst Freud (b. 1892), Sophie Freud (b. 1893), and Anna Freud herself.

The children's upbringing, according to the closest observers and best authorities, was liberal and lenient for those times. Discipline was nevertheless firm, and punctuality and other virtues were stressed at all times (M. Freud 1957, Jones 1955). Among Anna Freud's childhood friends in Vienna two later became child analysts also: Marianne Rie (b. 1900)—later Marianne Kris of New York—and Anny Rosenberg (b. 1898)—later Anny Angel and subsequently Anny Katan of Cleveland, Ohio. (Both were kind enough to correspond with this writer during the gestation period of his book.)[1]

There is some evidence to suggest that the young Anna Freud, as early as her 11th or 12th year, met and took an interest in some of her father's analytical patients (Zetzel 1966). Moreover, an early letter from Sigmund Freud to C. G. Jung makes it clear that Freud's daughters were free to peruse psychoanalytical publications and to comment on them (McGuire 1974, letter 166F). A close childhood friend of Anna Freud stated also that "I knew about psychoanalysis when I was a child" (Dyer 1980, letter of Anny Katan, March 15, 1978).

To be interested in psychoanalysis in the first decade of the twentieth century meant to be concerned with the writings and ideas of just one individual. That that individual was Anna Freud's father could not fail to place her in a special position with respect to those peers of hers who, themselves members of liberally minded and cultured families, had also shown an early interest in the new science of the mind.

Despite the great popularity of Sigmund Freud's *Interpretation of Dreams* (1900), others of his early works may have had more influence on the pioneers of child analysis. One work in particular, *Three Essays on the Theory of Sexuality* (1905), conveniently marks the inception in Vienna of what might be called the "first

---

[1]Facsimiles of the correspondence and questionnaires collected, from both Anna Freud and a number of her close associates, are reproduced in the appendices of my doctoral dissertation (1980).

period" of psychoanalytic child study. The significance of the theory of sexuality was that it gave us the first functional and adequate psychological theory or "model" of child development. This theory may naturally be traced to earlier works, and Anna Freud (1954e) indicated a "birthdate of psychoanalytic child psychology" somewhere between 1895 and 1900—in other words, after the *Studies on Hysteria* (Breuer and S. Freud 1895), which used such dynamic constructs as conscious and unconscious, but before *The Interpretation of Dreams* (1900), which added genetic propositions and traced the origins of psychic conflict to the individual's early development. We prefer 1905 as a more acceptable date for the beginning of child psychoanalysis, as it was then that the theory in a particularly well-developed form was shown to be capable of varied practical and theoretical application.

Sigmund Freud's notable theory of child development was based on his concept of infantile sexuality, its organized development through well-marked oral and anal phases, the transformations of puberty, the progress of the individual to genital primacy, and the discovery of a suitable love object. The neurological basis of this scheme is evident and is a superb example of Freud's ability to interweave his own neurological grounding with developmental observations. The resultant sequence or model of libidinal development was able to sustain psychoanalysts, analytical child psychologists, and others for almost half a century, until extended and revised by Anna Freud, Rene Spitz, and others.

A common criticism of Sigmund Freud's work is that his data on early childhood were obtained by simply reconstructing the analyses of his adult patients. Although reconstruction may be accepted as Freud's principal and original methodological approach to the child's mind, he also had many opportunities to supplement this reconstruction with actual observation. In 1886 Freud studied in Paris with the great psychopathologist Jean Martin Charcot and had witnessed the investigation of children suffering from hysterical fits. In the same period Freud studied children's diseases in Berlin and on his return to Vienna took charge of the neurological section of the Kassowitz Children's Institute (Jones 1953, chap. 10). Freud's own children provided him with many useful observations for his emergent psychological theories, in regard, for example, to childhood speech during sleep and dream states. In fact, the earliest reference to Anna Freud in the analytical literature concerns her dream utterances at 18 months (S. Freud 1900, 1950). Freud also included several other examples of children's dreams in his *Interpretation of Dreams*.

Freud also made other contributions to the study of early childhood. In his "Sexual Enlightenment of Children" (1907), he encouraged telling children what they wanted to know about sex. In "Creative Writers and Daydreaming" (1908a), Freud included an account of the dynamics of children's play, emphasizing its wish-directed nature and fantasy in contrast to the child's outer world of reality. He also discussed the primitive sexual theories held by children (1908b) and identified his three main sources of relevant data: (1) direct observation of what children say and do, (2) conscious recollections by adults, and (3) psychoanalytical reconstructions from the clinical material of adult patients. We believe that Freud was a good example of a competent empiricist-observer who worked within the constraints of a rationalist-theorist open to deeper levels of intuition and insight. We may add that such a balanced orientation was fundamental also to the subsequent methodology of his daughter Anna Freud.

Child analysis is frequently considered to have begun with Freud's publication (1909) of the historic case of Little Hans and his phobia, as noted also by a number of impeccable authorities (Klein 1932, M. Kris 1948). Anna Freud (1954a) stated that the Little Hans case material actually dated from 1905, as did Freud's *Three Essays on the Theory of Sexuality*, and the year thus becomes a watershed in the establishment of a science of child analysis. Despite the historic importance of the first psychoanalytic treatment of a child, there was as yet no distinctive child analytic technique or therapy. Freud's method still relied on the patient's verbalizations and his only other methodological innovation was to use the child's father as an intermediary. By this means more material of significance was made available than might otherwise have been volunteered by a very young patient.

Thus, before she had passed her tenth birthday, Anna Freud's father had begun to widen his original applications of psychoanalysis to encompass the particular area of interest that later captivated her interest also. For these first ten years or so of Anna Freud's life, her father's pervasive and enduring influence on her operated at three levels of relationship: (1) as a father per se, (2) as a father-figure physician-analyst whose consulting room was part of the family home, and (3) as a father-figure intellectual-mentor whose early publications were breaking new ground and arousing considerable scientific and social comment. Freud's influence on Anna was thus considerable from the start. It would never subsequently be surpassed, much in keeping with the fact that no single psychological thinker during her lifetime ever equaled or surpassed her father's intellectual achievement. There were, nevertheless, other factors that helped secure Anna Freud's lifelong loyalty to the discipline of psychoanalysis.

In 1907, when she was about 12, Anna Freud became more familiar with the world of psychoanalysis, in a period that Ernest Jones (1955) called the beginnings of international recognition for psychoanalysis. A number of visitors from abroad who had professional interest and standing in the fields of psychiatry and psychopathology visited the Freud apartment and incidentally made the acquaintance of the growing Anna Freud. Anna also became a secretary for the new International Psychoanalytic Association.

Arriving in January 1907, Max Eitingon was the Freuds' first foreign visitor and the first of the "Zurichers" from Eugen Bleuler's Swiss clinic, which for some years had been avidly studying Sigmund Freud's ideas. The Russian-born Eitingon became one of Freud's most loyal followers, and he later insisted on being symbolically adopted into Freud's family, thereby becoming an elder brother-figure for Anna. Eitingon and Anna Freud had many dealings together in subsequent years, especially with regard to the International Training Commission and the admission of candidates to psychoanalytic training. After leaving Berlin for Palestine during the political rise of the Nazi party some decades later, Eitingon's newly established Palestine Psychoanalytic Society was the first to offer an honorary membership to Anna in 1935. (The Detroit, Paris, and Swiss Psychoanalytic Societies followed in 1946, the American Psychoanalytic Association in 1950, and a number of others since.)

C. G. Jung, also from Zurich, arrived in February 1907, and he was immediately liked by both Freud and the family. Although Jung "much impressed the children" (Meng and E. L. Freud 1963, letter from S. Freud to Oskar Pfister dated July 12, 1919), this impression was all but obliterated by the break between Freud and Jung in the period leading up to the "dissensions" of 1913–1914. Anna Freud's rare published references to Jung came over 50 years later (1969k, 1982g). However, Miss Freud for many years safeguarded her family's half of the two men's correspondence and later helped in its publication (McGuire 1974). Anna Freud's sympathetic treatment of C. G. Jung, Wilhelm Reich, and Melanie Klein shows the same scrupulous honesty and scientific rigor with which she approached all of her work.

The third international visitor at the Freud apartment in 1907 was Karl Abraham, who had studied with Bleuler and Jung in Zurich and was now returning to Berlin. Abraham arrived just a week or two after Anna Freud's 12th birthday and was given the usual warm reception offered to guests at the Berggasse. Anna Freud later pursued her own contact with the Abrahams over the ensuing years, writing to the wife and daughter in a correspondence that has not yet been published. Abraham's daughter Hilda, like Anna Freud, eventually followed her father into a career in psychoanalysis. Over half a century later Anna Freud favorably reviewed Hilda Abraham's biography of her father Karl Abraham. In discussing the detached manner in which Hilda described "the man who, after all, dominated her childhood and growth and became the object of identification for her adult life" (1974b, p. 15), Anna Freud inevitably invites comparison with her own similar circumstances. Anna Freud's later acknowledgment of her own father's influence was somewhat different. Only twice, to this writer's knowledge, and each time on her father's birthday, did Anna Freud permit herself to offer an *Ansprache* in public celebration of her father (1936, unpublished paper read before the Vienna Psychoanalytic Society; A. Freud 1978d). This should not be interpreted negatively, however. Sigmund Freud often suffered the consequences of his own less cautious approach, and came to regret his many personal disclosures in the *Traumdeutung* and elsewhere. Freud's daughter thus strove to protect the privacy of the person as opposed to his works.

The first two English-speaking visitors to the Freud home were Ernest Jones of London and A. A. Brill of New York. Concerning one of these men, Ernest Jones, we have Anna Freud's own recollections of his early influence upon her. She first met Jones as a guest at the dinner table of her home in Vienna. He was a good-looking, personable young man, and she was a schoolgirl "quite impressed by him" (A. Freud 1979b).

As the first foreign visitors to speak English, Brill and Jones were instrumental in Anna Freud's decision to learn that language. Although her initial reason to learn English was one of personal gain—"so as not to be prevented from understanding their conversations in the future" (1979b, p. 347)—her decision to learn English led to enormous and beneficial consequences for psychoanalysis, the wider scientific community, and indeed all those interested in child development.

Of rather more significance as a pioneer in child study was Sandor Ferenczi of Budapest, though it is difficult to assess precisely his and Jones's relative influence on Anna Freud. If one uses the frequency of Anna Freud's citation of them as an index, then Jones is cited in ten papers and books, and Ferenczi is cited in 16. Ferenczi met the Freuds at their home early in 1908 and was an immediate success with the whole family, later vacationing with them at Berchtesgaden that summer (McGuire 1974, letter 106F). At the First International Psychoanalytic Congress, held in Salzburg that year, Ferenczi gave an important, though subsequently much neglected, lecture on psychoanalysis and education. The lecture appears to have been inserted into the congress's proceedings at a late moment and was followed by a discussion led by Ferenczi and entitled "What Practical Hints for Child Education Can Be Drawn from Freudian Experience?"

Ferenczi's paper was the first to argue for a "new education" that would take account of the findings presented in Freud's *Three*

Essays, especially as they concerned the predominance in infantile life of erotogenic zones (oral, anal, and so on). Ferenczi discussed mainly the reconciliation of sexual drives with the social mores. He opposed unnecessary repression and argued for greater personal freedom whenever biological impulses were found to be refractory to sublimation. This view was decades ahead of its time but was by no means unwisely libertine or morally biased away from the social group and society generally. Ferenczi recognized that unchecked gratification could not be permitted to the individual, especially to one with powerful instinctual drives, and so the master strategy was "to achieve the condition wherein transformation of sexual emotions, repressions etc. need have no more pathogenic effect" (Ferenczi 1908, p. 222). Personal insight, social and individual enlightenment, and the abolition of "hypocritical mysteriousness" were the major tactics by which Ferenczi sought to realize this strategy. He was critical both of correction and punishment and of spoiling and pampering. Ferenczi pointed to the importance of the reconciliation of sexual drives with social mores and to the development of speech and the symbolic thought processes, for it was by means of the new cathexis of instinctual drive that the child was thought to increase knowledge and self-control.

Ferenczi's pioneering educational work long remained in obscure Hungarian periodicals, lost to the wider world until retrieved some 40 years later by Ferenczi's pupil Michael Balint (1949). No doubt this obscurity helps explain the erroneous claim (Low 1929) that Ernest Jones had been the first to advocate the application of psychoanalysis to education. In a similar vein, Bruno Bettelheim (1969) identified Siegfried Bernfeld as having presented the very first psychoanalytic treatise on education and named Bernfeld, Aichhorn, and Anna Freud as being the very first psychoanalytic educators. Ferenczi's priority was clear, and Jones at least was present at the Salzburg congress at which Ferenczi first proclaimed his views.

In later years Ferenczi continued to be interested in the developments of psychoanalytic child psychology. Among his students and personal analysands were such prominent second-generation analysts as Alice Balint and Melanie Klein, both destined, like their tutor, to carry out pioneering studies in the field of child psychoanalysis. Klein, in particular, was grateful to Ferenczi for having convinced her of her aptitude for child analysis, and she noted "the remarkable rapport he had with the minds of children" (Klein 1932, *Preface*). On one early occasion Anna Freud (1927a, lecture 4) referred to Ferenczi's controversial "active therapy" initiatives, and elsewhere she stated that she had had access, "through the good offices of Ferenczi" (1928a, p. 174), to the notes of a teacher in a modern American school. Almost 50 years later Miss Freud once more recalled Ferenczi—in 1975 in London, at the I. P. A.'s Sixth Precongress Conference on Training—reminding her audience that it had been Ferenczi who, first among adult analysts, had been attracted to the child analysts' new techniques (Wallerstein 1976). Thus, there can be little doubt that the gifted and inherently child-oriented Ferenczi had an early and considerable influence on Anna Freud. There is little or no evidence to suggest that this influence was direct or in any way structured, but Ferenczi remains an important source of the ambience that favored and encouraged the professional self-awareness and growth of the child analysts of Anna Freud's generation.

A quite different and apparently more limited influence came from the Zurich pastor and pedagogue Oskar Pfister, who was introduced to Sigmund Freud through Jung. Pfister early began applying Freud's work to his own field of pastoral care in childhood and pedagogy and in April 1909 made the first of many visits to Freud's home in Vienna. We have Anna Freud's own recollection of Pfister, which was that he "enchanted the children of the household like a Pied Piper of Hamelin" (1963d, p. 11). Some years later Pfister reminisced about "the free and cheerful spirit of your whole family . . . and . . . the little girl who took care of the lizards, who now writes very serious papers for the International Psychoanalytic Association" (Meng and E. L. Freud 1963, letter to Freud, dated December 30, 1923). Pfister's own scientific work tended to support and broaden rather than creatively extend Freud's initiatives, and in later years Anna Freud preferentially cited her father's original works when acknowledging her own antecedents.

A follower of both Pfister and Freud was Ernst Schneider, director of the Teachers Seminary in Berne, Switzerland. Schneider later became a coeditor, with Anna Freud and others, of an important psychoanalytical journal, *Zeitschrift für Psychoanalytische Pädagogik*, from 1926 to around 1938.

Another Swiss, Hans Zulliger, visited Schneider in Berne around this time and, like Pfister, applied psychoanalysis to children in the regular state school system (Zulliger 1966). A recent commentator has referred to Zulliger, Anna Freud, and Melanie Klein as the *"drei Grossen der Kinderpsychotherapie"* (Bierman 1973).

In September 1909, Clark University in Worcester, Massachusetts, invited Freud to give a series of five lectures introducing his work, as part of the conference celebrating the 20th year of the university's founding. An important outcome of the Clark conference was the greater international support of psychoanalytic child study, both then and in the future. G. Stanley Hall was professor of psychology and pedagogies at Clark and a prime mover in extending the invitation to Freud. Although Hall's enthusiasm and support soon shifted to Alfred Adler, the link between Clark University and psychoanalytic child study was an enduring one, and over four decades later Anna Freud was invited to lecture at Clark (A. Freud 1951a).

Another important figure attending the Clark conference of 1909 was J. J. Putnam, professor of neurology at Harvard and destined to be Freud's most loyal early American follower. Both Ernest Jones (1955) and Anna Freud (1951a) recorded high opinions of Putnam. Interestingly, he also—like Freud and Abraham—had a daughter who later became a child analyst.

Sigmund Freud's work in America—together with its cultivation in England by such figures as F. W. H. Myers, Mitchell Clarke, Wilfred Trotter, Henry Havelock Ellis, David Eder, and Barbara Low before the First World War—can scarcely be ignored as an inducement for the largely Vienna-based child analysts of later years to turn their attentions to the English-speaking world.

German, as the original mother tongue of psychoanalysis, has certainly now been replaced by English as the main vehicle of worldwide psychoanalytic ideas, albeit with strong rivals in continental Europe, Latin America, and possibly elsewhere. The influential English language also increasingly, and in diverse ways, shaped the turnings of Anna Freud's life and work.

Figure 1 depicts the geographical and chronological spread of psychoanalysis in this first early international phase. The central European nucleus is clearly evident and it withstood all later world upheavals and vicissitudes. The same was not true of the psychoanalysis centers east of Vienna, though in the West, particularly in the United States, they were already beginning to make significant developments.

Anna Freud's desire to excel in languages, particularly English, may well have come from her father in the years immediately after his American lecture-visit in 1909. Vincent Brome (1967, p. 110) suggested that Freud responded negatively to America because of his "inadequacy with the language," which may have left him feeling at a disadvantage. Freud was fluent in a number of languages, though this apparently did not extend to a full command of English. Over a decade after his journey to Clark University, Freud confided to Ernest Jones that he had disliked using what he referred to as his "clumsy English" (Jones 1957, letter dated November 20, 1926). Freud frequently had Anna and some of his pupils and students translate scientific papers from English into German.

Anna Freud received her secondary education at the Cottage Lyceum in Vienna, and her academic curriculum included French, Spanish, and English. She also studied modern European literature. She was serious and hard working, as is evident from her father's letters of this period, which exhorted her to "take your duties less seriously" and "be a little happy-go-lucky" (E. L. Freud 1960, pp. 294–296). (This selection of Freud's general correspondence contains three letters dating from 1908–1912 to the youthful Anna, who her father addresses as "My dear little Anna.")

During her adolescence, Anna Freud continued to meet people who were destined to become important figures in and leaders of

Figure 1. The International Spread of Psychoanalysis, 1902–1914

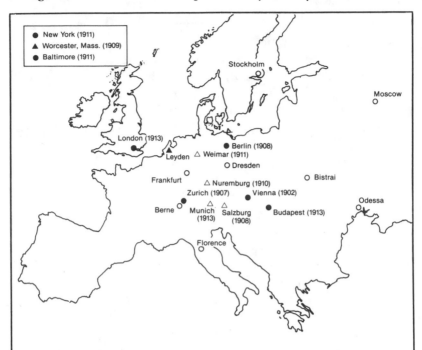

● Established Psa. Society
○ Groups/Individuals without status of branch society
△ Site of International Psa. Congress
▲ University Invitation to Lecture/Recognition

NOTABLE REPRESENTATIVES (c. 1913)

U.S.A.
NEW YORK—Brill, Frink, Oberndorf, Hinkle **BALTIMORE**—Jones, Burrow, Meyer, Putnam **WORCESTER**—Hall

ENGLAND
LONDON—Jones, Forsyth, Bryan, Eder, Low

CONTINENT
BERLIN—Abraham, Juliusberger, Eitingon **FRANKFURT**—Landauer **DRESDEN**—Stegmann (died, 1912) **BUDAPEST**—Ferenczi, Hollos, Rado, Levy **ZURICH**—Jung, Pfister, Maeder, Oberholzer **VIENNA**—Freud, Federn, Hitschmann, Rank, Sachs, Tausk, Sadger, (Adler, Stekel) **LEYDEN**—Jelgersma, Van Emden **MOSCOW**—Ossipov **ODESSA**—M. Wulff **BISTRAI**—L. Jekels **STOCKHOLM**—Bjerre **BERNE**—Schneider **FLORENCE**—Assagioli

the psychoanalytic world. In the summer of 1910 she vacationed in Austrian Silesia with her sister Sophie and her aunt Minna at the invitation of Ludwig Jekels. The Polish-born Jekels had been educated in Vienna and was working as a psychiatrist in his sanatorium in Bistrai (see Figure 1). Later he moved to Vienna to practice as a psychoanalyst. He was a gifted member of the Wiener Psychoanalytischen Vereinigung, and Anna Freud always considered Jekels, together with Nunberg, Federn, Hitschmann, and Helene Deutsch as respected members of that early generation of analysts which was more senior to her own (1969k).

In Vienna itself there was much activity concerning Freud and his work in the years just before World War I. This was literally true for those whose footsteps took them to Freud's home and place of business and symbolically true for those whose inclinations caused them to adopt a path and psychological model different from Freud's. Of the Viennese analysts loyal to Freud at this time, Otto Rank and Hanns Sachs were the most frequent visitors.[2] Of all Freud's colleagues in the prewar years, Otto Rank visited Freud the most often, and the reason was evidently the psychoanalytic business that this intellectually powerful figure took upon himself. As secretary of the now enlarged Vienna Psychoanalytic Society and coeditor with Freud of the newly established, nonclinical journal *Imago*, Rank was an essential coordinator of many important psychoanalytic affairs. Moreover, for the third edition of Freud's *Interpretation of Dreams*, Rank closely collaborated with Freud to incorporate new material and bibliographies, and this collaboration apparently continued through subsequent editions (from around 1911 onward. See James Strachey's editorial notes to S. Freud 1900). There seems little doubt that by the time Freud's famous inner "committee" came into existence,[3] Anna Freud already knew, by the age of 17, all the prominent

[2]Alfred Adler and Wilhelm Stekel were Viennese who broke with Freud. For Freud's polemic on the dissensions, see S. Freud 1914a.

[3]In the summer of 1913 was held the first meeting of what Ernest Jones viewed as Freud's "old guard" (Jones 1955). Each member received from Freud an antique Greek intaglio to be made up as a symbolic ring of fealty.

analysts—Ferenczi, Jones, Abraham, Rank, and Sachs—who were on the committee.

Otto Rank was the earliest and certainly the most prominent lay analyst who was not also a physician and he is said to have opened up the prospect of lay analysis for all later individuals, including Anna Freud, who lacked medical degrees. But Rank was by no means the only lay analyst even in these early days—Hermine Hug-Hellmuth and Oskar Pfister were also lay practitioners—although Rank was the first among them to join Freud in his work.

The importance of establishing the precedent of lay analysis was perhaps equaled by establishing the precedent of female analysts. The third international psychoanalytic gathering, held at Weimar in 1911, included at least seven women: Emma Jung, Antonia Wolff, Maria Moltzer, Martha Boddinghaus, Beatrice Hinkle, Lou Andreas-Salomé, and Mira Gincburg. In England the prewar London Psycho-Analytic Clinic was largely the result of the efforts of two women, May Sinclair and Jessie Murray (Boll 1962). In child study, sisters Rachel and Margaret Macmillan were exploring the ideas of Maria Montessori (Armytage 1975), ideas that Anna Freud also studied. In Berlin the young Karen Horney impressed Karl Abraham with a report on sexual instruction in childhood. And in Vienna around 1912 Hermine von Hug-Hellmuth, who had a doctorate in academic psychology and a wide grasp of her material, presented her first short studies of the child. She soon wrote a fuller monograph (1913) which quickly received Freud's approval and was published in a series on applied psychology that he himself edited.

But Sigmund Freud was the principal and enduring influence in all these early psychoanalytic works, whether theory or practice, and even the valuable educational applications in England contributed nothing of any significance to the stream of theory emerging from Vienna before World War I.

Freud developed both a dynamic theory of psychological functioning and a multistage model of the mind as a motivated filter mechanism frequently lacking conscious feedback control. (This would at least be a modern systems-analysis description of early psychoanalytic theory. Contrary to much recent assertion, Freud's language was more elegant and more personal than many of the later psychological languages employed by his critics.)

Following his psychoanalytic model of mind, as described in the seventh chapter of *Die Traumdeutung* (S. Freud 1900), Freud then conceived an elegant and still useful developmental framework (S. Freud 1905d), which proved to be particularly important to child study. Despite Ferenczi's prompt application of this work to childhood education—an application whose direction and form were completely in line with Freud's own thinking—and despite the many other pioneers who have been noted here as contributing to what we have termed the ambience of intellectual and professional preparedness, it was still Freud who dominated the scene. Cornucopialike in his creative and intellectual generosity to our scientific heritage, he also was the mainspring in shaping the working materials that his daughter Anna later used.

By 1914, Sigmund Freud's output had assumed prodigious proportions, even if limited to works related to child study. He discussed the role of secondary schools in preventing youthful suicides (1910g); he pointed to the ubiquity of masturbation in childhood (1912a); and in his important study of taboo (1912b) he touched again on the animal phobias that beset young children. This sort of phobia had figured in the Little Hans analysis, and data on children's fears of animals and other frightening figures were important in Anna Freud's subsequent development of her celebrated model of the ego's defensive denial and related activities for warding off anxiety (1936a).

Writing to Karl Abraham (Abraham and E. L. Freud 1965, letter dated May 2, 1912), Freud noted that a regular "children's corner" was planned for specialist contributions to the Vienna-based journal, *Zentralblatt für Psychoanalyse*. Shortly afterward this journal's editor (Wilhelm Stekel) broke with Freud, though the newer *Internationale Zeitschrift für Psychoanalyse* eventually set aside a *Kindersammlung* or special part for materials on childhood. The title of this section was *Aus dem infantilen Leben*, and the mental life of infants henceforward increasingly occupied the attentions of those who had previously been more concerned with merely the infantile mental state.

In a letter to Pfister (Meng and E. L. Freud 1963, letter dated January 1, 1913), Freud insisted on defending "the rights of educationalists to analysis" (p. 59), and a month later he contributed the introduction (1913b) to a book by Pfister, in which he noted that education and therapy had a definite relationship. The role of education was to ensure that neither individual nor society be harmed by the child's natural inclinations. Freud also warned that educators, insofar as they could mold children's minds, should proceed according to the possibilities inherent in the pupil, and not according to the adult's own personal ideals.

Elsewhere, Freud wrote a paper (1913d) on certain lies told by children, and in the new international journal *Scientia* outlined his own ideas regarding the "new education" (1913a). In particular, in warning against any unnecessary suppression of the child's socially unserviceable and perverse impulses, Freud did not go to the opposite extreme of advocating complete freedom of expression. Instead, he pointed to the educational significance of sublimation as a process that directed the asocial impulse into pathways leading to valued and acceptable contributions to character development. Such indeed was the "middle way" of philosophy that characterized Freud and the best of his earliest psychoanalytic theory and application. Despite the many later distortions of these ideas, Anna Freud adopted her father's own emphasis and tone, not the spurious extremism alleged by his critics.

The years immediately before the First World War witnessed the new science of psychoanalysis as a strong, vibrant growth with roots now well established and the future promising a rich harvest of new knowledge. There had been several applications of psychoanalysis to fields increasingly removed from the original narrow one of hysteria and certain other neuroses, and some of these newer applied fields provided valuable opportunities for talented lay analysts. As well, the early hostility to Freud's ideas about sex had begun to abate, and now several academic institutions were beginning to show interest in them. In addition to the invitation from Clark University, five years later Freud received an invitation from G. Jelgersma, Professor of Psychiatry at the University of Leyden in the Netherlands. The Freuds had in fact been visiting

Leyden since at least 1910 and had a good friend (and pupil of Freud's) there in the Dutch analyst van Emden.

All of these advances influenced Anna Freud and the early phases of her life and work as an analyst. But of far greater importance was the fact that she was now on the threshold of a new and closer relationship with Sigmund Freud himself.

FIRST MILESTONE— FATHER AND DAUGHTER

With the arrival of international recognition, Freud was soon in need of secretarial help. His oldest daughter Mathilde had married when Anna was 14, and so this task fell largely to the next daughter in line, Sophie. Freud's correspondence at the time records the dispatching of his scientific offprints by "my second daughter now my secretary" (McGuire 1974, letter 218F), and this state of affairs continued for three or four years until Sophie Freud married (Jones 1955).

The earliest indication of Freud's special attachment transferring to his daughter Anna was revealed around September 1912, shortly after Sophie's engagement, in several postcards sent by Freud from Rome to Anna. These cards were addressed to "my future travelling companion" (Jones 1955, p. 108), an allusion and significance that could scarcely be ignored. Elsewhere in his correspondence Freud confirmed that as early as 1912, Anna had indeed come to occupy a special place in his thoughts (Jones 1955, letter to Ferenczi dated July 9, 1913) and had influenced his ideas of love and death in *The Theme of the Three Caskets* (1913c).

After Sophie married in January 1913, Anna became the only unmarried daughter remaining at home. She also became her father's secretary and quickly came to have a special significance. The earlier promise of shared travels soon materialized, and Freud's correspondence mentions him in Venice with his "single little daughter, the only one still left at home" (Abraham and E. L. Freud 1965, letter to Abraham dated March 27, 1913).

The year 1914 began happily enough for Anna Freud, and even when the momentous events associated with World War I had been set in motion, none of them influenced her as much as did the enduring and now closer liaison with her father. There is some evidence to suggest that from the beginning, the older Freud was the more needful of and sought more from this liaison, whereas Anna was the more preoccupied with other interests and challenges. One letter written during this period showed Freud in a woeful mood—perhaps with some presentiment of his later dependence on his daughter—and he confided to Abraham: "We are no longer a family now, only three old people. Even my little daughter wants to go to England by herself this year" (Abraham and E. L. Freud 1965, letter dated February 15, 1914).

Early in 1914 Sophie Freud Halberstadt gave birth to a son, Ernst. Freud's remarks concerning this child nicely illustrate his daughters' familiarity with psychoanalysis. His grandson, wrote Freud (Abraham and E. L. Freud 1965, letter to Abraham dated September 22, 1914), was having "a strict upbringing by an intelligent mother enlightened by Hug-Hellmuth." The grandson's inclination and destiny were eventually to coincide, and he too became a psychoanalyst.

The science of psychoanalysis meanwhile continued to break new ground, and the most important territorial advances were still due to Freud. In a paper on the psychology of the schoolboy, Freud (1914c) assessed the manner in which the early parental images that are internalized by children continue to influence responses to their teachers. The ideas and concepts that Freud discussed here can be seen to presage, as did also the seminal paper on narcissism (S. Freud 1914b), his later structural theory of the 1920s. Perhaps because Anna Freud was at that time hoping to become a schoolteacher, Freud was persuaded to publish both of these papers in the same year. From these early theoretical concepts for handling the existence of part egos and their relationship to internalized objects in the psyche, our current mainstream object relations psychologies were developed. That Anna Freud and other "orthodox" analysts retained a structural viewpoint somewhat to one side of the object relations ideas associated with an influential modern group of theoreticians[4] is entirely in keeping with the manner in which science continually refines its tentative working models, based as they are on largely hypothetical constructs.

Meanwhile, Anna Freud, then 18, had her thoughts elsewhere, and in July 1914 she spent her first holiday in England, somewhat to her father's discomfort, as noted above. It seems unlikely that his nascent structural ideas occupied her thoughts, and her journey, moreover, demonstrated her disinterest in the wider political situation of that summer.

She was met in England by the ever attentive Ernest Jones, with bouquet of flowers in hand, and we are told that she was flattered and impressed, "though not without a lurking suspicion that his interest was more directed to my father than to myself" (A. Freud 1979b, p. 347), a circumstance to which, even at that age, Anna Freud had become accustomed. She stayed with friends of her family near Arundel in Sussex and also at a girls' boarding school on the south coast. With the outbreak of war she was temporarily marooned in England but remained safe at the boarding school where she had been staying. She kept in contact with friends in London and also with her father in Vienna via the Dutch analyst van Emden at the Hague (Jones 1955).

Anna Freud wrote that it was through the efforts of Loe Jones, Ernest Jones's former wife and a friend of hers, that she was included as one of the selected persons permitted to join the party of the returning Austrian ambassador (1979b). The journey was via Gibraltar and neutral Italy, and her impression of it as a "romantic trip" still vivid over half a century later reflects her youthful adventurousness. Sigmund Freud later wrote his English friends to thank them for "the clever and practical fashion in which you returned my little daughter. She is very well, but I suspect she sometimes pines for the country of our enemies" (E. L. Freud 1960, letter to H. Jones, n.d.). About the same time Martin Freud, now mobilized into the Austrian army, was also informed

---

[4]For example, O. Kernberg, J. Bowlby, R. Schafer, D. W. Winnicott, J. D. Sutherland, H. V. Dicks, H. Guntrip, M. Kahn, and so on, based on the earlier work of W. R. D. Fairbairn, M. Balint, M. Klein, and, of course, S. Freud.

that the important news of the day was that "Annerl" had arrived "surprisingly" (M. Freud 1957).

The English friends mentioned above were Herbert Jones and his wife Loe. Before she married, Loe (née Kann) had met Freud through Ernest Jones and had been in analysis with Freud in Vienna around 1912 or 1913. The close relationships among Loe, Freud, and Ernest Jones are evident from Jones's autobiography (1959) and have been the focus of at least one speculative foray (Roazen 1975, p. 356). The month before Anna Freud went to England, her father had been in Budapest to attend the wedding of Loe and Herbert Jones. It is apparent from these relationships that in a period in which divorce and remarriage were not as common as they are today, the Freuds were quite liberal, and placed personal loyalties above social appearances in their friendships.

Against the now swiftly changing events of late 1914, Anna Freud began her first career, as an elementary schoolteacher in Vienna. With her early training and experience as a schoolteacher, she established a lifelong interest in the problems of education, as seen in many of her later publications (e.g. 1930a, 1949d, 1952b, 1977d). She also was interested in children's literature—A. A. Milne, A. H. Burnett, and A. F. Johnston are cited in later psychoanalytical contributions—and she apparently was fond of reading Rudyard Kipling's *Jungle Book* to her pupils (Lobner 1975). In addition, her abiding interest and faith in Montessori's nursery school methods[5] were incorporated into her later observational day nursery run according to psychoanalytical methods.

With the worsening of the social environment in response to the wartime emergency conditions, Anna Freud, along with other teachers in Vienna, began "to collect children in play groups in order to keep them off the streets" (1955a, p. 141). Initiatives such as this drew attention to the effect on children of war conditions

[5]Maria Montessori (1870-1952) had from around 1907 used her talents as a pediatrician and innovator to introduce pedagogical methods relying on perception and sensorimotor integration in development. Sigmund Freud later wrote to Montessori that "my daughter, who is an analytical paedagogue, considers herself one of your disciples" (E. L. Freud 1960, letter 178).

such as the absence of fathers. From these same experiences, teachers and educators formed ideas about the impairment of learning caused by food deprivation, which was later extended to emotional deprivations as well. During the war years, Anna Freud witnessed firsthand the introduction in Vienna of an innovative school meals system (1952b, p. 563).

Although she was a schoolteacher, Anna Freud did not neglect psychoanalysis. On the contrary, teaching brought her into daily contact with young children and enabled her to make frequent observations regarding child development and behavior. It should come as no surprise that in her later work as an analyst she had an enduring interest in normal development, and she could hardly have had better experience with children elsewhere.

The second and third winters of the First World War were a milestone in psychoanalysis in the form of a historic series of "introductory lectures" delivered by Sigmund Freud (1916). These lectures were delivered in three separate courses at the Vienna Psychiatric Clinic to members and students of every faculty of the University of Vienna. Anna Freud was present at these lectures, as were several people who later figured in her personal and professional relationships—Helene Deutsch and Max Schur, for example (M. Kanzer 1971), though it seems unlikely that introductions were made there.

It has been said that Freud's *Introductory Lectures* are "the book with which to begin a study of psycho-analysis" (Jones, preface to S. Freud 1916). In the first two lecture courses, on the psychology of errors (parapraxes) and the psychology of dreams, Freud presupposed no previous knowledge of the subject and indeed took the view that his listeners needed instruction "even in its first elements." The eighth lecture was devoted to children's dreams, and the archaic and infantile features of dreams also formed the substance of the 13th lecture, as well as the oedipal and regressive nature of dreams.

The third series of lectures detailed the psychoanalytic theory of neurosis. In the first lecture of the new semester—the 16th of the series—Freud discussed the position of psychiatry. Psychoanalysis was to psychiatry, noted Freud, what histology was to anatomy, and he looked forward to a time when psychiatry would be based on a more rigorous science. Anna Freud's later work fulfilled this hope, insofar as she sought to give psychiatry—as well as child psychology, pediatrics, and a number of other disciplines—the two empirical instruments associated with her name: a developmental framework and a multistage metapsychological model emphasizing the ego. If we are correct in thus linking the early and late contributions of father and daughter, then it is an example of how much Anna Freud was influenced by her father's work.

The ego, as a concept and area of interest and study, is often neglected and missed by those—particularly nonanalysts—who read only Freud's publications before the 1920s. But his *Introductory Lectures* of 1916–1917 contain much discussion of the ego, following as they did Freud's breakthrough with the narcissistic neuroses two years earlier. Indeed—and professional critics of "Freud the depth psychologist" please note—in asserting his priorities, Freud made it clear that:

> The psychology of the ego, at which we are aiming . . . must be based, as is that of the libido, upon analysis of the disturbances and disintegrations of the ego. We shall probably think very little of our present knowledge of the fate of the libido . . . when that further, greater work has been achieved. (S. Freud 1916, lecture 26, p. 422)

It was in pursuit of that "greater work" that Anna Freud was for many years correctly classified in psychological circles as an ego psychologist, though in her later work the term *developmental child analyst* (or developmental child psychologist) was more appropriate.

In April 1918 Anna Freud took her final teacher's examination (Pfieffer 1972, letter to Andreas-Salomé dated April 21, 1918), thereby consolidating her initial career choice, or so it appeared to all but those closest to her. Even Freud's good friend Lou Andreas-Salomé believed that Anna might, because of her familiarity with the works of Rainer Maria Rilke and others, become "a poet-translator" (Pfieffer 1972, p. 62). But the youthful Anna was about to take up a new career: she entered a personal training analysis and subsequently changed her professional vocation.

SECOND MILESTONE—
ANALYST AND STUDENT

There is little information about this second phase of Anna Freud's life. When replying to my request for specific biographical information, she simply wrote that she was "trained as a psychoanalyst and began to practise" (Dyer 1980, letter dated July 29, 1976). Elsewhere, in her published writings, the most relevant autobiographical passages are in an address following the acceptance of an honorary doctorate at Jefferson Medical College. In essaying the curriculum vitae of a lay analyst Miss Freud stated that "we were trained by our personal analysts" (1967d). Although Anna Freud was one of the 70 or more surviving associates of Sigmund Freud who were interviewed in a major study undertaken in the mid-1960s, the interview yielded little new information and is nowhere cited in over 60 pages of detailed notes (Roazen 1975). But it is nevertheless possible to account for both the timing of Anna Freud's training and analysis and, which is much more significant, the identity of the training analyst.

There were bright prospects for psychoanalysis by 1918. Freud's work had been acknowledged by scientific, especially medical-military, authorities who were interested in treating the many cases of nervous disorder ("shell shock").[6] Moreover, an independent financial backer had appeared, the wealthy Hungarian brewer Anton von Freund, who planned to endow a new psychoanalytical publishing house (Verlag). Such were the new forces guiding Anna Freud's next important step toward becoming a psychoanalyst. Her close guide and tutor would again be her father.

[6]Even in England the authorities, faced with a possible breakdown of army discipline in the field, had to consider Freud's ideas in terms of their therapeutic efficacy rather than their country of origin. Both treatment centers behind the lines on the Western Front and consulting rooms in London reflected "a growing awareness of Freudian insights" (Armytage 1975, p. 317). In Dorset the Montessori Society set up a wartime reformatory for delinquents run according to psychoanalytic methods; Havelock Ellis, Bernard Hart, Ian Suttie, and other medical psychologists continued to read Freud's publications; and reading Freud became "the holy, if furtive, cult of the student 'counter culture'" (Armytage 1975, pp. 321–322).

Freud introduced his ideas to important medical authorities from the Austro-German armies at a congress of analysts held in Budapest in late 1918. Anna Freud stated that her intention to become a psychoanalyst preceded the Budapest Congress (Dyer 1980, letter dated March 28, 1977), and we should assume that her training analysis began soon after this decision. Once her analysis was under way she would not have interrupted it. Freud included his daughter in his plans to go to Budapest, and the two set out together in early July 1918 (Jones 1955, p. 222; Pfieffer 1972, p. 82). Anna's analysis probably had begun a short time before that. Certainly when Anna Freud and Kata Levy met in Budapest later that summer, Levy learned that her new friend's analysis indeed had begun (Roazen 1975, p. 433).

The knowledge that Freud had undertaken the training analysis of his daughter was at first confined to a relatively small circle of close personal and professional associates,[7] though analytical "outsiders" may well have been forgiven for inferring that no other was likely to have had the status or seniority required to analyze Freud's offspring. The first overtly public indication of this was the introductory remark made by Marie Bonaparte—"*Son père l'initia à la psychanalyse*" (1946, p. 180)—almost 30 years later when Anna Freud was in Paris attending a UNESCO conference. More recently, Roazen's insistent interviewing technique elicited the same information from Mrs. Eduard Hitschmann, Edith Jackson, Irmarita Putnam, and a number of others (Roazen 1969, chap. 4, n. 8) in this analytical fraternity, as well as Oliver Freud, Anny Katan, and Kata Levy (Roazen 1975), all persons having had a close relationship with Anna Freud both before and after this period. Finally, Eduardo Weiss, in his *Recollections of Freud* many years later, included a letter received in 1935 in which Freud admitted to having "succeeded well" in analyzing his own daughter (Weiss 1970, p. 81).

The commencement of Anna Freud's analysis coincided with new ideas regarding the formalizing of the training analysis re-

[7]The personal and the professional tended to be one and the same, a fact that Anna Freud described as "rather characteristic of the circumstances of my life" (1979b).

quirements for future analysts. In Vienna, Freud seems to have
again led the way and prompted Herman Nunberg to raise the
issue at the Budapest Congress (Nunberg 1969). A year earlier
Constance Long had made the same recommendation in London
(Long 1917). Freud's few student-analysands before Budapest
(ignoring the "analytical walks" that early pioneers such as Jones
and Eitingon had found as brisk as they were brief) included Rene
Spitz in 1910, Jan van Emden in 1911, and Ludwig Jekels around
1913. Kata Levy and Helene Deutsch both entered into analysis
with Freud at almost the same time as Anna Freud did. After the
war, Freud's personally trained students included David Forsyth,
Istvan Hollos, Elizabeth Rado-Revesz, James and Alix Strachey,
Joan Riviere, Abram Kardiner, Horace Frink, Jeanne de Groot,
Dorothy Burlingham, Marie Bonaparte, Eva Rosenfeld, Ruth Mack-
Brunswick, Edith Jackson, Maryse Choisy, Heinz Hartmann, and
many others. It is doubtful if a more distinguished group of
analysts has ever been privileged to share a training analyst of such
stature.

In regard to the duration of formal training analysis, it is
unlikely that Anna Freud's sessions continued for "a number of
years" (Roazen 1975, p. 433). In those days didactic analyses
tended to be measured in months rather than years. Helene
Deutsch, for example, had an analysis with Freud lasting from
October 1918 into 1919 (Roazen 1969, p. 98). Oliver Freud has
been cited as having reported that as late as the spring of 1921 his
sister was still going to their father's study for her analysis
(Roazen 1975, p. 433). But a letter from Freud to Ferenczi at that
time suggested that Oliver Freud did not spend much time in
Vienna that spring, having left for Rumania in March (Jones 1957,
p. 83). It is quite possible that when interviewed nearly half a
century later, the years had become merged in Oliver Freud's
memory.[8] He may also have misunderstood the technical nature
and purpose of many of Anna's subsequent sessions with Freud,
which would fall into the category of "lively interchange of ideas

---

[8]Interestingly, it is to Anna Freud that we are indebted for one of the clearest
accounts of the "telescoping" of events in the memory of the individual (1951b).

and discussions of problems with our elders" (A. Freud 1967d, p. 511), which she included as part of her early training.

Those of us who never knew Freud and who look instead to his scientific and therapeutic achievements may perhaps be forgiven if we assume that a personal analysis with such a figure must have inevitably led to a subsequent intellectual imprisonment within his specific doctrine. Fortunately, there is evidence to dispel such a harmful myth, and we are indebted to a forthright and discerning pupil of Freud's for revealing this to us. Eva Rosenfeld related that during her analysis with Freud, she had once tried to keep a certain matter from him in the belief that its disclosure would in some way sadden him. Freud immediately corrected his pupil's abuse of the fundamental rule of association with the words, "We have only one aim and only one loyalty, to psychoanalysis. If you break this rule you injure something much more important than any consideration you owe to me" (Jones 1957, p. 163). Ernest Jones confirmed that Freud was "deeply concerned with the transmission of his main function in life, the care of psychoanalysis" (1957, p. 46), and there is thus implied all the tendencies toward the progressive elaboration, corroboration, refutation, and eventual revision of doctrine that one would associate with any discipline claiming to share the *Weltanschauung* of science. Freud's *ancien régime* is thus rationally inspired, and though its influence is very real and profound, it is no more so than the roots of our own childhood, which too are capable of infinite and subtle variation and no small measure of self-direction.

That this is ideally the case is again shown by the example of Eva Rosenfeld, who was gracious enough to grant an extended interview to me. When she learned that I had come to London from Harrogate and Leeds in Yorkshire, she told me that she had visited them both and that a student of hers, R. E. D. Markillie, worked there. I commented that he now seemed to lean more to the object relations views of Ronald Fairbairn, along with Harry Guntrip and Henry Dicks who had also worked in Leeds. Rosenfeld then responded, "Well, I don't expect my students to keep to one place. Their training is a beginning. They go on from there" (Dyer 1980, p. 474). The evidence of Anna Freud's own work is a monument to the extent to which she herself went on from where her father took her.

Though nominally still employed as a schoolteacher during this period, several important events helped Anna Freud prepare for her later active role in psychoanalysis.

First was her attendance at the Fifth International Psychoanalytic Congress, held in Budapest in September 1918. This was Anna Freud's first presence at a meeting of the "International"—as it was also for another future notable, Melanie Klein—and they no doubt heard Sigmund Freud's paper on "Lines of Advance in Psychoanalytic Therapy" (1919b), which assessed and projected many current problems of therapy and technique. According to one commentator, the developments that Freud predicted in this paper eventually became possible, largely through "the new vistas that ego psychology opened up to the earliest and probably best systematized modifications of psychoanalytic technique, the development of child analysis by Anna Freud and the psychoanalysis of delinquents by Aichhorn" (E. Kris 1951).

Freud uncharacteristically read the paper from his prepared notes, and Anna and the other family members present criticized his having broken a family tradition of speaking from memory (Jones 1955, p. 223). This particular incident suggests a markedly independent—that is, a nontransference—aspect of Anna Freud's relationship at that time with her father-analyst. Later events likewise showed that Anna, though fully accepting all that seemed to her most valuable and reliable in her father's teaching, was by no means simply passive or dependent. Her technical innovations in particular (see chapter 2) would disregard some of Freud's strongest dictates, such as not promising the patient any certainty of cure.

The Budapest Congress, though attended mostly by Central Europeans, was by all accounts outstanding. There was an official reception and banquet, with high-ranking military and medical representatives of both Austria and Germany in attendance. Ernst Simmel was one and, according to his later work, clearly was impressed by the congress's scientific stimulus. Altogether, as Freud later wrote to his friend Lou Andreas-Salomé, it was "a great success" (Pfieffer 1972, p. 83) and could certainly be rated as a propitious moment for any newcomer to have considered entering the world of psychoanalytic affairs.

After returning from Budapest Anna Freud began attending the weekly scientific meetings of the Vienna Psychoanalytic Society. Until 1910 these meetings had been held at the Berggasse in Freud's own waiting room, but they now took place in a larger room of the College of Physicians at the University of Vienna. Anna's first guest attendance was on Wednesday, November 19, 1918, and the presenter was Siegfried Bernfeld, who read a paper entitled "Poetic Writing in Youth" (Nunberg and Federn 1975, p. 296). Among those present and voicing comments were Paul Federn, Victor Tausk, Theodor Reik, and, of course, Freud himself. About this time, too, Anna Freud translated from English to German a psychoanalytic piece by Ernest Jones on anal-erotic character traits (Jones 1918). Freud may well have given his daughter this task as part of her analytical training. The subject matter would thus have been of Freud's choosing, though it may well have influenced Anna's later emphasis on her own early case histories. The anal material concerning a 6-year-old obsessional girl is, for example, given some prominence in one of her important works on technique (1927a).

Miss Freud herself stated that her teaching career lasted "from age 19 to age 24" (Dyer 1980, letter dated July 29, 1976), and thus there were about 18 months between her decision to become a psychoanalyst and giving up her position as schoolteacher. The terrible economic situation of postwar Austria might have been responsible for that delay. Even Freud was having difficulties and was able to maintain his analytical practice during the first year after the war only on the strength of the few English and Americans referred to Vienna by Ernest Jones. During that year of privation and hardship, Anna Freud was also busy with relief collections and with the "children's trains" whereby starving Austrian children were sent abroad under the auspices of international aid agencies (Meng and E. L. Freud 1963, letter to Pfister dated December 27, 1919).

Late in 1919 Anna finally stopped teaching. Her father wrote in a letter to Abraham dated November 2 that "my daughter has begun work as an assistant in the English department of the Publishing House" (Abraham and E. L. Freud 1965, pp. 293–294). This publishing house was, of course, the Internationaler Psychoanalytischer (I. P.) Verlag of Vienna, having been recently endowed by the wealthy Anton von Freund. Ernest Jones at first viewed Anna Freud's role there as somewhat incidental and only later recognized its significance to her future career as a psychoanalyst (1957, p. 50). Miss Freud in turn acknowledged Jones's help in establishing a psychoanalytical literature in the English language, in directing the early work of translating by Joan Riviere and Alix and James Strachey, and "so far as it was done in Vienna, [she] was chosen to be their helper" (1979b). She also noted that harmony between the Vienna and London societies was then at its height, a happy situation that later changed drastically.

Although psychoanalysis had always attracted talented thinkers, this was especially true of the young intellectuals of the generation that survived the First World War. One of them was Siegfried Bernfeld, who after the war set up in Vienna the Baumgarten children's home as a residential venture for orphaned Jewish children and adolescents. These unfortunates were, as Anna Freud later reminisced, "running wild as victims of the . . . war" (1968, p. 7), and such a difficult undertaking inevitably produced mixed results, some of which she described as "disheartening" (1968d). Although not directly participating in the experimental home, she closely followed all such developments and, indeed, was an important participant-historian of psychoanalysis from World War I onward. Anna Freud quite legitimately viewed herself as "a historian of the psychoanalytic movement" (1976a, p. 178).[9] Both Bernfeld (1922) and his coworker Willi Hoffer (1965) de-

---

[9]Anna Freud's more important historical accounts are her obituary for Willi Hoffer (1968d), an appreciation of Herman Nunberg (1969k), a note on the *International Journal of Psychoanalysis* (1969t), her review of Hilda Abraham's biography of Karl Abraham (1974b), some reminiscences of Ernest Jones (1979b), and two short histories of child analysis (1966e, 1971b).

scribed the Kinderheim Baumgarten, which, though not unique, was in certain respects a precursor of all later residential infant nurseries. Other helpers and staff at the Baumgarten home included schoolteachers and social workers, one of whom was Eva Rosenfeld's mother. Eva herself had opened her own home in Vienna to war orphans in what she described as "an informal middle-class venture" (Dyer 1980, p. 472). However, Anna Freud and Eva Rosenfeld did not meet until some years later, and then with the help of Siegfried Bernfeld. Meanwhile Bernfeld continued to lecture regularly in Vienna, presenting to the Vienna Psychoanalytic Society papers such as "Psychoanalytic Problems in the History of Paedagogics" (Report of Vienna Psychoanalytic Society 1920, p. 123). It is probable that Anna Freud heard this and Bernfeld's other lectures, and in referring to her early days she observed that "many of us had for years been listening to the inspiring lectures for teachers and youth leaders given by Siegfried Bernfeld" (1974e, p. viii). Clearly, Bernfeld was influential during the crucial phase when Anna Freud was changing from a school-teacher to a psychoanalyst. It is unlikely, however, that Bernfeld contributed much to the deeper commitment to psychoanalysis that had already been planted by Freud himself.

THE SYMBOLIC RING

About two years after commencing her training analysis and about six months after giving up teaching to go to the Verlag, Anna Freud received in May 1920 one of her father's now renowned rings. The significance of this simple act is difficult to underestimate, as it carried with it all the implications of acceptance into Freud's innermost circle, and all but confirmed his approval of her future career.

Freud's rings contained a small, carved antique Greek intaglio from his collection, which had been set in a gold band. The only other individuals to have been so favored at this time were the members of the committee—Rank, Sachs, Abraham, Jones, and

Ferenczi—who were later joined by Eitingon. Anna Freud appears to have set a precedent as the first woman recipient, though there were other women later. Ernest Jones (1957, p. 18) mentioned that his own wife Katherine, Lou Andreas-Salomé, and Marie Bonaparte were among them, and Roazen (1975, p. 416) also listed Gisela Ferenczi, Jeanne Lampl-de Groot, Ruth Mack-Brunswick, Edith Jackson, and Henny Freud. Eva Rosenfeld bequeathed her ring to Hebrew University in Jerusalem, which now has a Sigmund Freud Chair of Psychoanalysis.

Freud's own ring depicted the head of the Greco-Roman Olympian Zeus (Jupiter), according to Jones (1955). The mythological parallel would suggest that Anna Freud's ring might portray the young goddess Pallas Athena, who sprang from the head of Zeus and became associated with wise counsel and healing cults.

With these important events, both actual and symbolic, there came the first of several tragedies in the Freud family. The First World War had spared all of Anna Freud's brothers, although Martin was captured and for long was feared lost, but now, in the great influenza pandemic which spread over the world a year or so after the war, her sister Sophie died. Writing to Ferenczi about his own feelings, Sigmund Freud added that "my wife and Annerl are terribly shaken" (Jones 1957, letter dated February 4, 1920).

Later that year came more cheering events with the marriage of Ernst Freud to Lucie Brasch. From this union Anna Freud became the aunt to three more nephews. Figure 2 shows the immediate generations of Anna Freud's family tree. In the summer of 1920 Anna Freud and her father were in Hamburg visiting the two nephews who were now motherless and who soon came to live with the Freud family in Vienna. Max Eitingon joined Freud and Anna, and all three then went to Holland, arriving at the Hague in time for the psychoanalytical congress. Writing to Lou Andreas-Salomé about this trip, Freud no longer referred to his "little daughter" but instead wrote, "I intend to take my daughter Anna with me to the Hague; she has long been anxious to meet you" (Pfieffer 1972, p. 105). But because of Andreas-Salomé's unavoidable absence from this congress, the important meeting between her and Anna Freud did not take place for yet another year.

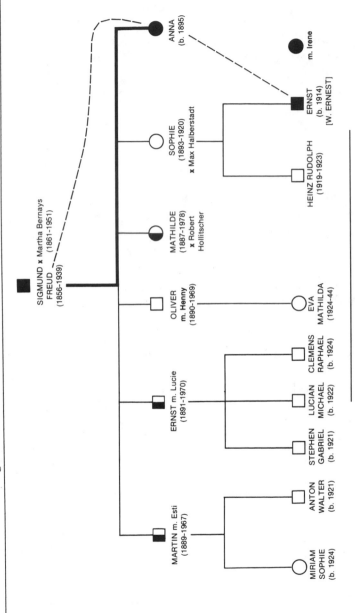

Figure 2. Three Generations of Anna Freud's Family Tree

SIGMUND **x** Martha Bernays
FREUD   (1861-1951)
(1856-1939)

MARTIN m. Esti
(1889-1967)

MIRIAM
SOPHIE
(b. 1924)

ANTON
WALTER
(b. 1921)

ERNST m. Lucie
(1891-1970)

STEPHEN
GABRIEL
(b. 1921)

LUCIAN
MICHAEL
(b. 1922)

CLEMENS
RAPHAEL
(b. 1924)

OLIVER
m. **Henny**
(1890-1969)

EVA
MATHILDA
(1924-44)

MATHILDE
(1887-1978)
x Robert
Hollitscher

SOPHIE
(1893-1920)
x Max Halberstadt

HEINZ RUDOLPH
(1919-1923)

ERNST
(b. 1914)
[W. ERNEST]

ANNA
(b. 1895)

m. Irene

■ =Psychoanalyst or analytical child-therapist.
■ =Involved with analytic publishing/translating.
----- =Probable training-analyst/analysand relationship.

34

The Sixth International Psychoanalytical Congress was held at the Hague from September 8 to 12, 1920 (*International Journal of Psychoanalysis* 1920). The congress is of special interest for Anna Freud's formative years, as it fell between her decision to train formally as an analyst and her actual entry into the Vienna Society. She was one of 57 guests who attended, and the increased numbers revealed the surge of academic and professional interest in psychoanalysis in the postwar years. Guests from England included James Glover and John Rickman, and the contingent of full members numbered another 62 persons (Jones 1957, p. 28). This meeting, moreover, was truly international in a way that had been quite impossible for the Budapest meeting two years earlier. Miss Freud recorded the great pleasure she earlier experienced at being "in contact with the outer world again" and listed two tasks for the postwar Central European group in the Netherlands, namely, "to learn to communicate again and also to begin to tolerate the proper food to which Central-European stomachs had become unused" (1979b, p. 348).

No doubt we may accept as true for the Hague Congress the statement by Ernest Jones who, in noting that Sigmund Freud always made a point of listening to every single paper at all the congresses he attended, added that this was "an example followed in later years by his daughter" (1957, p. 106). The complete list of scientific papers is given in Figure 3, and we may point to three or four of the 20 as having particular, though widely differing, impacts on the budding Anna Freud. Five of the main presenters were also women, a proportional representation that was improved in the years to come.

First was Freud's own paper, a supplement to dream theory (1920b) in which his attention was directed to the then unpublished work of the psychologist J. Varendonck of Ghent, who had studied daydreaming and related chains of thought processes. When this was published in 1921 as an English-language book, Anna Freud immediately prepared a translation for a German edition (Varendonck 1921). The content of Varendonck's work was certainly relevant to Anna Freud's own first psychoanalytic paper, which was also in preparation, though his work was not

Figure 3. List of Papers Presented to the Hague International Psycho-analytic Congress, 1920

SIXTH CONGRESS OF THE INTERNATIONAL PSYCHO-ANALYTICAL ASSOCIATION.

DR. K. ABRAHAM: Forms of Expression of the Female Castration Complex

DR. HELENE DEUTSCH: On the Psychology of Suspicion

DR. A. STÄRCKE: The Castration Complex

DR. VON HATTINGBERG: Transference and Object Choice; their Significance as regards the Theory of Instinct

J. C. FLÜGEL, B. A.: On the Biological Basis of Sexual Repression

PROF. G. JELGERSMA: A Psycho-Analytical Contribution to the Theory of Feeling

DR. HANNS SACHS: Day-Dreams in Common

DR. THEODOR REIK: The strange God and one's own God

DR. GÉZA RÓHEIM: Central Australian Totemism

DR. ERNST SIMMEL: Psycho-Analysis of the Gambler

PROF. SIGM. FREUD: Supplements to the Theory of Dreams

DR. S. FERENCZI: Further Extension of the Active Technique in Psycho-Analysis

EUGENIA SOKOLNICKA: On the Diagnosis and Symptomatology of the Psycho-Analytical Theory of the Neuroses

DR. GEORG GRODDECK: On the Psycho-Analytic treatment of Organic Illnesses

DR. L. BINSWANGER: Psycho-Analysis and Clinical Psychiatry

DR. A. STÄRCKE: The Relations between Neuroses and Psychoses

O. PFISTER: The Significance of Psycho-Analysis for Constitutional Law and Political Economy

DR. SABINA SPIELREIN: On the Question of the Origin and Development of Speech

DR. MARGARETE STEGMANN: Form and Content in Psycho-Analysis

DR. HERMINE HUG-HELLMUTH: On the Technique of the Analysis of Children

---

From the *International Journal of Psychoanalysis* 1920:1.

actually cited (A. Freud 1922a). It seems likely that by then Anna Freud had adopted the critical attitude of her father toward Varendonck's term *foreconscious*, and viewed daydream processes as "freely wandering or phantastic" thinking rather than intentionally directed thinking (S. Freud 1921b, p. 271).

Ferenczi's Hague paper concerned his innovative "active technique" in psychoanalysis, which Anna Freud (1927a), as noted earlier, was quite prepared to consider sympathetically and on its merits. Much more controversial and varied in its impact was the contribution by Georg Groddeck. This was not a carefully prepared and closely reasoned presentation, as most of the others were, but was a spontaneous performance before the gathered audience. Beginning with the provocative statement "I am a wild analyst," Groddeck proceeded to offer a rambling and, to some listeners, a brilliantly insightful and original account of the analytical work with patients (C. S. and S. Grossman 1965, p. 13). Anna Freud was shocked and offended by Groddeck's presentation, which to her may well have seemed to threaten the scientific rigor of the psychoanalysis she knew best and to which she had only recently committed herself. Her attitude here differed markedly from her father's, who had been "amused rather than offended" (C. S. and S. Grossman 1965, p. 97) by his analytical colleague, and who continued to defend Groddeck after his speech. Anna Freud's antipathy to Groddeck persisted, despite the more accommodating stance taken by her father, Andreas-Salomé, and certain others of importance to her. This was, therefore, one of those instances in which Anna Freud showed herself capable of assuming an independent attitude, despite the obvious closeness and rapport with such a monumental father figure.

The final paper of note here was that by Hermine Hug-Hellmuth entitled "On the Technique of the Analysis of Children" (1921). There is little doubt that Hug-Hellmuth was the leading exponent of this speciality at that time, and our attention is inevitably drawn to her ideas concerning new developments for analyzing young children. Both Anna Freud (1927a, lecture 1) and Melanie Klein (1948, p. 38) acknowledged Hug-Hellmuth's priority in their own early publications.

In the same year as the Hague congress Hug-Hellmuth published an English translation of her important early monograph
(1913) on child development, regarding which reviewer Barbara
Low noted the "extraordinary close and detailed observation of the
infant and young child" (1922, p. 236). More contemporary publications then existed, forming a primordium of analytical-obser-
vational empiricism from which the new play analysis and other
techniques would shortly emerge. Hug-Hellmuth's collective review offered over 40 titles dealing with the new child psychology
(1920), including names such as Abraham, Freud, Pfister, Putnam,
and Bernfeld. Almost forgotten today are the many other participants who gave academic and scientific respectability to Anna
Freud's chosen new field.[10]

A strong educative influence pervaded Hug-Hellmuth's work
and was present in her paper given at the Hague Congress. She did
not confine her analytical approach to the relief of suffering and
symptoms but went on to advocate moral and aesthetic values also.
She drew wider attention than had previously been given to those
peculiarities of the child's psyche that necessitated "a special technique for its analysis" (Hug-Hellmuth 1921, p. 287). But if Meng
(1939, p. 175) was correct in writing of Hug-Hellmuth that *"eine
exakte Technik der Kinderanalyse bemühte,"* then clearly Hug-
Hellmuth strove for an illusory goal. We accept here the fundamental dictum of A. N. Whitehead, that in science "exactness is
fake."

Hug-Hellmuth favored educational methods based on psychoanalytical knowledge for treating those children considered too
young—under 7 or 8 years—to warrant a "proper" analysis. A true
pioneer, she dispensed with the "lying-down" technique and moved
analysis and the educative therapy into the child's own home. No
doubt it was there—perhaps incidentally—that she observed how a
child's own toys and games could be used in the analytical work.

---

[10]Rarely mentioned today are Erwin Lazar, Otto Mensendieck, Hermann V.
Muller, Lindworski, Blüher, Diettrich, and others. Between 1922 and 1945 Anna
Freud considered it worthwhile to offer a kind of "honorary bibliography"
(1974f), which included many names likewise unknown to later generations.

Certainly Hug-Hellmuth herself joined in such play and came close to recommending play as an important medium throughout the whole treatment. She also made positive, "active therapy" requests of the patient, and free association and dream-analysis became merely techniques in a wider repertoire of techniques. Willi Hoffer, who had personal experience of Hug-Hellmuth's work, stated that she "spent most of her efforts in finding out secrets that the child had intentionally withheld from educators—and thus she opened the door to the child's phantasy life" (1945, p. 296).

Hug-Hellmuth, however, overemphasized Freud's Little Hans analysis, which she viewed as "the" method and "the basis of psycho-analytic child therapy" (1921, p. 289). She thus underrated and failed to capitalize on her own initiatives, tending instead to see them as means to "pave the way" in the early stages of treatment. Although she did mention symbolic acts and nonverbal behavior, she did not follow up this new area of study.

Nevertheless, by 1920, albeit for only a brief period,[11] Hermine von Hug-Hellmuth was, without question, the most prominent figure in the field of child analysis. Her contribution to the Hague Congress reflected the contemporary state in regard to the analysis of children, and it could hardly have failed to interest even those who later outgrew her ideas. Roazen (1975, p. 437) asserted that as early as 1922 Hug-Hellmuth's work was overshadowed by that of Anna Freud, though we do not agree and recommend instead a somewhat later date for even the earliest emergence of any significant ascendancy of Anna Freud, the child analyst.

FRAU LOU AND THE FIRST PATIENT

Both the personal friendship and the professional encounter between Anna Freud and Lou Andreas-Salomé began when Anna was 25. It would be difficult to rank these two events in order of their importance. Fortunately we are spared this task, for they are

[11]She was murdered in 1924 at the age of 53 by her own nephew, who had been in analysis with her.

complementary and supportive in character. The friendship was a powerful formative influence at the time and endured for almost two decades until Andreas-Salomé's death. Nevertheless, it could not accurately be described as essential, and in its absence no doubt alternative influences would have emerged. On the other hand, though it was relatively brief and quickly outgrown in the span of life and work, Anna Freud's first professional analysis can be described only as unique and essential—a *rite de passage.*

Lou Andreas-Salomé—"Frau Lou"—attended the Weimar Congress of 1911, and in the following year she began an extended correspondence with Freud, whom she always addressed as "Professor." Though Freud and Lou soon met, Lou regretted that Freud's youngest daughter had "escaped me" (Pfieffer 1972, p. 62). Lou did not meet Anna for four more years. In the meantime, however, the correspondence between Freud and Lou showed how well qualified the gifted Frau was to help shape Anna Freud's understanding of her own first psychoanalytical case material.

In a wartime letter (Pfieffer 1972, letter dated November 28, 1917), Lou confessed to Freud that the classic Little Hans method had failed her in analyzing a 6-year-old girl referred with *pavor nocturnus.* Although ostensibly asking for advice and help, Lou's letter already showed a high degree of originality and methodological initiative in regard to gaining access to the child's mind. Thus, by posing as a fellow sufferer, the analyst contrived to elicit a number of dreams from the young child. And by writing and drawing on cards that they then exchanged, Lou and the child established a system of indirect communication. In a later letter (Pfieffer 1972, letter dated December 15, 1917), Lou reported the use of "mutual confessions" as another technical method.

Freud's reply was reminiscent of the advice he had offered to C. G. Jung ten years earlier when Jung had also been caught in a therapeutic impasse (McGuire 1974, letters 241 and 257). Lou could, wrote Freud, wait until a stronger attachment was formed and the child began communicating more, i.e., became more amenable to analysis. But if she had confidence in her interpretations and surmises, she could just "tell it to the child yourself" (Pfieffer 1972,

p. 70), with the expectation that the child would acknowledge the essential accuracy of the revelation.

In her subsequent correspondence Lou reported to Freud that her little patient now regarded her "much more as a kind of fellow-child than as a threatening adult" (Pfieffer 1972, p. 73), and clearly she had used great skill and empathy to achieve such an acceptance, without abrogating the actual responsibility of being the adult. Freud's view was that Lou's technique of putting herself on the child's level, though skillful, had nevertheless reduced the educational possibilities of the analysis. The founder of psychoanalysis then reminded his correspondent of a point that has great consequence for teachers, therapists, and all who work closely with children, namely, that "in education, as in analysis, one partner must be the unassailable and the superior" (Pfieffer 1972, p. 74). Freud also pointed out, en passant and with masterful theoretical acuity, that the child's general inaccessibility corresponded to his or her narcissism.

Our interest is naturally excited by this wartime exchange between two people who were important influences on Anna Freud's own handling of early analytical childhood case material. Sigmund Freud's views on the relative distribution of authority and responsibility between adult and child inevitably will appear entrenched and conservative after more than half a century of intervening liberalization and progress in the social sciences. Nevertheless, it is our view that although the adult who deals with children can often and with advantage reduce his or her authoritative role aspect, that adult can in no sense lessen his or her corresponding responsibility. The successful separation of these two intertwined role aspects will therefore continue to present a dilemma to all those who aspire to greater levels of mutuality and reciprocity in their relationships with children.

Before the memorable first meeting between Frau Lou and Anna Freud, the latter had finished the analysis of her first patient. This was a 15-year-old girl who offered many daydreams and other materials associated with her beating fantasy. The treatment was "rather thoroughgoing" (1922a, p. 138), and both the nature and quantity of the material suggest an analysis of frequent sessions and prolonged duration. In all probability this inaugural treatment occupied most of the year (1921) between the meeting of the International Association at the Hague and Anna's eventual introduction to Lou. By that time—and not without good reason—Anna Freud considered herself a psychoanalyst and recently admitted, "I collected the material for my first paper already as a psychoanalyst" (Dyer 1980, letter dated July 29, 1976). Since that same first paper was also Anna Freud's candidacy presentation to the Vienna Psychoanalytic Society, its detailed examination is left to the next chapter.

Lou Andreas-Salomé, at Freud's invitation, stayed at the Berggasse apartment from early November until late December 1921. During that time she continued to keep her diary (Pfieffer 1972, pp. 229–231), to which we are indebted for much detail. There can be little doubt that meeting and coming to know Lou well was a great highlight of Anna Freud's life, and a firm bond soon was established between them. One outcome was the shaping of Anna Freud's first published case history and scientific communication from their long discussions. Another was their voluminous correspondence, which remains as yet unpublished, although many of the letters are cited or alluded to in the volume of published correspondence between Sigmund Freud and Lou (Pfieffer 1972).

Lou arrived in Vienna on a Wednesday evening, just in time for Anna Freud to take her along to the weekly meeting of the Vienna Psychoanalytical Society.[12] There were some 50 members and guests at the meeting, and the power of the past was strongly in evidence. Lou could not help noticing the absence of her late friend Viktor Tausk—"I looked for him everywhere" (Pfieffer 1972, p. 229)—although he had been dead for over two years (Roazen 1969, S. Freud 1919c). The lecturer was Eduard Hitschmann, and his presentation was entitled "Pedagogic Methods in Psychoanalysis" (Report of the Vienna Psychoanalytic Society 1922).

---

[12]These had continued to be held on the same day as Freud's original "Wednesday Psychological Society" of 1902–1908. Even today, the Hampstead Clinic holds its "Open Case Conferences" on a Wednesday.

Many years later Anna Freud mentioned Hitschmann as belonging to that older generation of analysts who were her seniors in the Vienna days (1969k).

During the ensuing days and weeks of Lou's visit, she and Anna spent much time together discussing psychoanalytic topics, a fact noted in a letter from Sigmund Freud to Anna's brother Ernst and his wife Lucie, (E. L. Freud 1960, p. 341). Lou apparently assisted with the interpretation of the beating-fantasy material that was currently occupying Anna Freud, and her help was acknowledged in a footnote to the title page of its publication (A. Freud 1922a). Lou thus appears to have functioned in much the same capacity as a modern supervisory analyst would. There seems to be no grounds for the statement by Roazen that for a time in the 1920s, "Lou became Anna's psychoanalytic therapist" (1969, p. 52). Entries in Lou's diary kept at the time support the view that she was a consultant only, and she wrote that "Anna and I used to sit with him [i.e. Freud] in his back room to talk about our theme in which we were immediately and involuntarily absorbed." And during the earlier part of the day, "Freud would come in after every analytic hour for a few minutes and talk with us and share in our work" (Pfieffer 1972, p. 230). This same reliable source makes it clear that Anna Freud invited other of her most valued Viennese colleagues to come and share certain of their discussions, particularly Bernfeld and Aichhorn.

Paul Roazen (1969) offered what can only be described as an unreliable and highly distorted view of the relationship between Anna Freud and Lou Andreas-Salomé. Without citing any specific sources he suggested that in later years Sigmund Freud wrote to Lou and discussed with her "the emotional problems of his daughter Anna . . . [and] . . . asked Lou to help loosen Anna's ties to him" (Roazen 1969, p. 52). The published correspondence between Freud and Lou contains no evidence for Roazen's contention (Pfieffer 1972), and the editor of that correspondence observed that "nothing of significance would appear to have been lost" (Pfieffer 1972, p. 241). This issue was part of a talk between Professor Ben Morris and myself, and our conclusions were that there was little importance here "except to suggest still further that Roazen is not entirely to be trusted and has a not too well hidden animus against Freud" (letter from Ben Morris dated April 7, 1980).

If a more general argument were required to refute the validity of Roazen's position, it could be found in the evidence presented above for the early development of the various practical, symbolic, and indissoluble bonds between Freud and his youngest daughter. Moreover, and as will be apparent in later chapters, there is no other reason that the father would tire of his daughter's fealty and certainly no evidence that the daughter was in any way dependent or neurotic and clinging. The evidence of later years shows that as the physical and corporeal Freud waned, his daughter Anna grew in strength and stature, both personally and professionally, and served to fill most of the gaps in his life left by the loss or defection of others or by his own increasing infirmities. In later years the psychoanalytic Zeus had no intention and no reason for relinquishing his daughter to lesser mortals.

After the years of postwar economic chaos and relative professional stasis, the close of 1921 brought a further good omen for psychoanalysis, and hence for the burgeoning Anna Freud. In December 1921 Sigmund Freud was made an honorary member of the Dutch Society of Psychiatrists and Neurologists. As his biographer Ernest Jones remarked, from then on it was common to recognize that some of his work, despite its many alleged errors, "was of outstanding importance, and that Freud himself was a man of scientific eminence" (1957, p. 86). But it is to the development of the eminence of Anna Freud in her own right that we shall next direct our attention.

CHAPTER TWO

The Vienna School
of Child Analysis

The Vienna Psychoanalytic Society (Wiener Psychoanalytischen Vereinigung) heard the candidacy paper of Anna Freud after a period of three and a half years during which time she had attended their meetings as "a silent listener," as she herself much later confessed (1969k, p. 195). This extended hospitality granted by the society to their inactive (*untätig*) candidate was acknowledged at the time by the candidate herself in her opening remarks. These remarks have, until now, been available only in the German original, but their interest merits inclusion here in an unauthorized translation:

> Ladies and Gentlemen, for several years I have enjoyed your hospitality, though I have not presented any contribution here so far. I know from a very good source [*guter Quelle*] that the society is not very keen on inactive guests who only observe. I suppose I might have continued to be inactive if your strict rules and regulations had not demanded a direct contribution from anyone applying for membership. Thus, my application for membership of the Vienna Society is the motivation as well as the excuse for my lecture today. ("Schlagephantasie und Tagtraum," p. 317)

Anna Freud's presentation took place in the spring of 1922 (Report of the Vienna Psychoanalytic Society, scientific meeting of May 31, 1922), and her election to membership of the society followed within a month (business meeting, June 13, 1922). We are reliably informed that this turn of events was "much to her father's gratification" (Jones 1957, p. 90). The successful overcoming of this obligatory obstacle would appear to have had for Freud a significance scarcely less than it had for his daughter. Her membership contribution was heard and commented on by an audience that included Bernfeld, Federn, Rank, Reik, Helene

Deutsch, Walter Schmideberg, Silberer, Fenichel, and, of course, Freud himself (*Imago* 1922, note p. 247).

The publication of Anna Freud's paper—her first scientific contribution—followed in the same year (A. Freud 1922a). It was clearly derived from Sigmund Freud's "A Child Is Being Beaten" (1919a) of three years earlier, and she acknowledged this in her introductory remarks. The paper consisted of a detailed presentation of an elaborate daydream and its numerous variants, together with an analytical demonstration of the roots of the daydream in a masochistic beating fantasy. In particular, she sought to test the view that the daydream superstructure permitted the gratification of excitation in the absence of actual masturbation. But she went beyond this and indicated that the very act of verbalization in the analytical setting served as a powerful source of pleasure for her patient.

In "A Child Is Being Beaten," Freud outlined in three stages the ontogenesis of the beating fantasy in the young child. In "Beating Fantasies and Daydreams," Anna Freud extended this scheme to show significant developments in the patient's fantasy material at around 8 to 10 years of age and around 14 to 15 years of age, the latter being the time of the patient's analysis. Although Anna Freud's contribution thus may be considered a longitudinal study, it could also be argued that the methods used were not fully longitudinal. In other words, this child was apparently not studied at age 8 or 10 years and again at age 14 or 15 years. Rather, the data on earlier ages were obtained by personal introspection, recall, or analytical interpretation. This in no way reduced the analytical elements of the author's contribution, though academic psychologists would no doubt argue for a more precise longitudinal design. In later years Anna Freud and other child analysts did comply with this methodological refinement.

The merit of Anna Freud's first psychoanalytical study did not go unrecognized at the time. Indeed, it has become a respectable and oft-cited part of the analytical literature. Lampl-de Groot (1928) was perhaps the first to cite Anna Freud's early clinical observation that at the climax of the masochistic fantasy, excitement is resolved into a feeling of happiness. A few years later Otto Fenichel (1932), with the clarity that soon became the hallmark of Anna Freud's own written style, described the beating-fantasy paper as demonstrating "in model fashion" the manner in which the daydream, though originally devised to suppress masturbation, changed in function to become a distorted expression of the old recurring masturbatory fantasies. Twenty years later Ernst Kris (1953) used Anna Freud's study in discussing the origins of narrative art and revery in masturbatory fantasy, and her 1922 paper continues to be quoted in the more recent literature of psychoanalysis.

In the close of her paper, Anna Freud referred to certain of Bernfeld's observations regarding creative story writing in adolescents. Her own adolescent patient had taken to writing just such similar accounts of her fantasy and daydream-based elaborations, and it was through the mediation of such literary efforts and their necessary greater attention to wider social reality considerations that the girl attained an important developmental step. As Anna Freud put it, "she has found the road that leads from her fantasy life back to reality" (1922a, p. 157). Interestingly, in the same year as Anna Freud published her work, the English psychologist Cyril Burt came to much the same conclusion with regard to the role of fairy stories as a bridge or stepping-stone enabling the child to reach over from daydreams to contact with reality (1922).

Anna Freud was 26 years old when she was elected to membership of the Vienna Psychoanalytical Society, and in the same year she became a published psychoanalytic writer. With these public acknowledgments of increased scientific and professional stature, there was a less widely known indication of her special standing with her father. From 1922 onward there was much discussion of Anna Freud in the correspondence between her father and Lou Andreas-Salomé. It was around this time that Freud introduced the epithet "Anna-Tochter" (Daughter Anna) (Pfieffer 1972, letter dated March 13, 1922), which both Freud and Lou henceforth used in an affectionate, though restrained, manner. Lou herself was elected to membership in the society that year, in the month following her friend Anna. Although Lou was not in Vienna at the time, Anna Freud attended the meeting and afterwards wrote immediately to Lou with the news of her successful election.[1]

Many interesting people were members of the Vienna Psycho-analytical Society at the time of Anna Freud's joining. The complete list is presented in Figure 4, and we should note that Anna never considered herself the equal in every respect of all these analysts, largely owing to the tactful discrimination on grounds of seniority. For example, in an appreciation of one of these analysts, written many years later, she stated that "Nunberg and I are not of the same analytic generation" (1969k). Along with Nunberg in the older and more senior generation she included Paul Federn, Helene Deutsch, Eduard Hitschmann, and Ludwig Jekels, whereas her own contemporaries included the Bibrings, Hartmann, Kris, Wilhelm Reich, and Robert Waelder.

Anna Freud observed that her analytical training was by no means completed simply with the successful presentation of her candidacy paper. Training in Vienna, even in those days, was both varied and lengthy, and novices had to continue for "five or ten years before our colleagues considered us full-grown members" (1967d, p. 513). Clinical work with patients comprised the major source of learning during this phase of training, and five, six, seven, and even eight cases were taken at one time.

Anna Freud learned psychiatric symptomatology by attending ward rounds in the hospital department of the distinguished Julius von Wagner-Jauregg. The department's first clinical assistant in the postwar years was the gifted Paul Schilder, and Anna Freud remembered his ward rounds as being particularly valuable (1967d, p. 512). Schilder also lectured at the University of Vienna, and it was here in 1923 that the pediatrician Josephine Stross first came to know Anna Freud (Dyer 1980, letter dated May 4, 1977). Half a century later the two women lived in North London and together ran the Hampstead Child Therapy Clinic.

---

[1] Anna Freud's letter, as yet unpublished, was discussed by Lou in her own letter to Freud, dated June 26, 1922, in Pfieffer 1972, p. 115. Anna visited Lou in Gottingen three times between April and August 1922.

Figure 4. Membership List of the Vienna Psychoanalytic Society, 1922–23

August Aichhorn, Wien, V., Schönbrunnerstrasse 112.
Lou Andreas-Salomé, Göttingen, Herzberger Landstrasse 101.
Dr. Siegfried Bernfeld, Wien, XIII., Suppégasse 10.
Dozent Dr. Felix Deutsch, Wien, I., Wollzeile 33.
Dr. Helene Deutsch, Wien, I., Wollzeile 33.
Dr. Paul Federn, Wien, I., Riemerg. 1.
Dr. Otto Fenichel, zurzeit Berlin-Halensee, Johann-Georg-Strasse.
Dr. Walter Fokschaner, Wien, VI., Kasernengasse 2.
Anna Freud, Wien, IX., Berggasse 19.
Prof. Dr. Sigm. Freud, Wien, IX., Berggasse 19.
Dozent Dr. Josef Friedjung, Wien, I., Ebendorferstrasse 6.
Dr. H. v. Hattingberg, München, Ainmillergasse 62.
Eric Hiller, Wien, VII., Andreasgasse 3.
Dr. Eduard Hitschmann, Wien, IX., Währingerstrasse 24.
Dr. Wilhelm Hoffer, Wien, IX., Liechtensteinstrasse 65a.
Prof. Dr. Guido Holzknecht, Wien, I., Liebiggasse 4.
Dr. Hermine Hug-Hellmuth, Wien, IX., Lustkandlgasse 10.
Dr. Ludwig Jekels, Wien, IX., Bergg. 29.
Dr. Robert Hans Jockl, Wien, III., Sechskrügelgasse 2.
Dr. Michael Kaplan, Wien, XVIII., Cottagegasse 48.
Dr. Salomea Kempner, Berlin W. 30, Barbarossastrasse 32, II.
Prof. Dr. Levi-Bianchini, Nocera Inferiore (Salerno).
Dr. Karl Landauer, Frankfurt a. M., Kettenhofweg 17.
Dr. I. Marcinowski, Bad Heilbrunn, Isartalbahn, Bayern.
Dr. Richard Nepallek, Wien, VIII., Alserstrasse 41.
Dr. H. Nunberg, Wien, VIII., Florianigasse 20.
Prof. Dr. Otto Pötzl, Prag, Psychiatrische Klinik.
Beate Rank, Wien, I., Grünangerg. 3–5.
Dr. Otto Rank, Wien, I., Grünangerg. 3–5.
Dr. Wilhelm Reich, Wien, XIX., Barawitzkagasse 12.
Dr. Theodor Reik, Wien, IX., Lackierergasse 1a.
Dr. Oskar Rie, Wien, III., Esregasse 5.
Dr. I. Sadger, Wien, IX., Liechtensteinstrasse 15.
Dozent Dr. Paul Schilder, Wien, II., Taborstrasse II.
M.-U.-C. Walter Schmideberg, Berlin W., Rauchstrasse 4.
Eugenia Sokolnicka, Paris VI., rue de l'Abbé Gregoire 3.
Dr. Maxim Steiner, Wien, I., Rotenturmstrasse 19.
A. J. Storfer, Wien, IX., Porzellangasse 43.
Frieda Teller, Prag, III., Plaska 14.
Dr. Karl Weiss, Wien, IV., Schwindg. 12.
Dr. Eduardo Weiss, Trieste, S. Lazzaro 8.
Dr. Alfred Winterstein, Wien, I., Augustinerstrasse 12.

From the *International Journal of Psychoanalysis* 1924:5, p. 267.

Heinz Hartmann, the second clinical assistant in Wagner-Jauregg's department, also became part of Anna Freud's personal and professional circle at this time. A cordial and mutually respectful relationship between the two lasted for nearly half a century, and although each followed rather different interests, their work was always essentially complementary.

Felix Deutsch, Sigmund Freud's personal physician during the early 1920s, gave seminars on psychoanalysis and related topics which were attended by Anna Freud, Hug-Hellmuth, Hitschmann, and others (Flagg 1966). The Dutch physician Jeanne de Groot came to Vienna in 1922 for an analysis with Freud. At a Wednesday meeting of the Vienna Society she met Anna, and the two quickly became friends (Dyer 1980, letter dated April 4, 1977). After her marriage to Hans Lampl the couple remained close and loyal to Anna and her father.

The training that Anna Freud received was broadly based and highly stimulating, and she had some of the best medical psychologists of the day as teachers and instructors. There was a mood of satisfaction, excitement, and pioneering that they all experienced. "We felt," she wrote, "that we were the first who had been given a key to the understanding of human behaviour and its aberrations . . . [and that] . . . apart from suggestion and hypnosis we had no rivals in the field of mental treatment" (1976a, pp. 177–178). In the realm of nonorganic mental illness there were few serious contenders for the crown that Anna Freud claimed for the science of psychoanalysis.

The Seventh International Psychoanalytic Congress took place in Berlin a few months after Anna Freud read her candidacy paper to the Vienna Society. Father and daughter traveled to the congress from Obersalzburg, Berchtesgaden, where they had been vacationing.[2] It was Anna Freud's first attendance as a member rather than

---

[2]Berchtesgaden was where, 23 years earlier, Sigmund Freud wrote his crucial theoretical chapter of *The Interpretation of Dreams* (Jones 1957, p. 90). In 1916 Anna Freud had also stayed at the Hotel Bristol, Salzburg, scene of the historic First Psychoanalytic Congress of 1908.

as a guest at a meeting of the congress. Conversely, for Freud, it was his last attendance at a major congress before the onset of his final illness.

NEW PSYCHOLOGY OF THE EGO

The year, 1922, that Anna Freud became a member of the Vienna Psychoanalytical Society and attended as a member the Berlin International Congress was also the year that Sigmund Freud completed his elegant tripartite model of mind. This paper, delivered at the Berlin Congress, was the public début of his new superego concept, though it was not published until 1923 (S. Freud 1923). James Strachey, translator and editor of *The Complete Psychological Works of Sigmund Freud,* noted that whereas the book portraying the new structural model did not appear until the third week of April 1923, the ideas contained in it had been in Freud's mind since at least the previous July (S. Freud 1923, editor's introduction). The year, 1922, that Anna Freud formally became a psychoanalyst thus inaugurated what Ernest Jones later termed "the new psychology of the ego" (1957, p. 92). In due course Anna Freud made her own substantial contributions to her father's psychology, whose basic model of id-ego-superego is well known in the literature of psychoanalysis. Many people believe that personal greatness goes hand in hand with the coincidence of great moments. For Anna Freud there could have been no greater moment to make her own début on the public stage of world psychoanalytic affairs. Needless to say, her father's new theoretical model profoundly influenced her own future work, though for the first half decade or so her principal concern was with technical rather than theoretical issues.

The distressing personal events associated with her father's illness, the onset of which followed within a few months of the Berlin Congress, were apparently responsible for an uncharacteristic lost memory by Anna Freud. In a letter to me she stated that "I attended the Berlin Congress of 1922. As far as I remember my father was prevented by illness" (Dyer 1980, letter dated March 28, 1977). But there can be no doubt that Freud did attend the congress, as noted by a number of eyewitnesses (Jones 1957, S. Freud 1923, Reich 1967). Reich in particular emphasized Freud's commanding figure and paid tribute to his impressive presentation of his paper (1967, p. 73). Lou Andreas-Salomé also met Freud and Anna again at the Berlin Congress (Pfieffer, p. 119).

Some may argue that the events surrounding her father's illness must have professionally affected Anna Freud, surpassing perhaps even the significance of her formal recognition as a psychoanalyst and easily outweighing the importance of such events as her attendance at scientific congresses. But it obviously is difficult, if not impossible, to separate one's professional and private lives. Nonetheless, it is certain that Freud's new theoretical model, and not his state of illness, was the essential shaping influence on Anna Freud's psychoanalytical awareness and theoretical grasp for the next and subsequent decades.

The Swiss educational psychologist Jean Piaget also attended the Berlin Congress, presenting there a paper entitled "Symbolic Thought and the Thought of the Child" (1945). However, Anna Freud did not remember meeting Piaget then, nor did she ever subsequently have any direct involvement with him (Dyer 1980, letter dated March 28, 1977).

Work as a translator of scientific publications continued to occupy Anna Freud's time, and within a year of joining the Vienna Society she translated a third important psychological paper from English into German. The subject matter concerned some problems of adolescence (Jones 1922), and this fact, together with the translator's role now as a practicing analyst in her own right, may have meant that the work was done on her own initiative rather than that of her father. By now Anna Freud had her second patient, a fact which her father proudly disclosed in a letter to Frau Lou (Pfieffer 1972, pp. 121–122). The case was one of a severe obsessional neurosis in an adolescent girl (A. Freud 1967d, p. 513). Anna Maenchen, later one of the leading child analysts in the United States, also entered into analysis with Anna Freud about this time and later trained more formally as a child analyst. She does not, however, on the strength of her early personal analysis, consider herself to be one of the historic first group of child analysts who trained with Anna Freud in the Vienna period (letters of Anna Maenchen dated May 19 and June 9, 1977). Those indicated as having seniority in this respect included Editha Sterba, Edith Buxbaum, Jenny Waelder-Hall, and Marianne Kris.

April 1923 saw the onset of Freud's severe and ultimately terminal illness with cancer of the jaw, the details of which have been sufficiently well documented by others (Jones 1957, Schur 1972). Apparently, and quite understandably, Anna did not immediately accept that her father's condition might be malignant. Writing to her friend Lou on this matter, she noted merely "Growths which apparently occur sometimes with smokers . . . something quite benign" (Pfieffer 1972, p. 232). In this respect she was probably misled by her father's physician Felix Deutsch, who initially strove to keep the true nature of the condition from his patient. During their summer holiday, taken at Gastein that year, the entire inner committee, together with Deutsch and Anna, convened in Freud's absence in order to discuss the situation. Afterwards, while walking together back up the mountain to where her father was resting, Anna Freud's questioning finally wrung from Deutsch his true opinion of the illness (Jones 1957, chap. 3).

Once reconciled to the facts, Anna Freud became her father's only nurse for the remaining 16 years of his life. Freud "made a pact with her at the beginning that no sentiment was to be displayed" (Jones 1957, p. 101), and the daughter's complete success in this difficult role was revealed by Freud in a letter to Lou: "Anna is splendid and self-assured" (Pfieffer 1972, pp. 124–125).[3]

---

[3]Letter of Freud, August 5, 1923. Freud's attitude at this time does not support the contention, discussed in Roazen 1975, that the father was at this time seeking to loosen his daughter's ties to him. Indeed, the opposite would seem to have been the case.

Apparently during these difficult times Anna Freud's several qualities and abilities—as colleague, companion, secretary, nurse, and business and personal courier—greatly aided Freud in the painful matter of breaking with Otto Rank. The circumstances of the break between Freud and Rank, including Rank's controversial technical and theoretical views and his eventual paranoia and psychotic collapse, have been discussed elsewhere (Jones 1957, Brome 1967). Roazen, often unreliable when interpreting his material, was nearer the mark than usual when he stated that Anna Freud became a psychoanalyst "shortly before the struggle with Rank began, and served to fill the gap he left. Eventually she performed all the functions of Rank's substitute" (1975, p. 445). We should add that such a successful "substitute role" was by no means the sine qua non of Anna Freud's acceptability to her father. Rather, it was her competence in her own right that enabled her to fill so readily the place left by another.

Anna Freud's own view regarding Rank's break with her father is contained in an unpublished letter to her friend Lou. There she wrote that "one is almost sorry for him, as if he didn't really know what he is doing and what an incision he is making in his life" (Pfieffer 1972, p. 234 and n. 171). Between 1913 and 1915 and 1918 and 1921 Anna Freud was in almost daily contact with Rank, either at the Berggasse or at the Verlag. Her comments indicated Rank's close acceptance before his dissent with Freud, and many years later when writing for the 50th anniversary of the *International Journal of Psychoanalysis* Miss Freud quoted Jones's biography of her father in such a way as to acknowledge Rank's strenuous endeavors in the early days on behalf of the psychoanalytic press (1969t).

In September 1923 Freud carried out his "long cherished plan" of showing his daughter Anna around the historic city of Rome (Jones 1957, p. 98). Writing to Lou from Rome, Freud admitted that he realized for the first time what good company his daughter was, and a later letter from Lou to Freud also disclosed the special closeness that she sensed between the father and daughter. "Perhaps it will be evening when this letter reaches you," she wrote, "and you will be sitting at your writing desk, with Anna perched on the library steps" (Pfieffer 1972, pp. 126–128). Some years later Lou jokingly reproached Freud with the reminder that one of the few ways in which Anna could not help him was by taking a spring holiday for him.

Meanwhile, Anna Freud had begun establishing her own scientific groundwork and experience. First was the collection of her own string of individually analyzed cases. It is no exaggeration to say that from the very beginning of her work as a psychoanalyst, she showed an appreciation of the necessary checks and balances of the scientific process, matched the theoretical and applied aspects of her field, and continually sought to improve both her conceptual model and her experimental-observational techniques. The roots of her attitude and orientation lay in the therapeutic and observational-interpretive approach of orthodox psychoanalysis and thus ultimately in the strict empiricism of 19th-century physiology and anatomy.

EARLY CHILD CASES

Anna Freud published only one scientific paper in 1923, a short piece describing observations related to her by Hilda Sissermann, the mother of a 27-month-old boy. The method used was still essentially the Little Hans technique (A. Freud 1923a), though in effect it foreshadowed her later interest in the role of the parents in the development, normal or pathological, of their child.

From that time onward Anna Freud accepted more and more child patients. Between 1923 and 1926 she carried out ten long analyses of children, thereby grounding herself in the practical technique which would provide the foundation for all of her later innovations and theoretical suggestions. The children's ages ranged from 6 to 11 years (the basic data are recorded in Table 1). Some of these cases deserve to be more widely known—the 6-year-old obsessional girl, for example—as they were important to the development of the new subspeciality of child psychoanalysis (*Kinderanalyse*). At the time there was no immediate publication of the results of this work nor of the recommendations based on

Table 1. Summary of Ten Early Child Cases, 1923–1926

Sex	Age in Years	Salient Features
F	6	Obsessional; high I.Q.; the most prominent early case
F	11	Delinquent (thieving, lies, etc.); difficult home with stepmother
M	10	Perversions; very diverse anxieties; semi-delinquent
M	10	Behavior problem; attacks of rage and defiance; sister already in analysis with same analyst
F	7	Difficult; neurotic; admitted her "bad self" when analyst confronted her with it
F	8	Sensitive; self-critical; attachment to over-strict nanny undermined by analyst's strategy; most successful of early cases
—	—	Low I.Q.; largely analyzed through dream material
—	—	Low I.Q.; largely analyzed through dream material
F	9	Masturbator; fire dreams
M	9	Anxiety; castration fears; prominent day-dreams

This sequence of cases is not necessarily chronological; see A. Freud 1927a.

her experiences with technical problems. With one exception this was a phase during which Anna Freud gained little acclaim or recognition beyond her own close group of professional specialists. The exception was the appearance in 1924 of Freud's *Gesammelte Schriften*—three volumes were on display for preview in April 1924 at the Eighth International Psychoanalytic Congress, held in Salzburg[4]—edited by Anna Freud and A. J. Storfer. The appearance

[4]Despite the historic importance of Salzburg as the site of the very first analytical congress, Anna Freud was unable to attend "to the best of my knowledge . . . because of my father's illness at the time" (Dyer 1980, letter dated March 28, 1977). Freud's illness on this occasion was influenza, and Anna accompanied him on an all too rare convalescent break (Jones 1957, p. 107).

of these volumes could scarcely have failed to draw the attention of readers far beyond Vienna to the rising stature of Anna Freud in the academic world of psychoanalysis, though merely on the strength of the evidence of the collection itself (S. Freud 1925) many could be forgiven for assuming that, apart from purely editorial labor, Anna Freud was simply illuminated in the reflected success and achievements of her father. Such was not the case, though it took some time for this fact to percolate beyond the confines of Vienna.

In Vienna itself, new technical views and insights evolved over a number of years during which Anna Freud organized regular seminars attended by Bernfeld, Aichhorn, and a few other close colleagues. The wider presentation of Anna Freud's technical innovations, which she later referred to as "my first independent move" (1967d, p. 514), was delayed a few years and then took the form of a series of lectures given before a general audience of the Vienna Psychoanalytic Society. The lectures were then published, and quite unexpectedly launched their author into the noisy arena of scientific divergence and controversy.

The small group that, from around 1924, was formed around Anna Freud probably began with the informal discussions during Frau Lou's stay at the Berggasse some three years before. A particularly interesting early case for discussion one day was that of "Minna," a difficult 15-year-old female patient. Anna Freud asked Bernfeld whether he knew of a suitable woman or family who might take Minna into their home. Bernfeld suggested Eva Rosenfeld, in the 13th District of Vienna, with whose sympathetic disposition he had become familiar from the Kinderheim Baumgarten period. Anna Freud then visited Eva at her home and succeeded in obtaining her help. The first meeting between the two women was described in Eva Rosenfeld's own words: "One Sunday morning in November 1924 she arrived at my door and explained what she wanted. This was the turning point of my life. I knew that this was forever. I have never altered my view since about Anna Freud" (Dyer 1980, interview on May 31, 1977). Eva Rosenfeld went on to have a personal analysis with Sigmund Freud and became a close friend of the family. Despite her association with some of Anna Freud's early initiatives, however, she did not consider herself a child analysis pioneer and worked as an adult rather than a child analyst.[5]

The nucleus of what would later be known as the Vienna School of Child Analysis had by now been formed, and it attracted both qualified analysts and others. An important factor in this was Anna Freud's appointment to the important training committee of the Vienna Institute.

The earliest formal position held by Miss Freud as a member of the Vienna Psychoanalytic Society was training secretary to the then newly formed training committee and later the training institute (*Lehrinstitut*). The precise dating of this event is well documented.[6] In a letter to me, Anna Freud stated, however, that "it is difficult to remember when I was what. I am sorry I cannot give you exact data about the positions held in Vienna" (Dyer 1980, letter dated July 29, 1976).

Anna Freud's colleagues on the influential training committee were Helene Deutsch (president), Siegfried Bernfeld (vice-president), Eduard Hitschmann, Herman Nunberg, Wilhelm Reich, and Theodor Reik. Students and prospective candidates applying for analytical training in Vienna naturally went to the official training committee, and many had their first meeting with Anna Freud there. One of the earliest to apply, in around 1925, was the graduate child psychologist Edith Buxbaum (Dyer 1980, letter dated July 19, 1977). Others included Editha Sterba, Jenny Pollack (later Jenny Waelder-Hall), Annie Reich, and Marianne Kris, all of whom graduated as associate members of the Vienna Psycho-

---

[5]Eva Rosenfeld died barely six months after granting me a long interview in her London home. She had recently written her own memoirs, though the manuscript was still in its original draft and "for my family to do with it what they will" (Dyer 1980, interview on May 31, 1977).

[6]Ernest Jones (1957, p. 107) wrote that as early as December 1924 Anna Freud became "Secretary to the Training Institute in Vienna," though this seems a little premature both in date and title (Institute). Jones may have known of an earlier, informal decision. The official I. P. A. Bulletin recorded that "Fraulein Freud" became secretary of "the Training Committee" in January 1925 and again in October 1925 (Report of the Vienna Psychoanalytic Society 1926, p. 285).

analytic Society on December 28, 1928 (Report of the Vienna Psychoanalytic Society 1929, p. 551). Although Anna Freud probably functioned as supervisory case analyst for most of these and similar trainee child analysts, their personal training analysts varied. Edith Buxbaum identified Herman Nunberg as her personal analyst (Dyer 1980, letter dated July 19, 1977), and Marianne Kris's analyst was Franz Alexander of Berlin (Dyer 1980, letter dated April 19, 1977).

It is difficult to overestimate the importance of Anna Freud's new position as secretary to the training committee, for here she was placed at the very hub of those affairs relating to the intake of fresh new minds into the Vienna Society. Over the ensuing years many talented young candidates were attracted to Anna Freud's personality and work and were recruited into her emerging "school" of child analysis. That she was well qualified and energetic enough for the additional work is without question, and her new rank proved to be only the first of a number of such secretarial posts that she eventually accepted.

We also should note that Anna Freud's rapid acceptance into the Vienna Society's business hierarchy—coming less than three years after her candidacy paper before the society—largely coincided with her father's partial eclipse and withdrawal from such affairs. It may well have been no mere piety to the absent founder of psychoanalysis but, rather, an urgent desire to keep fully abreast of his thinking that encouraged many of Anna Freud's more senior colleagues to accord her such rapid promotion. In any event, the choice was well made, and the daughter demonstrated her ability not only to substitute for her father but also to pursue her own line of thinking.

During this time Anna stood in for her father on many occasions. At the next gathering of analysts at the Ninth International Psychoanalytic Congress at Bad Homburg, she read her absent father's paper, "Some Psychological Consequences of the Anatomical Distinction Between the Sexes" (1925), which was warmly received by the membership. Sending the paper had not been Freud's idea, and he described it as "a last minute idea of my daughter's" (Abraham and E. L. Freud 1965, letter dated September 11, 1925). Karl Abraham acknowledged the daughter's warmly received presentation, which he had witnessed at the congress (Abraham and E. L. Freud 1965, letter dated September 8, 1925). In referring to her as "Miss Anna" he indicated the personal and professional standing of one whom he had, after all, known since she was 12 years old. Abraham had, the previous year, also been responsible for suggesting that Anna should join her father's inner committee, thus replacing the dissenting Otto Rank (Jones 1957, p. 78). Abraham's proposal was accepted—the names of A. A. Brill and August Starcke had also been proposed but were rejected—and Anna Freud formally became a member of Freud's private committee, together with Abraham, Ferenczi, Jones, Sachs, and Eitingon.

Henceforward, Freud entrusted his daughter to carry his greetings to the congresses and to read important scientific papers on his behalf. "Anna and the typewriter" also increasingly assisted him with his voluminous correspondence (Pfieffer 1972, letter dated May 10, 1925). By the time Anna Freud's relatively little known ten cases were analyzed, she had acquired, in addition to her own analytical method and technique, a formal position of influence in her local psychoanalytic society, an enthusiastic and talented group of close associates prepared to accept her direction, and an increasingly influential position as spokesperson for Sigmund Freud himself. But her labors did not cease there, and she continued the task of translating works from English into German: a book by I. Levine was published in 1923, a philosophical study that had received strong approval from Freud when read in the original (translated as *Das Unbewusste* [1925]).

The 6-year-old obsessional girl patient mentioned above was possibly the most prominent and analytically instructive case taken by Anna Freud during this period before her true worth began to be recognized beyond the small group of analytical colleagues in Vienna. The patient was staying with friends of her family at the time, and her perverse and antisocial anal "naughtiness" had all but alienated her from her playmates, who refused to sleep in the same room with their little guest. The little girl's otherwise difficult and silent nature prompted her referral to Anna Freud for three weeks of observation to determine whether there was any "defective disposition and unsatisfactory intellectual development, or whether we had here a case of an especially inhibited, dreamy, and withdrawn child" (1927a, pp. 8–9). Close observation showed the child to be highly rational and intelligent, but with a severe obsessional neurosis centering on the control of her "devil"—the patient's own term for the unruly part of her personality.

The child had two friends who were already in analysis with Anna Freud (it was also almost always true of these earliest child patients that they had parents who were analysts or friends of analysts and were consequently familiar with psychoanalysis), and she met Anna Freud when she went along with one of these other children. On the second visit, in answer to what in effect was the young patient's demand for a guarantee of cure, the therapist reversed the orthodox disclaimer by saying "Certainly . . . but it would be no light work" and making an agreement with her young charge. With the analytic situation thus established, the little girl's anal conflicts were manifested through a variety of channels, though verbalization predominated and largely focused on the child's fantasy and daydream material. Dream analysis proper was also used, though without much in the way of associations—the latter being the most fundamental technical problem to be overcome in this early pioneering phase—and drawing and playing with toys completed the therapist's repertoire.

Acting out was not discouraged by the therapist, and for this obsessional patient it inspired a most instructive episode. Over a period of time the analytic hour was "entirely given over" to anal material, largely verbal, and gradually the girl began carrying this behavior even into the home. The adults there were naturally perturbed and asked the analyst for guidance. When Anna Freud "inexperienced as I was," advised them to "simply let it pass unnoticed" (1927a, p. 62), the effect was unexpected. In the absence of adult condemnation, and of support for the child's own superego demands, the latter proved ineffectual for the task. A massive verbal and behavioral outpouring of her anal preoccupations now became the norm, much to the disgust and concern of the other members of her household. But the little girl greatly

enjoyed and "completely revelled" in the material thus made manifest. The new freedom from any restraint, internal or external,
quickly spread to other areas of personality and behavior, and
within days "she had become transformed into a cheerful, insolent,
and disobedient child, by no means dissatisfied with herself" (1927a,
p. 63). The retransformation of the child and the salvaging of the
analytic situation were achieved only by the analyst's presentation
of an ultimatum, namely, that the child choose between keeping
her analyst and saving the "dirty" disclosures for the analytic hour
or continuing as she was at home in which case she clearly had no
further need for the analyst. The child decided to cooperate with
the analyst and was again transformed into an inhibited and apa-
thetic individual. We are told that such transformations and retrans-
formations had to be accomplished several times during the course
of treatment. Thus the therapist steered a middle path between
alternately liberating the patient from her severe obsessional
neurosis and reinstating her "devil." Finally, the child herself
became capable of steering her own middle course between excessive inhibition and excessive license.

This example of the 6-year-old obsessional girl illustrates many
of the important characteristics of child analysis raised by Anna
Freud in this early period of her practice. In particular, it demon-
strates the relative weakness of the child's superego, the dependence of that part of the child's personality on the external adult
figures in his or her environment, and the consequent dual role of
the therapist-educator who had simultaneously to "allow and for-
bid, loosen and bind again" (1927a, p. 65).

The exquisite balance shown by Anna Freud both in her treatment of this young child and in her philosophy of approach to
childhood was by no means common among the avant garde of
those interested in child study. England at that time was a case in
point. The year 1920 has been seen as a turning point for England's
acceptance of psychoanalysis by educational and related institutions, with Percy Nunn and J. J. Findlay noted as contributing good
work (Low 1929). Nevertheless, certain practitioners cannot es-
cape criticism with regard to their exposition and interpretation of
Freudian ideas in the decade immediately following the First World
War.

Although admitting the existence of infantile sexuality and its manifestations, educators were initially inept at helping their pupils cope with their now progressively conceptualized biological drives. Fragments of psychoanalytic findings and teachings tended to be used piecemeal and misguidedly, and often in extreme forms to the detriment of other analytic knowledge. Some of the analytic pedagogy and experimental schooling of the period—for example, that associated with A. S. Neill at Summerhill and Bertrand Russell at Beacon Hill—is difficult to accept as a viable alternative education. The behavioral extremism allowed to these children was far removed from the fine balance between necessary repression and permissible gratification as early advocated by Freud, Ferenczi, and possibly others, and as demonstrated and emphasized by Anna Freud after the First World War. The more anarchical pedagogical experiments may well have reflected an overzealous reaction to the prevailing social mores, and the pioneering postwar educational applications of psychoanalysis have been described as "an expression of protest, a demand for the new" (Ekstein and Motto 1969), with specific techniques being evaluated only later.[7]

Misapplications of psychoanalysis to teaching, with inevitably poor results, were by no means confined only to enthusiasts with insufficient training in analysis.[8] Hoffer (1945) observed similar difficulties in the early experiments conducted by Bernfeld, Aichhorn, Schmidt (1924), and Zulliger. Hoffer, as noted above, also had personal experience of the 1919 Baumgarten Children's Home in Vienna and so was in a position to state that it was "to the surprise of those who had advocated it" (1945, p. 302) that psychoanalytically based education yielded such poor results. Many of the children, subjected to the early techniques founded too one-sidedly on freedom from repression, still went on to develop character disorders, behavior disturbances, poor concentration, and intoler-

---

[7]Observers with firsthand experience have, however, noted the practical brilliance of some of the early workers. For example, Ben Morris knew A. S. Neill and witnessed his work with children. Although a poor theoretician, Neill was apparently very good with his pupils (Personal communication, February 6, 1980).

[8]The well-known study by Green (1922) has been criticized on these grounds by the less well known but more knowledgeable review by Low (1923).

ance of routine, authority, and so forth. Concealed anxiety was usually the reason for such antisocial and related peculiarities, and the difficulties inherent in the early applied pedagogy were caused "not by an erroneous but by an incomplete" application of psychoanalysis (p. 303). A prominent British worker of the time was also critical of the early experimental schools, particularly in their attempts to apply only certain psychoanalytic theories and findings (Isaacs 1933, p. 408).

Despite these drawbacks, we may still assert that Freud's psychology, with its far-reaching structural revisionism of the 1920s, proved capable of providing the necessary understanding of personality to a degree whereby interested workers could apply a coherent and viable theory of mind to the various areas of experience and behavior. By advancing such psychoanalytic ego psychology, together with its educational and other applications, Anna Freud was destined to play an active and integrative role. She was among the first to point out that in the then "widening scope" of the applications of the classical psychoanalysis designed originally for neurotics, child analysis shared the enlarged field with Sadger's treatment of perversions, Aichhorn's work with delinquents, Federn's experiments with psychotics, and Alexander's and Staub's studies of criminals (A. Freud 1966e).

During Anna Freud's years of intensive analytical casework coupled with public restraint prior to the announcement of her independent technical recommendations—a period in which, as we indicated, her professional position was inadvertently, though inevitably, strengthened by, among other factors, the death of Hermine Hug-Hellmuth, the onset of her father's illness, and her appointment to the influential training committee in Vienna—a quite different though equally consequential event took place. This was the appearance in her life of an individual who became her close personal and professional mainstay, loyal friend, and industrious colleague for over 50 years.

Dorothy Burlingham arrived in September 1925 in Vienna from the United States, bringing her son with her for a consultation with Anna Freud (Dyer 1980, letter dated March 23, 1977). She had heard of psychoanalysis from friends, and when she became convinced of its value and benefit, her son became one of Anna

Freud's first patients. Eventually all four of Dorothy Burlingham's children received analytic treatment (Kennedy 1980). Burlingham herself trained with Sigmund Freud and became one of the earliest and staunchest members of Vienna's "Child Analysis School."

The connection between Anna Freud and Dorothy Burlingham was, in the words of the latter, "a simple and direct one" (Dyer 1980, letter dated March 23, 1977), and she added that "in many discussions with her on child development, my own interest grew and I was fortunate to be at the first discussion groups which she organised on child development and child psychoanalysis, and from then on I became part of the growing child analysis movement." This she considered to have been her child analysis training. Of particular note here is Burlingham's remark that all meetings in which Anna Freud took part were important "because she clarified the subject under discussion" (Dyer 1980, letter dated March 23, 1977).

A significant but relatively unknown development that occurred shortly after Dorothy Burlingham arrived in Europe was the opening in Vienna of a small private school associated with Anna Freud's analytical child education group. The following account relies on the testimony of Eva Rosenfeld, who was a member of the group. A slightly differing version—which, for example, ascribes an exclusive role to Dorothy Burlingham—appeared recently, though its sources were not named (Kennedy 1980).

Sometime during 1926 there was a meeting in Eva Rosenfeld's house in Vienna. Present were Anna Freud, Dorothy Burlingham, Eva Rosenfeld, and a schoolteacher named Peter Blos, who later also became a prominent psychoanalyst. "At that meeting," stated Eva Rosenfeld, "no one knows by whom. . . . It was decided to go ahead and form a nursery school" (Dyer 1980, interview dated May 31, 1977). Funds were provided by Dorothy Burlingham for a timber house to be built in Eva Rosenfeld's garden, and Peter Blos became the teacher in charge. Fifteen children were recruited, largely from those undergoing analytical treatment with Anna Freud, Burlingham, Aichhorn, Buxbaum, and others in the Vienna group. The school operated until the rise of Hitler in Germany, when many of the analysts left for the United States or England.

The nursery school of the Viennese analysts of the 1920s cer-

tainly deserves to be better known, as it was perhaps the most
formative precursor of later endeavors that similarly reflected the
close interactions between clinical and educational work and between pathology and normality, which would henceforth characterize both the Vienna child analysis "school" and all subsequent
ventures associated with Anna Freud and Dorothy Burlingham.

A short time after her first meeting with Dorothy Burlingham,
in January 1926 Anna Freud replaced Max Eitingon as the general
secretary of the International Psychoanalytic Association, or I. P. A.
(Jones 1957, p. 126). The arrangement was no doubt provisional at
the time and was not ratified until almost two years later at the
next I. P. A. congress. Nevertheless, the move was significant in
the world of psychoanalytic affairs and was a valuable preparation
for the "climate of response" before the wider announcement and
publication of the technical recommendations stemming from
Anna Freud's early experiences with her ten celebrated child cases.

Appointment as general secretary in this growth period of the
international movement carried with it the "understanding" that
the holder of the post would be next in line for the post of I. P. A.
president. Such had been the case when Karl Abraham, as secretary, replaced Ernest Jones as president in March 1924 and when
Eitingon as secretary then replaced Abraham as president in
January 1926. But for several reasons, Anna Freud never became
the I. P. A. president. By the time the next congress convened, the
I. P. A. statutes decreed that new presidents were to be first nominated and then popularly elected by each new congress (Report of
the Tenth I. P. A. Congress 1928), thereby eliminating the automatic succession of general secretary to the office of president. In
any case, Anna Freud's modesty in public life restrained her from
ever accepting any official position higher than that of joint vice-
president of the I. P. A.[9]

Sigmund Freud's 70th birthday was celebrated quietly at the

---

[9]As happened in 1934, 1936, and the late 1940s. On one occasion, in 1955, Miss
Freud was actually proposed for president but declined to accept the nomination
(Report of the 19th I. P. A. Congress 1956), a gesture quite in keeping with her
general character. A few years prior to her death she did finally permit her analytical
colleagues to elect her to an honorary presidency of the I. P. A.

Berggasse apartment on May 6, 1926. Those present included his daughter Anna, the other members of the committee, Paul Federn, and a few other close followers. It was at this meeting that Freud announced his retirement from any active role in the psychoanalytic movement (Jones 1957, p. 131). Clearly, and with good reason, Freud could now count on Anna to keep him informed of all relevant developments. The close personal and professional understanding between father and daughter was further shown in a letter to Marie Bonaparte a few days after the birthday event. No doubt with his birthday meeting in mind, Freud wrote that "Anna . . . shares my feeling that it is embarrassing to be publicly exposed to praise" (E. L. Freud 1960, pp. 369–370).

CHILD ANALYSIS LECTURES

Following her appointment as training secretary, in 1926 Anna Freud presented a formally recognized course of lectures on child analysis at the *Lehrinstitut* (training institute) of the Vienna Psychoanalytic Society. The talks were by invitation of the society, and they were attended by most of the members "as was the habit then" (A. Freud 1966e, p. 50). There were four lectures (*vier Vorträge*), dealing with the following technical aspects of the psychoanalysis of children: (1) preparation for analysis, (2) methods of child analysis, (3) the role of transference in child analysis, and (4) child analysis and child upbringing. Within a year the successful lecture course had been published in German, and a year later the first English translation appeared in the United States. With this book—*Einführung in die Technik der Kinderanalyse*, or *Introduction to the Technique of Child Analysis*—Anna Freud became, in her own right, a public figure open to scientific controversy.

The publication of Anna Freud's technical lectures was a personal, professional, and public milestone for her as well as for the development of child analysis as a prominent subspeciality of psychoanalysis, and of child psychology and child study generally. Her earlier papers had not been sufficiently comprehensive to have greatly influenced the overall theoretical structure and orientation of psychoanalytic child study, nor even its technical procedures. Indeed, one advantage of her early analytical training was that "no one was expected to produce theoretical papers at the beginning" (A. Freud 1967d, p. 514).

In contrast, Melanie Klein viewed the year 1920 as marking a new trend in child analysis study, 1922 and 1923 as beginning her own evolution of play analysis, 1920 to 1932 as representing more considerable work along two main lines, "one represented by Anna Freud and the other by myself" (Klein 1932). My view is that the years from 1920 to 1926 were a gestation period for child analysis and that the relatively late date of 1926 to 1927 was the actual beginning of the wider, and henceforward more vigorously debated, developments in modern child analysis. The debate began immediately, with the appearance in England of a critical symposium devoted entirely to the discussion of Anna Freud's technical recommendations. With this famous divergence of opinion and approach, the era of current psychoanalytic child psychology began.

Writing to Pfister, Sigmund Freud noted that of all the applied fields of psychoanalysis, "the only one that is really flourishing is that initiated by you in the field of education. It gives me great pleasure that my daughter is beginning to do good work in that field" (Meng and E. L. Freud 1962, p. 106).

The "good work" to which Freud alluded was now part of Anna's lectures. In her new introduction to the latest edition of the work—now known as the *Four Lectures on Child Analysis* (1927a) —she admitted that "If I now look back to my first book from the vantage point of almost half a century of psychoanalytic experience . . . a number of statements made . . . have to be modified" (1974a, pp. xi–xii). Although these modifications are important— being alterations in Anna Freud's views concerning the analyst's nonanalytic role in relation to parents and teachers, the preparation for analysis and means of achieving it, and her more sympathetic stance on the question of children showing transference phenomena—the lectures are still significant in their original form because they illustrate an essential stage in the author's thinking and indeed in the evolution of child analytic technique in general.

The first lecture was entitled "Preparation for Child Analysis," opening with the indications for analysis, a theme to which Anna Freud returned at least three other times (1945a; 1965a, chap. 6; 1968c). She contrasted the views of Melanie Klein in Berlin and the shared views of most of the members of the Vienna group. The latter advocated analysis only when there was a genuine infantile neurosis, whereas Klein believed analysis was beneficial for any disturbance of intellectual or emotional development and "goes still further in maintaining that an analysis also greatly benefits the development of any normal child" (A. Freud 1927a, p. 4) and would eventually become an essential part of all child care and upbringing. Although over the ensuing decades many orthodox analysts agreed with Klein, it is true that she invariably argued beyond her objective data and beyond any capacity to assess her hypotheses adequately. Klein's rapid and intuitive style of theory making, though exciting and stimulating, was less reliable, valid, and enduring than Anna Freud's more rigorously controlled approach to the formulation, testing, and reformulation of ideas.

In preparing her young patients for analysis Anna Freud needed to refute some of the accepted shibboleths in the orthodox technical approach. For example, she was quite prepared to encourage a child with the promise of a certain cure and did so in the case of the 6-year-old obsessional girl, albeit emphasizing the long time necessary for such a cure. In the case of an 11-year-old delinquent girl, following the recommendation of Aichhorn (1925) she sided with the girl in her conflicts with her parents. With a 10-year-old boy suffering from diffuse anxieties and perverse habits, she used many subtle ways to make herself indispensable to him. She typed letters for him and made all sorts of little things for him during the analytic hour. With another little girl needing similar preparation, Anna Freud "zealously crocheted and knitted during her appointments, and gradually clothed all her dolls and teddy bears" (1927a, p. 13). The reader might well ask where in all this is the restraint expected of the analyst, the caution with which the uncertainty of "cure" is held out, the scrupulous discretion in all personal matters, and the full freedom of the patient to terminate the analysis whenever so desired? In fact, asserted Anna Freud, she was merely extending in the new situation of child analysis certain elements and attitudes already implicit in the established adult-therapist technique, though there they were not especially stressed.

Although present-day practicing child analysts and analytical child therapists now have superior means of gaining access to the child's inner world, for example, in the analysis of defenses, largely because of Anna Freud[10] (see Chapter 3), there would nevertheless seem to be much of value to others in these early preparatory insights and recommendations. Teachers, child-care officials, prospective adopters, and all who need to meet difficult, anxious, and distrusting children may benefit enormously from these methods which, though no longer preferred in the realm of analysis proper, may still be valuable whenever actual analytical or prescribed therapeutic intervention is not required.

In her second lecture, "The Methods of Child Analysis," Anna Freud reviewed the technical means available to the adult analyst: conscious recollection, dream interpretation, free association, and the interpretation of transference phenomena. She saw some of these methods and their utility for child analysis as viable and efficacious, though she rejected others. Conscious memory, for example, could not be used with child patients to supply details, and with the rarest of exceptions, children simply do not enter into the fundamental rule of free association. On the other hand, children's dreams are easier to interpret than are those of adults, while in many instances extensive daydreams and related fantasy productions may be available, including serialized or "continued daydreams." She also considered drawings as another valuable source of analytical material in childhood.

It is perhaps in the interpretation of their dreams that children come the closest to the adult analyst's requirement for associations. Anna Freud was in the habit of telling her young dreamers that the dream could not come out of nothing, that "it must have fetched every bit from somewhere" (1927a, p. 25). The child then usually cooperated in the search for origins "and with great satisfaction

[10]Berta Bornstein must also be acknowledged as pioneering deliberate defense analysis.

follows up the separate images or words . . . into real life situations" (1927a, p. 25). Even two children of limited intellectual means were able thus to maintain a viable analytical stance.

According to Anna Freud, it was the child's refusal to enter into free association that ultimately led everyone concerned with analyzing children to seek substitutes of one kind or another. The celebrated play techniques of Hermine Hug-Hellmuth and Melanie Klein were just such alternative measures and, in one form or another, quickly achieved wide applicability with all those specializing in child analysis, and indeed with child psychologists and educationalists generally.

In her third lecture, "The Role of Transference in the Analysis of Children," Anna Freud examined the theoretical basis of the Kleinian play technique. She acknowledged Klein's great contribution to and advance over the method whereby Hug-Hellmuth studied the child in his or her own home. By offering to the child many toys and little or no adult intervention, the whole of the child's significant world was established under the analyst's eye. This and related merits make the Kleinian play technique "virtually indispensible to us for familiarising ourselves with small children, for whom action is more natural than verbal expression" (1927a, p. 37).

Where Anna Freud disagreed with Melanie Klein, however, was over the latter's assumption that the child's play actions were equivalent to the verbalizing adult's free associations, and also with regard to Klein's procedure of accompanying the child's play activities with a stream of verbal interpretations, which must have had what Anna Freud termed "a directing influence" on the individual's further psychological processes. Anna Freud refused to ascribe a symbolic significance to every action performed by the child, and, as was the habit of her father before her, she argued against her own standpoint: the child's play might be open to nonsymbolic interpretation, or it was the symbolic significance that caused certain actions, rather than others, to be reproduced. Her conclusion was that theoretical controversy would not resolve the matter and that the issue "must be left to be reviewed in the light of practical experience" (1927a, p. 39).

We should point out that even a belief in strict determinism need not imply a necessary causal significance for predominantly inner psychological processes. There is both an inner world and an outer world in all human experience, except perhaps the most regressed psychosis, and in the developmental phases of childhood in particular there is a strong element of intellectual curiosity directed at the outer world. It thus is quite legitimate, even for a psychoanalytical psychology, to posit for the events of that outer world an independent sphere of influence largely free from the emotional determinism of neurotic conflict. In other words, the child's play and related actions may sometimes have a significance related to a dominant and emotionally tinged inner world process or may at other times and with other actions have a significance not emotionally tinged but largely related to the random or systematic exploration of outer world processes. As common sense and everyday observation would lead us to expect, children may play and behave in stereotyped, repetitive, and essentially neurotic forms, or in intelligent, exploratory, and essentially conducive-to-learning forms.

The refusal of the child to indulge in free association has apparently not been fully or satisfactorily explained. Anna Freud listed two differing, but perhaps complementary, possibilities, namely, that the child resists suspending censorship of its thoughts because it does not trust its own ego strength or, alternatively, that the child may not sufficiently trust adults to be honest with them (A. Freud 1965a, p. 33). The second possibility holds open the prospect that under suitably encouraging circumstances, free association may be forthcoming, and Anna Freud was able to illustrate this with three examples, though still emphasizing their general rarity (1927a, pp. 32–34). The alternative, that the child does not trust its own ability to control and direct its associations, is in accord with the view that there is in the ego a "dread of the strength of the instincts" (A. Freud 1936a, pp. 58–60). In this view, the child sees free association as a threat to its ego security or, following Robert Waelder, as such a danger that "the ego's whole organisation may be destroyed or submerged" (A. Freud 1936a, p. 59).

Spontaneous and undefended free association is rare in normal childhood encounters, as, for example, in primary school. Typically, children need to be thrust suddenly and unexpectedly into startling situations, as with the many physical activities taking place on the school playground. The undefended association is often a single word, socially taboo, and is quickly followed by signs of alarm, guilt, and denial. A more deliberate and extended chain of free association was observed only on a single occasion by this writer. An 11-year-old girl with a low IQ and poor mental ability was chanting rhymes and jumping rope with friends who all had taken turn at demonstrating their rope-rhyme coordination. When pressed to take her turn, the girl in question, after several silent turns followed by jeers or encouragement from her friends, produced the following chant that she claimed to be "making up": "Nickey, pickey, pickey nose. Ackey, cackey. . . ." (child dissolved into laughter). The term *cacky* or *cackas* was a local dialect word for feces in the child's region, and the general trend of the rhyme is clear. As the chain of associations proceeded, it showed a deteriorating degree of conscious ego control and became increasingly regressive until the last stage when the distortion was so gross that censorship was rapidly and suddenly reinstated and laughter provided a substitute and partial gratification. The final and unspoken association, with its forbidden pleasure, was recognized and appreciated by the girl's circle of friends, who also joined in the half-suppressed laughter.

The divergence between the Kleinian and the Viennese views of the symbolic content of play was, in the same third lecture of Anna Freud's technical series, broadened into the discussion of the role of transference in play and in child analytic therapy generally. It was this issue, the role of transference as a technical aid, that comprised the single most important topic in the early technical lectures and that largely served to distinguish those who stood with Klein and those who stood with the Vienna group, that is, Anna Freud.

Anna Freud did not doubt the importance of the child's positive transference to the analyst, pointing to her own initiatives in establishing a strong affectionate attachment and dependence in her young patients. This positive transference became "the pre-requisite for all later analytic work" (1927a, p. 40). In contrast to the analytical work with adults, however, Anna Freud believed that negative transference phenomena disrupted work with children, as the latter inevitably contained a reeducational element and the child would make its best efforts only for those with whom it had a strong and positive bond.

Even though she offered examples of instances in which the child analyst could become, as in the case of adult analysts, "the target of the patient's friendly or hostile impulses" (1927a, p. 43), Anna Freud nonetheless refused to accept that the child had thereby made "a good transference" to the extent of forming a transference neurosis. She listed a number of reasons why the child patient could neither be said to give up its attachment to the old objects that had been the center of its fantasies nor to shift its neurosis onto the analyst. There are essentially two reasons. First, the child is nearer to the original objects or parents who are still present in reality to satisfy the child's emotional life. Second, the child analyst cannot remain a shadowy and aloof partner in the therapy, a *tabula rasa* on which the patient may project—and learn to recognize the projection of—his or her own inner world of loves and hates. In Anna Freud's technique, carrying as it does certain educational implications, the analyst must alternately allow or disallow and approve or disapprove, and such a figure "is un-fortunately a poor transference object, that is, of little use when it comes to interpreting the transference" (1927a, p. 46). It follows that the child will continue to act out his or her difficulties and conflicts primarily in the home; that the therapist will constantly need to upgrade the information from that sector; and the child's behavioral acts in the therapy situation will not be strictly in-terpretable, as recommended in Klein's technique.

Twenty years later Anna Freud still doubted that the child formed a transference neurosis along the lines shown by adult patients, and in a now classic contribution (1945a) she argued that part of the child's neurosis remained centered on the original parent figures and that only part therefore remained available, at best, for the formation of genuine transference relations. After another 20 years, Anna Freud reviewed her initial standpoint, pointing out that "taught by experience, by the elimination of the introductory phase . . . and by the deliberate use of defence analysis [Bornstein] . . . I have modified my former opinion that transference in childhood is restricted to single transference reactions" (1965a, p. 38). Even in this later work, however, there is still the qualified acceptance of only a partial transference neurosis in the child, as opposed to the adult. Moreover, and with characteristic clarity, the author now pointed to two other factors that had been identified as effectively refuting any possibility of successfully asserting for children a full-blown transference neurosis. These were that (1) the analytical observer, lacking the child's verbal free associations, failed to secure all the evidence necessary for a full assessment of the transference situation; and (2) the transference reactions of the child overemphasized the aggressive content, as opposed to the libidinal one, owing to the child's facility for acting out rather than verbally associating.

In the fourth lecture of her technical series, "Child Analysis and the Upbringing of Children," Anna Freud returned to the role of the parents in the child's development. The interest and sympathy of parents with the aims and teachings of psychoanalysis were, from these early lectures onward, of fundamental importance to her, for only thus could there be a smooth "transition from the analytic education in the course of treatment back to education in the parental home", (1927a, p. 66). With this early acknowledgment of the "analytic education" aspect of child therapy, Anna Freud became a powerful ally of teachers, educators, parents, and all who studied normal children, their development, social provision, and so forth. This realistic appreciation of the complementarity between treatment and education, between normal and psychopathological processes, and between the individual and society was always a hallmark of Anna Freud's work. Apart from her technical analytical and later theoretical contributions, this alone has identified her as an eminent psychological and pedagogical prophet in our time.

The hostile reception accorded to Anna Freud's published lectures by certain incredulous sections of the psychoanalytic com-

munity outside Vienna could scarcely have been foreseen at the
time and was probably largely due to the existence of two contrasting technical schools of child analysis. For the past few years
these schools had been developing along divergent lines in London
and Vienna, and their differences now began to show publicly. In
response to the appearance of Anna Freud's *Einfuhrung in die
Technik der Kinderanalyse*, a number of papers appeared before
the British Psychoanalytical Society in London,[11] virtually amount-
ing to a critical symposium aimed at the views of the Vienna
school of child analysis. The papers, by Melanie Klein, Joan Riviere,
Nina Searl, Edward Glover, Ernest Jones, and Ella F. Sharpe, were
immediately published in the *International Journal of Psychoanalysis*. Anna Freud's response was an unpublished communication to the Vienna Society on January 25, 1928 (Report of the
Vienna Psychoanalytical Society 1928).

Elsewhere the reception was less hostile. Anna Freud's book
appeared in February 1927, and she sent a copy to her friend Lou
Andreas-Salomé in Gottingen. In March, at Max Eitingon's invitation, Anna Freud attended a discussion of her book at a meeting of the Berlin Psychoanalytic Society. Lou regretted having been
unable to attend the Berlin discussions and wrote to Sigmund
Freud that Eitingon had described them to her as "truly stimulating" (Pfieffer 1972, letter dated May 4, 1927).

In regard to the technical divergences between the two major
child analysis schools of this period, both their a priori theoretical
assumptions and their practical methods influenced the therapist-
patient dynamics, and consequently the material elicited in the
treatment situation. For Klein, the assumption of equivalence
between the child's behavioral acts and missing verbal associations,
and the practical elimination in treatment of prohibitions and
restraints—"If the analyst, even only temporarily, becomes the
representative of the educative agencies, if he assumes the role of
the super-ego, at that point he blocks the way of the instinctual

---

[11]On May 4 and 18, 1927. The paper by Klein (1927) is available in her later
collected *Contributions* (1948, pp. 152–182, with a postscript dated 1947). For
other papers in the critical symposium, see Symposium on Child Analysis 1927.

impulses to Cs" (1948, p. 182)—inevitably led to the manifestation and recognition of a much fuller transference situation. The concomitant danger, however, was that in relinquishing any "superego stance," together with those related aspects of prohibition and restraint that were realistic and egosyntonic, the analyst's a priori empirical skepticism was reduced, as were the a fortiori experimental checks and counterchecks during the therapeutic-observational situation. Klein's genius lay in her ability to see more of the child's psyche than almost anyone else could, but her paramount weakness was her poor validatory procedures and the consequent inability to distinguish the real from the merely inferred or imagined in her perception of the child's inner world.

Conversely, Anna Freud assumed only a partial equivalence between behavioral and verbal acts, together with a practical emphasis on educative and reeducational techniques in the therapy situation, which constrained the child's uninhibited behavior. Less of the transference neurosis—if one existed—would be seen. However, what was observed could be better assessed against objective criteria, the child's openness to rational direction, and so forth. By assuming that the child was capable of both transference and nontransference reactions, the analyst would be better able to distinguish between these two types of phenomena, even though transference reactions might not be as prolific as with those using the Kleinian technique.

Anna Freud's genius thus is her balancing of imagination and skepticism with conjecture and validation. She was, in short, a rational scientist and a powerful ally of psychoanalysis, which has often been criticized as leaning too far toward the intuitive and poorly validated in its theoretical and experimental studies.

The ailing older Freud could now leave the public world of psychoanalytic affairs to his daughter Anna, who had scientifically come of age. After his 70th birthday pronouncement regarding his "retirement" noted above, Freud dispatched a circular letter stating that he could no longer attend the meetings of the Vienna Psychoanalytical Society (Jones 1957, letter dated November 23, 1926). Instead, a small number of carefully chosen analysts were invited to the Freud apartment on the second Friday of each month for an evening of scientific discussion. These meetings continued for the next year or two and, without doubt, offered to Anna Freud an invaluable opportunity in scientific statecraft.

Ernest Jones (1957) wrote that around this time Freud considered Heinrich Meng and Franz Alexander to be the most promising of the younger analysts, though in Freud's letter to Pfister, cited above in regard to Anna Freud's child analysis lectures, we saw that the father also had a high opinion of his daughter's abilities and early achievements. Both Meng and Alexander remained in contact with Anna Freud and her work over the years. The Swiss-born Meng, eight years older than Anna Freud, had trained in Vienna with Paul Federn and in 1926 became, with Ernst Schneider, a founding editor of the important new *Zeitschrift für Psychoanalytische Pädagogik*. Anna Freud made a number of contributions to the journal over the years (1929a, 1931a, 1935a) and between 1931 and 1937 was herself a member of the editorial panel. Many years later Meng continued to secure Anna Freud's contributions (1957c), and he also was a coeditor of the Freud-Pfister correspondence to which Anna devoted a preface (1963d).

Franz Alexander trained with Hanns Sachs in Berlin after World War I and emigrated to the United States in 1930. His studies of psychosomatics, criminality, and technique received frequent and sympathetic citation by Anna Freud over the years.

THE CHILDREN'S SEMINAR

In Vienna, Anna Freud's original course of technical lectures was quickly followed by the organization of a *Kinderseminar* which, many years later, she described as "a first seminar on child analysis," with regular meetings at which "cases were presented, technical innovations described, and theoretical conclusions put up for discussion" (1966e, p. 50). She also observed that "from 1927 onwards, a group of analysts . . . held regular meetings with me to discuss the child analytic technique I had suggested, to report on cases treated with this method," and so on (1974e, p. viii).

The seminar at the Vienna *Lehrinstitut* may be regarded as the direct heir of those informal discussion groups earlier convened by Anna Freud in her home, involving Bernfeld, Aichhorn, and no doubt occasional others. But the broad scope of work that the children's seminar covered was not widely recognized, even in the Vienna Society itself. Paul Federn, then president of the society, reported on the scientific work of his colleagues, referring somewhat perfunctorily to "the so-called children's seminar [that] reviews the literature" (Report of the Tenth I. P. A. Congress 1928, p. 144). Much later Anna Freud recalled that this discussion group was officially known as the "children's seminar," not because of the kind of material discussed, "but because the discussants themselves were considered to be in analytic infancy" (1967d, p. 513).

Nevertheless, many talented students of psychoanalytic child study—many of whom later became leaders in the field in the United States and Britain—joined the child study seminar. Edith Buxbaum frequently attended during the decade after 1927, as did Dorothy Burlingham, Marianne Kris, and Anny Angel Katan (Dyer 1980, letters dated July 19, 1977; April 19, 1977; and March 15, 1978). Other members of the seminar included Editha Sterba, Jenny Pollack, Robert Waelder, Hedwig and Willi Hoffer, Wilhelm Reich (before 1930), and Grete and Edward Bibring. Over the next ten years the Vienna Children's Seminar became better known, attracted many students and visitors from abroad and, for many, epitomized the best work of the now ascendant Continental School of Child Analysis associated with Anna Freud. Twenty years later the impact of these early seminars remained fresh in the minds of participants. Otto Sperling, for instance, in reviewing the case history of 3-year-old Rudy, pointed out that he first presented the material in Anna Freud's seminar in 1931 (1954).

The *Kinderseminar* was not unique to Vienna in this period, though Anna Freud's group was both longer lived and more authoritative than any other group. In Russia there was an active interest in the progressive new child psychology, and two to three years before the introduction of the Children's Seminar in Vienna, the Russian Psychoanalytic Society began a *Kinderseminar* in

Moscow, conducted by Sabina Spielrein-Scheftel and having 30 members (Report of the Russian Psychoanalytic Society 1924). Other prominent child analysts in Russia at that time were Tatiana Rosenthal, Moshe Wulff, Vera Schmidt, and J. Ermakoff. Though relatively unknown today, the contributions of the Russian group were considered important at the time, and Anna Freud acknowledged in particular Schmidt's experimental residential home run on analytical lines (1930a, pp. 113–114).

There was a casual and apparently incidental meeting that was crucial to the development of psychoanalytic child psychology. During the summer of 1927 while Anna Freud and her father were on holiday on the Austrian Semmering, with Dorothy Burlingham and her children in an adjoining house, the young tutor to the Burlingham children made his first acquaintance with Anna Freud. The young teacher, a Danish-German artist named Erik Homburger, was encouraged by Peter Blos to join the analytic school set up in Eva Rosenfeld's Vienna garden. While working at the school as a teacher, Homburger became a pupil at the Vienna Psychoanalytic Society and trained in psychoanalysis with Anna Freud and in case analysis with Aichhorn, Helene Deutsch, and Edward Bibring as his supervisory analysts. During his formal training period, between 1929 and 1933, Homburger—who in later years became better known as Erik Erikson—recalled that as part of training he attended all "required seminars," including Anna Freud's *Kinderseminar*, Deutsch's adult seminar, and Hartmann's and Kris's theory seminar (Dyer 1980, letter dated November 1, 1977). Graduating from the Vienna Society in 1933, Erikson almost immediately emigrated to the United States. His highly original work was not confined to early child analysis but embraced anthropology and sociology before turning to a solution to the psychoanalytic study of the human condition. Erik Erikson has been, without doubt, the most gifted and influential child psychologist to come out of the Vienna Children's Seminar.

The differences between the child analysis schools of Vienna and London continued to cause occasional academic sparks, though these were largely confined to confrontations at the various meetings of the International Psychoanalytic Association. At the Tenth

Congress, held in Innsbruck, Austria, on September 1–3, 1927, Anna Freud opened the scientific proceedings by reading to the gathering her absent father's paper on humor (1927b). Of even greater interest from our viewpoint, was Anna Freud's own paper, *"Zur theorie der Kinderanalyse"* (1928a). This was the first scientific contribution she ever offered at a meeting of the International and it was read at the third scientific session along with the papers by Melanie Klein and Mary Chadwick from London. Klein's paper examined the early stages of the oedipus complex, and she reiterated her view that this nuclear personality constellation became operative "earlier than is usually supposed" (1948, p. 202), i.e., around three years of age. By this Klein presumably meant earlier than Anna Freud and the Continental School believed. Differences such as this, concerning the status of the young child's developing superego and related aspects of personality, were one of the areas of contention and divergence between the two child analysis schools.

The thrust of Anna Freud's Innsbruck paper on the theory of child analysis was that the infantile neurosis not only derives its existence and continuation from internal forces, as in the case of adult neurosis, but also is linked to external forces, like parents and perhaps other environmental variables. Interwoven in this view of the essential difference between the adult and the infantile forms of neurosis was Anna Freud's corresponding stand in relation to the differences in the relative degree of independence and autonomy achieved by the superego in the adult and in the child. Thus, whereas in the analysis of the adult, "we are dealing with a situation in which the superego has achieved full independence and is no longer subject to external influences"; in the analysis of the child, the therapist is faced with situations "where the superego has not yet achieved full independence; where it operates all too clearly for the sake of those from whom it received its commands, the parents and persons in charge of the child, and is swayed in its demands by every change in the relationship with these people" (1928a, pp. 171–172).

Anna Freud's theoretical views were supported by observations from her own clinical practice, in particular the 6-year-old obsessional girl discussed previously, and by observations published by others. Moshe Wulff is cited as having intervened in one case to advise parents that their demands for early toilet cleanliness were too excessive and could not be met by their little infant daughter. When the parents then lessened their demands and at the same time offered the child reassurances that she was still loved, even though wetting herself, the child's anxiety symptoms improved dramatically. Anna Freud pointed out that Wulff actually carried out a therapeutic experiment that demonstrated the source of the little girl's phobic anxiety attacks. That source was an external rather than an internal one. If the child's neurosis had been caused by a strict and largely autonomous superego, then the parents' reassurances could have had little effect on it (1928a, p. 173).

Anna Freud's view of the relatively plastic nature of the child's superego can be widely applied, not only to mental health care workers and psychotherapists, but also to teachers, parents, and all who deal with children, especially at the behavioral level. But this range of normality, as opposed to pathology options, is not available with Klein's differing theoretical model, for instance. Although Anna Freud revised her model of the infantile neurosis, especially in regard to the place accorded to transference phenomena, she never fundamentally changed her mind on the question of the child's superego, as was made clear in some later correspondence (Dyer 1980, letters dated November 7, 1976, and March 28, 1977). She also established in her early works her appreciation of the complementary roles of the internal and external in human life, the relative place of the somatic and environmental with the mediating psyche, and the crucial appreciation of psychological as opposed to outer world reality. Moreover, and in the best tradition of a scientific researcher assigning probability rather than certainty to provisional theoretical models, she continued to leave open the extent of significant differences and implications between the two major therapeutic strategies, that is, between the analyzing and influencing of psychological conflict and compromises, on the one hand, and the modification of external and environmental factors, on the other hand (1971a).

Anna Freud's Innsbruck paper was published in 1928 in the *Internationale Zeitschrift für Psychoanalyse* and republished the following year in the second edition of *Einführung in die Technik der Kinderanalyse*, along with the four technical lectures. That same year the paper also appeared in the *International Journal of Psychoanalysis*, translated into English by Nancy Procter-Gregg. Thereafter this important short paper became an integral part of the composite volume of Anna Freud's technical recommendations, which had several editions (1946d, 1974e). At the close of the Innsbruck Congress, at Eitingon's proposal, Anna Freud was unanimously elected to the office of general secretary to the I. P. A., thus confirming her occupancy of the office. The official report of the Innsbruck Congress was itself edited and produced by Miss Freud in her first term as general secretary, and here too she broke new ground and established the model for all subsequent congress reports. Earlier reports had been meager productions: that of the previous congress, edited by Eitingon, had been less than one page (Report of the Ninth I. P. A. Congress 1926). The Innsbruck report, by contrast, had more than 20 pages and for the first time presented detailed coverage of congress events, in a framework of headings that separated business affairs, scientific proceedings, and reports from component societies (Report of the Tenth I. P. A. Congress 1928, A. Freud 1928b).

After Innsbruck the structure of Sigmund Freud's inner committee was altered so as not to seem so exclusive a group. It thenceforward consisted of officials of the International Psychoanalytic Association. The first "official" committee was composed of Anna Freud in her capacity as I. P. A. general secretary; the I. P. A. president, Eitingon; the two vice-presidents, Jones and Ferenczi; and one new member, van Ophuijsen, who was currently treasurer of the International Association (Jones 1957, pp. 143–144).

In April 1928 the monthly discussion group meeting at the Berggasse apartment considered Freud's recently published *Future of an Illusion* (1927a), which emphasized the "renunciation of instinct" necessary for the emergence of civilization and religious thought. After the meeting Anna Freud wrote to the absent Lou to criticize the poor quality of the discussion comments (Pfieffer 1972, pp. 173–174). Her father apparently shared her opinion, as suggested by his own letter to Lou written the following month (Pfieffer 1972, pp. 174–175). The scientific meetings at Freud's apartment were temporarily suspended about this time because of his poor health. But, by the early 1930s, a regular "Wednesday circle" of close associates was once more convening regularly, and it was then that Robert Waelder became a closer colleague of father and daughter (Guttman 1969).

Anna Freud's work at the Vienna Training Institute now required her each Monday to chair the seminar on the technique of child analysis (Report to the Vienna Psychoanalytic Society 1929), and she also regularly gave a recapitulatory paper on "The Technique of Child Analysis Compared with the Analysis of Adults" (Hitsch-mann 1932). On their return from a visit to Berlin, Anna Freud and Siegfried Bernfeld jointly presented to the Vienna Society their "Report of a Discussion Held in Berlin on the Psychoanalytical Training of Teachers" (Report of the Vienna Psychoanalytic Society 1929). In her comments Anna Freud compared the changes in a teacher's work after undergoing a personal analysis with the changes in patients undergoing psychoanalysis. In commenting on a future "analytical pedagogy," she acknowledged that her views drew heavily on her father's recent publication. In the absence of other information, this presumably meant that she viewed the process of education, and indeed therapy, as requiring some "re-nunciation of instinct," much as Freud (1927a) had argued for religion and civilization in general.

For a period in the late twenties, Berlin was almost a second home for the Freuds. Ernst Simmel ran the Sanatorium Schloss Tegel there, and on a number of occasions Freud received medical treatment there. Tegel was the second great service rendered to Freud by Simmel, who, at the Budapest Congress in 1918, had been one of the influential medical-military authorities interested in the latest psychoanalytic findings. Here too, at Tegel, he offered a meeting place where child analysts working in Berlin could meet and exchange views with Anna Freud. Berta Bornstein and Annie Reich were "Berliners" too at this time, and they all often met and discussed technical problems. The Polish-born Bornstein had been drawn into psychoanalysis by the influential home-seminars of Otto Fenichel in the early twenties. After 1929 Bornstein moved to Vienna to work. Brody (1974) maintains that Anna Freud early recognized Bornstein's talent, and her publications were included by Anna Freud in a recent bibliography of early child analysis pioneers (1974e, pp. 189–194). Although no formal school is associated with her name, Bornstein's technical innovations and method rank with those of Anna Freud and Melanie Klein.

The emergence of Anna Freud as an independent and commanding analytical figure was by now established, at least in continental Europe. The Berlin Psychoanalytic Society invited her to speak at the opening of their new premises and noted that "Fraulein Freud hailed the extension of the Berlin Institute as a new and logical step forward in the development in which the psychoanalytic organisation reposes its hopes for the future" (Report of the Berlin Psychoanalytic Society 1929, p. 533). The next year the South-West German Psychoanalytical Society also invited Anna Freud to attend their inaugural celebrations for the opening of a new institute in Frankfurt. As a contribution to the events there, she presented to an audience of several hundred a public lecture on "Pedagogy," which unfortunately was never published. Other speakers were Bernfeld, Sachs, and Federn. The Frankfurt press was especially appreciative of Anna Freud, "both of her personality and the subject matter of her lecture" (Report of the Frankfurt Psychoanalytic Institute 1930, p. 246). Key figures involved at that time with the work of the Frankfurt Institute and with Anna Freud were Karl Landauer, Frieda Fromm-Reichmann, and Heinrich Meng.

Important personal encounters continued to color Anna Freud's life. The visits to Tegel, for example, often coincided with meetings with Frau Lou who came from Gottingen, and Dorothy Burlingham—perhaps by now Anna Freud's closest confidante—generally accompanied her. Then, in March 1929, a new relationship was formed, though a more detached and less intimate one than the other two. In that month Marie Bonaparte was instrumental in introducing to Sigmund Freud a new personal physician, Max

Schur. The choice for such a position proved wise, and Jones remarked that for the ailing Freud, Schur and Anna "made an ideal pair of guardians" (1957, p. 154). Anna Freud later confirmed that "in the nurse-doctor relationship with him, I have met him at his best. . . . We formed a bond between us then which will last for our lifetimes" (1971e, p. 6).

INVITED LECTURES
TO NURSERY TEACHERS

Unlike her father's work, to which the academic world in Austria had a shocked and negative reaction, Anna Freud's work early received wide public acclaim, as did that of her close colleague August Aichhorn. During 1929, at the invitation of Vienna's education authorities, both Aichhorn and Anna Freud were invited to give courses of lectures on psychoanalysis to the city's teachers and child-care workers, a development that drew appropriate recognition from Helene Deutsch in her report on the activities of the Vienna Training Institute (*Bulletin of the International Psychoanalytic Association* 1929).

Among the numerous *Pädagogen* attending Anna Freud's lectures were several notable Montessori-trained teachers. Thesi Bergmann, for example, eventually published a work on childhood with Anna Freud (Bergmann 1965). Of even greater standing was Lili Peller, who made important contributions of her own, nonetheless acknowledging the influence of Anna Freud on her thinking and practice (Ekstein and Motto 1969).[12] As Lili Roubiczek she was listed as an associate member of the Vienna Psychoanalytic Society in 1931. Peller was also influenced by the Viennese academic child psychologist Charlotte Buhler (Ekstein and Motto 1969), and apparently many of the younger generation of students attended lectures and seminars at both the Institute of Psychoanalysis and the

---

[12]Peller was one of the first to start a model nursery unit based on Montessori's and psychoanalytic principles.

University of Vienna's psychology department. During the next decade or so several of Buhler's postdoctoral associates, for example, Liselotte Frankl and Ilse Hellman, were drawn into a close and lasting involvement with child analysis.

In the next major contribution of her Vienna period, addressed specifically to teachers and educators, Anna Freud dealt with several areas of psychoanalytic observation and theory, for example, "Infantile Amnesia and the Oedipus Complex" (lecture 1), "The Instinctual Life of Early Childhood" (lecture 2), and "The Latency Period" (lecture 3). The metapsychological framework she used, as in most of her Vienna-based writings and teachings, leaned heavily on Sigmund Freud's structural approach developed after 1920. Anna Freud's own strong developmental framework also was already much in evidence.

Her lectures began with certain directly observable and apparently simple phenomena in children's behavior and proceeded to explain them by applying psychoanalysis as a coherent and systematic model. Children, for example, were observed as bringing with them to school[13] a number of preformed behaviors. They might thus approach the teacher "with the suspicion, defiance or wariness which they have acquired in their earlier dealings with other adults" (1930a, p. 76). Using a scheme of child development involving early dependence on the mother, rivalry and aggression in relation to siblings, a crucial love-hate relationship with the father, and repression of early conflicts at an oedipal stage because of fear of parental rejection, Anna Freud was able to show that what teachers[14] see enacted "are really only repetitions and new editions of very old conflicts of which you are the target but not the cause" (1930a, p. 88). Thus was devised a general paradigm of the basic psychoanalytic proposition regarding the infantile roots of behavior, i.e., the assumption that later behavior and experience are based on what occurred earlier in life.

---

[13]The school situation could also be replaced by the juvenile court, the probation office, the therapy room, the interview building, and so on.

[14]Besides teachers, these could also be youth leaders, police, care officers, foster parents, and the like.

Between the two world wars, the father was of great importance as a figure in child theory: "He is hated as a rival. . . . But he is also loved and admired" (1930a, p. 86), and the 4- to 5-year-old child's typical response to this dilemma is twofold, namely, to repress negative ambivalent responses and to introject and set up internally an admired father-figure representation. This superego, identified by Sigmund Freud as "the heir to the oedipus complex" (1923, pt. 5), was given by Anna Freud a quite specific applied value for teachers and others who deal with children. Thus, between the age of 5 or 6 years and puberty, the child confronting the adult is "divided within himself"—structurally his or her personality may be viewed as possessing an id, ego, and superego —and "his superego, the successor to his parents, is on the side of the educators" (1930a, p. 119). The lecturer recommended to her audience of educators that they recognize this split within the child, and assume for each child the role of superego, thus becoming, for the school or class, "the ideal of the group" (1930a, p. 120). The advantages that should then follow are (1) voluntary self-discipline replacing forced obedience, and (2) social and group bonds being encouraged among children.

Anna Freud presented similar views three years later at a Congress of Early Childhood Educators (1934a), and on both occasions her advice to educators followed her previous advice and recommendations to child analysts, whom she also had encouraged to assume "the place of the child's ego ideal for the duration of the analysis" (1927a, p. 60). The underlying philosophy of harmony and balance is evident too in her lectures to educators, and in a manner entirely Greek in its ideal, Anna Freud took a middle road between views of the child as wholly good or wholly bad. She thus achieved a significant rapprochement between the apparently divergent fields of education and psychopathology, though her basic source of case material was now decidedly the realm of clinical psychoanalysis. Here too the fundamental quality of balance was evident, as when she stated that "a fixation and subsequent neurotic illness may occur either when the impulse is allowed full expression, or, conversely, when it is entirely denied expression. The path to mental health lies somewhere between these two extremes. Evidently the problem is to find a middle course" (1934a, p. 182).

Certain progressive educationalists of the day represented the antithesis of much that the Vienna child analysts taught. A. S. Neill, for example, "raged against the father principle" because of his own unhappy childhood relationship, and with the children with whom he worked, he became "one of the gang" (Ilan 1963). Neill's professional activities were principally determined by his childhood fear of his father and by his anxiety in the presence of anything symbolizing the father figure. His emphasis on such curricular interests as games, handicrafts, and story telling reflects the typical habits of the prepubertal boy, and his extreme emphasis on democratic procedure in his work was, in effect, antiauthoritarianism bordering on anarchy. That freedom may become license and expression mere acting out are of consequence to all who attempt to educate and teach, and the paradox of "freedom versus authority" is at the heart of all the affairs of childhood.

Though maintaining that the time, around 1930, was yet too early for a detailed exposition of the "new analytic type of education" (1930a, p. 128), which was mostly still restricted to analytically trained parents and teachers, Anna Freud identified three major contributions that psychoanalytic child study had made to education: (1) it offered the means to criticize existing methods; (2) it extended the adult worker's knowledge of adult-child relationships and their dynamics; and (3) as a therapeutic method, psychoanalysis could "repair the injuries inflicted on the child during the process of education" (1930a, p. 129). If one wished to extend the list in the light of subsequent progress in child analysis, then it would certainly come to include: (4) a thoroughgoing developmental theory with important implications and applications at all stages of the child's growth from infancy to adolescence; (5) a multistage hierarchical model of the mind relevant to studies of learning theory and cognitive function; and (6) an increasingly exhaustive coverage of what may be termed "the pathology of normal schooling," studies of school phobia, learning failure, delinquency, and so forth.

To return to the language of psychoanalytic metapsychology, the task of educating the child is, in Anna Freud's synthesis, "to find for each stage in the child's life the right proportion between drive gratification and drive control" (1930a, p. 128; 1934a, p. 182). It is the child's and future adult's sanity and equilibrium that is at stake, and "which educational goals are compatible with mental health" must be clear (1934a, p. 179).

Anna Freud's invitation lectures to pedagogues were soon published (1929a, 1930a), and like her technical lectures to analysts three years earlier, the *Einführung in die Psychoanalyse für Pädagogen* had several editions over the next 30 or 40 years and were translated into several languages including Dutch, French, Italian, Spanish, and Japanese. An English edition, translated by Barbara Low, appeared in 1931 with the title *Introduction to Psychoanalysis for Teachers and Parents*. In her own latest revision of the lectures, Anna Freud entitled this work *Four Lectures on Psychoanalysis for Teachers and Parents*. Both sets of her early lectures, together with one or two shorter pieces, make up the first volume of her collected writings.[15]

The acceptance of much of Anna Freud's work continued, and in 1931 she sent a contribution to Carl Murchison's eminently respectable *Handbook of Child Psychology*. For some reason, possibly to avoid duplication elsewhere, she did not include this essay in her later collected writings. The essay's bibliography cited Abraham, Aichhorn, Freud, Ferenczi, and Hug-Hellmuth and is of interest in indicating the authors of greatest value to Anna Freud in this early general discourse on child analysis (1931a). In the same year she became one of the editorial leaders of the foremost child study journal of that time.[16] In October 1931 the town council of Freiberg, Moravia, in Czeckoslovakia, placed a commemorative plaque on the house where Sigmund Freud had been born. Anna Freud went there and read the letter of thanks that her father had written to the town's mayor (Jones 1957, p. 172).

[15]*The Writings of Anna Freud*, 8 vols. New York: I. U. P.; London: Hogarth Press and the Institute of Psychoanalysis, 1968–1982.

[16]The journal being the *Zeitschrift für Psychoanalytische Pädagogik*. Anna Freud was also one of the editors of the *Psychoanalytic Quarterly* from 1932 to 1939.

From 1931 to 1933 Anna Freud was the secretary of the Vienna Psychoanalytic Society. This was a joint post that she shared initially with Robert Jokl and later with Herman Nunberg (Report of the Vienna Psychoanalytic Society 1931). During the same period she was also secretary to the important training committee of the Vienna *Lehrinstitut* and general secretary of the International Psychoanalytic Association. As psychoanalytic business secretary par excellence, she thus had the opportunity of gaining an almost unparalleled insight into the organized world of psychoanalytic affairs, at both the local and international levels. It was a professional apprenticeship that would not be wasted in later decades, and on more than one occasion Anna Freud demonstrated her ability to manage business affairs so as to avoid damaging the good growth of psychoanalysis as she saw it.

Having evolved its technical method and established its seminar of international repute, and led by a figure of rapidly growing stature and professional rank, the Vienna School of Child Analysis was now ready to offer the scientific world something more: Anna Freud's theoretical study of the ego and its defensive operations.[17]

[17]The high point of the Vienna child analysis group, before the publication of *The Ego and the Mechanisms of Defence* (1936a) was the publication in January 1935 of a special "Child Analysis Number" of the *Psychoanalytic Quarterly*. The issue was organized by Anna Freud (1935b), and her cocontributors included Anny Angel, Edith Buxbaum, Editha Sterba, and Dorothy Burlingham, as well as Bernfeld, Homburger, Berta Bornstein, and Steff Bornstein. The catalytic effect of such material, particularly in the United States, was more noticeable as the 1930s progressed.

CHAPTER THREE

Defense Theory of The Ego

With the publication of *The Ego and the Mechanisms of Defence* in 1936, it is widely acknowledged that Anna Freud gave us both her most celebrated work and her most significant theoretical contribution. Though the former view is a matter of proven record, we reject the latter as no longer tenable in view of her monumental contributions to the developmental field after 1960 (see chap. 6).

Recognition of the importance of Anna Freud's analysis of the ego's defensive activities was virtually immediate, with reviews appearing in the foremost analytical journals (French 1938, Hendrick 1938, Reik 1941). The reviews in the *International Journal of Psychoanalysis* were grouped into what amounted to a critical symposium on the subject (Jones 1938, Fenichel 1938, E. Kris 1938), a phenomenon with which we are by now familiar in this account and one that should effectively refute any idea that Freud's daughter was, in these early days, accorded any undue "special consideration." Over the decades the discussion of defense processes in the psychoanalytic literature has continued, though conversely, and, as one notable analyst who trained at the London Institute in the late 1930s, asserted, Anna Freud's book was not on the student reading list at that time (Zetzel 1969). In April 1973 the Philadelphia Association for Psychoanalysis hosted a special panel (Slap 1974) on "The Ego and the Mechanisms of Defense." Here Anna Freud, returning to the subject more than 30 years later, discussed her work with Erik Erikson, Hans Loewald, Jacob Arlow, Arthur Valenstein, Eli Marcovitz, and Jenny Waelder-Hall. The interest in defense processes appears to be in no danger of waning, and even now the London clinic associated most closely with Anna Freud has begun an extensive series of discussions on this subject and is, moreover, closely following the original plan of presentation (A. Freud 1980d, 1981a, 1981b, 1981c).

Almost a decade before *Das Ich und die Abwehrmechanismen* (1936a) as a whole was published, key elements of Anna Freud's argument had appeared as short pieces in technical journals, and many of the earliest presentations of the material were verbal contributions at major international meetings.

The first public indication that Anna Freud was developing radically new theoretical ideas came in July 1929 when she went to England to attend the 11th International Psychoanalytic Congress, held in Oxford. At the third scientific session, following papers by David Eder, Melanie Klein, and Nina Searl, she read a paper entitled "A Counterpart to the Animal Phobias of Children." In its original form this was first published only in German (1929b), but it was reread before the Vienna Psychoanalytic Society on February 26, 1930 (Report of the Vienna Psychoanalytic Society 1930), and was eventually incorporated into the now classic book dealing with the ego and its defense mechanisms. The congress paper received a somewhat hostile reception from certain sections of the gathering at Oxford, though whether this was because of its new theoretical initiative or more personal reasons is not entirely clear. Sigmund Freud's correspondence at that time to his friend Lou observed that "According to her telegraphic reports Anna is having rather a hard time in Oxford" (Pfieffer 1972, letter dated July 28, 1929).

That Anna was indeed having a difficult time was confirmed by Eva Rosenfeld who, although not present at the Oxford Congress, nevertheless "knew it for sure" (Dyer 1980, interview) that Klein in particular had contested Anna Freud's views at every opportunity. Anna Freud's comprehensive official report of the 11th I. P. A. Congress (1929c) characteristically made no issue of these difficulties. Such acrimony as existed may well have been related to events at the Innsbruck Congress two years earlier, when the question of admitting candidates to training was debated, leading to what Eitingon called the "venting of affects" (A. Freud 1929c, p. 509). Undoubtedly, however, the major problem was the rivalry between the child analysis schools of Vienna and London, with Oxford providing a convenient venue for the latter's members to appear en masse.

After publication of the important book of lectures to teachers and parents (noted in the previous chapter) Anna Freud attended the 12th I. P. A. Congress in Wiesbaden, September 4–7, 1932, and read a paper entitled *"Die neurotischen Mechanismen unter dem Einfluss der Erziehung"* (neurotic mechanisms under the influence of education). This paper was not published separately. But thanks largely to the review by Ernst Kris (1938), we know that this piece marked another step in the slow gestation of Anna Freud's ideas concerning ego defensive processes. Pedagogical-analytical themes appear to have been especially well represented at the Wiesbaden congress, with Alice Balint and Gertrud Behn-Eschenburg among others giving relevant papers. Less well known was Anna Freud's short paper, entitled "Infantile Methods of Overcoming Anxiety."[1] Though missing from Kris's review, it is likely that this paper also was on defense mechanisms as ego processes of fundamental importance, which by now were one of Anna Freud's principal theoretical considerations.

Around this time Anna Freud also had planned to deliver what was to have been her leading paper, "Psychotherapy of Developmental Crises," for the Seventh Congress of Psychotherapy. Though the congress was intended to take place in Vienna in April 1933, it too was affected by the sham parliamentary victory of the National Socialist (Nazi) Party in the spring elections that year. With the abrupt political success of Adolf Hitler the future was clear, for most of the analysts were Jewish. The depression in intellectual circles caused by these events quickly spread beyond the native confines of Germany, and Sigmund Freud confided to Frau Lou that in those mad times, "Even Anna is depressed at moments" (Pfieffer 1972, p. 200).[2] From our own vantage point we doubly

[1] Unpublished communication to the Vienna Psychoanalytic Society, January 11, 1933. Anna Freud's unpublished papers and similar materials will eventually be included in the Sigmund Freud Archive at the Library of Congress, Washington D.C. (Dyer 1980, letter dated May 11, 1976).

[2] The significance of the word "even" should not be missed. Clearly, Freud now looked to his daughter for strength and example, if not for himself, then at least for others.

regret that Anna Freud's paper to the Seventh Congress of Psychotherapy was never heard (Thoma 1969). Other contributors were to have been Kretschmer, Paul Schilder, Heinz Hartmann, and Charlotte Buhler, and the whole event would almost certainly have been a memorable *tour de force*. Not all of the year's events were bad, however, and at a historic meeting of the Vienna Psychoanalytical Society on October 18, 1933, Anna Freud was elected to be vice-president of the society, a position that she held jointly with Paul Federn. In effect, the joint vice-presidents now directed the society's work, though the presidency was still nominally held by Sigmund Freud.

From 1904 onward, Federn had been one of Freud's earliest followers in Vienna. A gifted analyst, he had personally trained Fenichel, Reich, Weiss, Bibring, and Aichhorn and was to Anna Freud a commanding, albeit difficult, figure. Federn was best known for both his pioneering studies in psychosis and his own unpredictable personality. In 1938 when fleeing Vienna for refuge and safety in New York, Federn was entrusted by Freud with the *minutes* of the early meetings of the Vienna Society (Nunberg and Federn 1962). References to Federn's work are widely scattered throughout half a century or more of Anna Freud's publications. For example, in her work on defense she cited Federn's notion of "sympathetic identification" and compared it with her own view (1936a, p. 126). Later she followed Federn's important "ego boundary" concepts (A. Freud 1958b, p. 161), and to this day the prospectus of Anna Freud's Hampstead Child Therapy Clinic includes on its student reading list Federn's difficult but valuable work on ego psychology and the psychoses (1952). During her first United States lecture tour in 1950, Anna Freud visited the now ailing Federn in his apartment in New York. When he spoke of a debt he still felt he owed to Freud, Anna replied that her own debt to Federn far exceeded any obligation on his part (Weiss 1966).

Next in the important series of scientific contributions that led to the eventual publication of her ego defense book was Anna Freud's paper to the Lucerne Congress in August 1934. In her paper "The Problem of Puberty" (Report to the 13th I. P. A. Congress 1935), she covered much of the ground that later formed the final chapters of her major work on defense theory (1936a). The congress also elected Anna Freud to the vice-presidency of the International Association, with Edward Glover replacing her as general secretary.

The Lucerne Congress provided the setting for the culmination of a now famous internal wrangle concerning the expulsion from the International Psychoanalytic Association of one of its members, the enigmatic and controversial Wilhelm Reich, whose earlier and much respected work was by then widely considered to have strayed beyond the bounds of scientific credibility. As the secretary to the International Association, Anna Freud was obliged to play a formal part in the whole affair and apparently chaired a somewhat secretive precongress committee that met, ostensibly to hear Reich's views but allegedly to simply ratify an earlier decision to expel him from the I. P. A. (Higgins and Raphael 1967, pp. 221–222). Anna Freud's correspondence with Reich at this time, as reproduced in the same pro-Reich account, shows that she handled the problem correctly as the I. P. A. Secretary (Higgins and Raphael 1967, p. 220), and Reich himself attributed "that mess in Lucern" to others, notably Ernest Jones and Paul Federn, who supposedly were jealous of Reich. Reich was undoubtedly a powerful and original thinker, who helped advance the new ideas concerning the ego's defensive organization. Anna Freud herself always maintained a high opinion of Reich's "exciting and promising beginnings of so-called strict defence analysis" (1954c, p. 357), which helped stimulate the emergence, albeit in a radically different technical form, of her own approach to the analysis of defenses.[3] Reich was included, many years later, in a short list of Anna

[3]The defense techniques of Reich and of Anna Freud were contrasted by Richard Sterba (1953). Whereas Reich concentrated on resistance, Anna Freud had a wider concept of defense; and whereas Reich viewed the ego narrowly and suspiciously, largely in its attitude toward the analysis-analyst per se, Anna Freud viewed the ego more broadly, considering also its relations with the id and superego and observing it in a neutral, nonaggressive, and more objective manner. Both she and Sterba discarded Reich's term "character resistance," as it implied that what was actually a major defense mechanism was somehow synonymous with a wider totality of the individual's character.

Freud's most memorable peers of that period—the others being Heinz Hartmann, Ernst Kris, Robert Waelder, and Edward and Grete Bibring (1969k)—and his important and enduring psycho-analytical contributions (those before around 1932) are still recommended reading for the students of the latter-day Hampstead Child Therapy Course and the Cleveland Center for Research in Child Development.

It seems reasonable to assume that the new ideas concerning the analysis of defenses and the ego's wider defensive organization were discussed in the child analysis seminars of the Vienna school of analysts, and this is confirmed by a number of footnotes in *The Ego and the Mechanisms of Defence* (1936a) that cite suggestions and similar contributions made during the work's formative phase. Those noted were Jeanne Lampl-de Groot, Helene Deutsch, Jenny Waelder, and Margit Dubovitz.

Since its inception in 1927 as a formal technical seminar, the Children's Seminar had spread its influence far beyond Vienna and far beyond the initial technical material presented for discussion. Anna Maenchen attended regularly from 1933 onward (Dyer 1980) and also trained in analysis with Anna Freud. Members came from Budapest and Prague (A. Freud 1974e, p. viii), for example, Alice Balint and Annie Reich,[4] as well as Margaret Schoenberger Mahler and Esther Menaker, and students from the United States or elsehwere: Marie Briehl, Julia Deming, Edith Entenmann, Margaret Fries, Elisabeth Geleerd, Margaret Gerard, Mary O'Neal Hawkins, Rosetta Hurwitz, Edith B. Jackson, Estelle Levy, Marian C. Putnam, Margaret Ribble, and Helen Ross (A. Freud 1966e).

With this growing following confirming Anna Freud as a gifted and untiring training analyst and seminar teacher; with her official status secure in the vice-presidencies of the local Vienna Society, its training institute, and the International Association; and now, with her increasing theoretical grasp and sureness, the aegis of her father-mentor had become largely nominal. The older Freud him-

---

[4]Annie Reich and the Bornstein sisters are noted by Jacobson (1971) as being outstanding members of the Berlin Kinderseminar run by Otto Fenichel and Schultz-Hencke immediately before 1931. Jacobson also was a member of the Berlin group.

self by now viewed his daughter in legendary terms, and in a letter to the novelist and friend Arnold Zweig, he described her as one "who, in tragic circumstances, would not have fallen short of Antigone" (E. L. Freud 1960, p. 420). In another letter to Zweig, Freud used the phrase "my faithful Anna-Antigone."[5] There were few if any serious contenders to now challenge Anna Freud's unique and close position to the father of psychoanalysis, and certainly not such comparative newcomers as Ruth Mack Brunswick, as Roazen asserted (1975, p. 416). In addition, Anna Freud's theoretical model of the ego was now in its final stages and perhaps more than any other piece revealed the clarity and conceptual rigor of her metapsychological thinking. This in turn ensured that in psychoanalytical child psychology, Anna Freud would have few real contenders for the title of child psychologist par excellence.

In January and February 1935, Anna Freud began to outline her theoretical views concerning the id, ego, superego, and their interrelations in the defensive activities of the wider personality. She first presented this material to her colleagues in the Vienna Society as "The Application of Analytic Technique in the Examination of Psychic Institutions" (Report of the Vienna Psychoanalytic Society 1935). This also became the second chapter of her later book (1936a). After discussing this material at subsequent meetings, Anna Freud then began preparing the manuscript for publication. If her industry at this stage was particularly marked, there was good reason, as she herself pointed out many years later. Her own deadline was May 1936, her father's 80th birthday. The finished book was to be her special birthday gift (Slap 1974), and it was ready on time, as Lou Andreas-Salomé mentioned in a letter to Freud at that time (Pfieffer 1972, p. 209).

In the final revision of *The Ego and the Mechanisms of Defence*, Anna Freud was assisted by Ernst Kris, which she acknowledged almost 40 years later (Slap 1974). This disclosure helps explain Kris's great insight into the book's historical "building blocks," as shown in his early review (1938).

[5]Antigone was a daughter of Oedipus Rex. Her loyalty to her family under duress caused her great suffering.

Ernst Kris, one of the best analytical thinkers in the decades since Sigmund Freud's death, was not analyzed by Anna Freud, as Roazen erroneously stated (1975, p. 441). Rather, on the advice of Freud himself, Kris went to Helene Deutsch for his analysis and afterwards married the child analyst Marianne Rie (S. and L. B. Rivto 1966), one of Anna Freud's childhood friends. Some years later, during the exodus and diaspora of the Viennese group of analysts, Ernst and Marianne Kris initially joined Anna Freud in London but then moved on to the United States. There, in 1950—the same year that Anna Freud first visited America—Ernst Kris set up the Yale Child Study Center as the first experimental laboratory devoted to a psychoanalytic approach to human development. From the 1950s onward Anna Freud's publications show her agreement with Ernst Kris's observations and views (A. Freud 1950a, 1951a, 1951b, 1954a, 1958a, 1965a, 1967a, 1969g, 1971g). Kris was also often in agreement with her work (1975).

PRECURSORS IN THE FIELD OF DEFENSE

The term *defense* was first used by Sigmund Freud in 1894 and was, in effect, "the earliest representative of the dynamic standpoint in psychoanalytic theory" (A. Freud 1936a, p. 42). As is widely known, Sigmund Freud soon virtually abandoned the term defense—only a single citation is catalogued in his *Interpretation of Dreams* (1900)—and he replaced it with the more specific term *repression*. In February 1926 when *Inhibitions, Symptoms and Anxiety* came out, Freud revived the term defense.[6] By defining his

---

[6]Freud's abandonment of the term defense was by no means total in the period between 1899 and 1925. In a letter to Jung dated March 3, 1908, he agreed with him that "your ideas about defense are certainly correct, but not only for paranoia. I believe that they apply to all neuroses and psychoses" (McGuire 1974, letter 76F). And in his notable Winter Lecture Series of 1915–1916, attended by Anna, Freud spoke of the principle of "defense against unpleasant memory by forgetfulness" (1916, lecture 4). His classic work of 1914, *on Narcissism*, used the term *defense formation* as a means of relieving anxiety in the neuroses by "further mental 'working over'" (1914b).

concept of defense as "a general designation for all the techniques which the ego makes use of in conflicts which may lead to a neurosis" (1926, appendix A[c]), Freud was able to satisfy most requirements, including those of the clinical therapists and of the biologists, with the widest possible theory of adaptation. Freud's language is simple and clear, a point not lost on his daughter, though the same cannot be said of others who attempted to clarify his definition (Eidelberg 1968, p. 92).

With Freud's reintroduction of a respectable notion of defense in the ego's operations, the way was clear for others to concentrate on this topic. Reich, as noted above, had pioneered the new approach (1935), to the delight of the young Anna Freud, though she quickly surpassed Reich's "character armor" synthesis of the biological notion of membrane and the psychological idea of boundary. Though somewhat an exaggeration, Reich's notion of a defensive armor does have some validity, as the following observation shows:

> Helen, a nine-year-old girl of average abilities, chose to paint, on a winter's day when she was beginning to show the first symptoms of flu which subsequently kept her away from school. After depicting a bold snowman in strong white she then mixed an ochre and encased the snowman in an outer thick shell of colour. When asked why she did that, she replied "I don't feel well." The expression "to withdraw into one's shell" inescapably comes to mind in similar contexts, especially of social rejection and hurt. (Dyer 1980, personal observations)

The 1929 Oxford Congress was Anna Freud's first public foray into the realm of defense, and it also produced a number of other papers on the same theme, ranging from the unsystematic and premature treatment of the theory by Pfieffer (1930), to the useful contribution by Edward Glover (1930). In pointing to the concept of "preliminary stages of defense" and its presence in Sigmund Freud's work and in indicating denial as an early ego technique of this kind, Glover helped prepare the way for the surer treatment of these matters by Anna Freud. Interestingly, around this time Melanie Klein also came to the view that anxiety situations affecting the child called forth "special mechanisms of defence on the part of his ego and determine the specific character his psychotic disorder will assume" (1932, p. 202). Twenty years later Klein maintained that her interest in the ego's defense activities had begun with her 1932 book (1952).

The massive study of primitive cultural types by Geza Roheim included a long discussion of the ego, with—four years before Anna Freud's published book—a section specifically reserved for defense mechanisms (1932, chap. 6, pt. II [a]). Roheim viewed displacement as the prototypic transformation, a position quite in keeping with Freud's turn-of-the-century model involving a primary process essentially based on displacement.[7] Roheim also listed as examples of specific mechanisms, repression, regression, and projection. More systematic and thorough than Roheim in his treatment of defense was Nunberg, who also published his major work in 1932.

Regrettably, *The Ego and the Mechanisms of Defence* does not consider or acknowledge the earlier study by Herman Nunberg on *Die Abwehrvorgänge* (Nunberg 1932, chap. 7). Nunberg's list of defenses compares most interestingly with Anna Freud's list in that the first eight comparisons are identical, and in his concept of "defence as narcissistic protection" (*Abwehr als narzisstischer Schutz*) Nunberg also implied and utilized important ideas on ego boundaries and stimulus barriers. Some consideration and discussion of his work would certainly have enhanced the value of *The Ego and the Mechanisms of Defence* in regard to, for example, the nature of any fundamental process underlying defense mechanisms generally.

Nunberg's ideas enjoyed wide currency in Viennese analytical circles, as did those of Paul Federn, another pioneer of ego boundary concepts. The theoretical ideas of both these analysts were not complete at this time, however, which may well explain why Anna Freud preferred to defer consideration of this material. In

---

[7]Freud's fundamental distinction (1900, chap. 7) between a displacement-based primary process and a logic-based secondary process has, with good reason, been named his greatest discovery and his most important contribution to human psychology (Peters 1965; Strachey, in S. Freud 1900).

later years Anna Freud often acknowledged and cited the work of both Federn and Nunberg.

Some idea of the mental effort required to grasp or conceptualize their ideas was given by Erik Homburger Erikson, who listened to Federn lecturing in 1930 on ego boundary concepts. Erikson depicted his teacher, at the end of the difficult presentation, gazing quizzically into the distance and asking himself aloud, "Now, have I understood myself correctly?" (Erikson 1968, *Preface*).

THE EGO PSYCHOLOGIST

From its beginning, psychoanalysis was concerned with "the ego and its aberrations . . . and . . . the proper field for our observation is always the ego" (A. Freud 1936a, chap. 1, pp. 4, 6; 1980d). Moreover, as is self-evident, "the ego itself is the object of analysis, in that the defensive operations in which it is perpetually engaged are carried on unconsciously" (A. Freud 1936a, p. 30). Anna Freud thus sought to focus on the ego per se. The defense mechanisms, so widely publicized by others, she considered primarily on the basis of their function in mediating the threefold relations of the ego with the id drives, the superego, and the external world. We fully agree with her allocation of priority to the ego, and we criticize those who focus on the mechanisms of defense per se, in relative isolation from the defending ego. Some err more grossly in appearing to attribute their own orientation in this respect to Anna Freud.

Goodenough's influential text on child development, for example, stated that one of Sigmund Freud's contributions was to identify and name many defense mechanisms; however, the only reference to Anna Freud was that she "elaborated them in some detail" (Goodenough and Tyler 1959, p. 486). MacKinnon and Dukes, in a distinguished article on repression, asserted that the fullest and clearest relegation of repression to a position of one among many mechanisms came in Anna Freud's *The Ego and the Mechanisms of Defence*, and after the publication of this influential book psychoanalysts focused their attention increasingly upon the problems of defense (1962). Other psychologists have similarly emphasized Anna Freud's contribution to a psychology of defense, rather than her contribution to a more comprehensive and meaningful psychology of the ego (Miller and Swanson 1960).

We do not deny that Anna Freud advanced the study of defense processes (mechanisms); however, her most important contributions are often missed or obscured, and she is credited for what is neither original nor hers.

Consider, for example, the widely celebrated list of ten classic defense mechanisms—repression, regression, introjection, projection, reaction-formation, turning against the self, undoing, isolation, reversal, and sublimation—which are accepted in psychology generally and are attributed by many psychoanalysts (French 1938, Wyss 1961, Rycroft 1968, Rangell 1975) to Anna Freud. Actually, Anna Freud attached relatively little significance to the mere itemization of defense mechanisms, and relegated to a mere sentence in parentheses these "nine methods of defence which are very familiar in the practice," to which she added sublimation as "a tenth which pertains more to the study of the normal than to that of neurosis" (1936a, p. 44). With her allusion to the familiarity of practicing analysts with this material, together with the location of the sources for individual defenses in the earlier writings of Sigmund Freud, Anna Freud underlined the fact that this material was the least original and most recapitulatory of her entire book. Paradoxically, the wide familiarity with this same section of Anna Freud's book has tended to obscure her real contribution. This misplaced attention is perhaps readily explained by the convenience and "focal quality" of the neat and accessible list of defense mechanisms.

An early reviewer of *The Ego and the Mechanisms of Defence* warned against the mere enumeration of defenses (French 1938), and more recently the supposedly fundamental list has been criticized for staying too simply at the taxonomic level (Schafer 1968) and further as having a certain arbitrariness (Suppes and Warren 1975). However, in the light of what has been presented here, we can safely maintain that Anna Freud did not need to defend herself on the issue of enumeration of defenses. Other analysts are less fortunate, however. Hendrick (1938) extended the list of basic defenses by adding flight from an object, avoidance of an object, and motor inhibitions, though without describing them in detail. Grete Bibring, Arthur Valenstein, and their coworkers, in attempting to reclassify the defense mechanisms, listed 26 "basic or first order" defenses and 19 "complex or second order" defenses (Bibring et al. 1961). Ludwig Eidelberg (1968) named 18 mechanisms of defense. But possibly the most extreme example of such enumerative progression was provided by Suppes and Warren, who used mathematical combinatorial methods to generate 29 possible defense mechanisms, as well as another 15 so-called elementary mechanisms specifically termed *identifications*. Although such methods may be recommended for statistical surveys of individual variation and other population-related parameters, their efficacy for clinical work is doubtful.[8] We believe that, like trait listing and the later mathematically sophisticated factorial analysis of personality and cognitive functions, enumerative and replicative techniques of this kind are not valid for the study of individual persons in dynamic-interactional and essentially meaningful contexts.

In a later general article on defense mechanisms written for the *Encyclopedia Britannica* Anna Freud herself added the further defense of intellectualization and referred also to other minor mechanisms (1964a). But she also criticized her own "foregoing enumeration," pointing out another drawback, that "it includes under one heading a number of heterogeneous processes" (1964a, p. 172).

IDENTIFICATION WITH THE AGGRESSOR

With her now famous account of this important defensive process Anna Freud gave us a clear description of a phenomenon that is not only complex and involves a combination of defenses

---

[8]A valuable comparison of clinical and statistical methodologies is that by Meehl (1954). Thanks largely to analysts such as Ernst Kris, Anna Freud, and their coworkers, it is no longer valid to equate the clinical-statistical distinction with that of psychoanalytic-experimental psychology.

but also can be applied to both internal and external anxieties. Moreover, as a normal stage in the development of the child's superego, it is a common psychological constellation in early personality formation (1936a, chap. 9).

Identification, important to superego formation and hence to the mastery of internal drives, was shown by Anna Freud to be one of the ego's most powerful devices for combating external anxiety situations. For this latter role to be achieved, identification must operate with other defensive processes, principally projection. Anna Freud offered graphic case material of Aichhorn and Jenny Waelder-Hall, as well as some examples of her own, in order to demonstrate the processes involved. Some of this material is well known, for example, Aichhorn's elementary schoolboy who involuntarily grimaced in a pathetic caricature of the angry face of his teacher (A. Freud 1936a, p. 110); Waelder-Hall's 5-year-old boy patient who became a roaring lion in the analytic hour, carried a "Krampus rod" with him and laid about him with it in a most aggressive fashion, especially in the presence of adults, from whom he expected condemnation for his forbidden masturbatory fantasies (1936a, pp. 114–115); and Anna Freud's own little girl patient who, afraid of crossing the hall in the dark for fear of meeting ghosts, one day discovered the secret of pretending to be the ghost herself (1936a, pp. 110–111). Far from being idiosyncratic, Anna Freud noted that such behavior was "one of the most natural and widespread modes of behaviour on the part of the primitive ego" (p. 111). Exorcism of spirits, primitive religious ceremonies, and certain games of childhood all are examples supporting her view that identification is a common mechanism by which objective anxiety is converted into a feeling of safety and pleasure.

Bettelheim confirmed Anna Freud's ideas in a disturbing but psychologically relevant vignette of the way in which certain Jewish inmates of the concentration camps imitated their S. S. captors (1943). That the imitation was by no means superficial and did indeed take on the dimension of an unconscious mechanism of identification is indicated by the fact that the involved individuals defied the S. S. guards while at the same time using their own torturous practices on their informers. Fashioning of bits of camp clothing into uniforms completed their identification with the aggressor.

The complete process of identification with the aggressor has at least three distinct stages: (1) introjection of the characteristics or forces in the outside world that are perceived as threatening, (2) transformation of the threatened into the threatening within the individual by impersonation-identification, and (3) projection of the threatening and aggressive aspects back into the outside world. Other defenses may operate generally, as with the denial of aspects of reality. By the use of well-chosen examples—for instance, the 6-year-old boy who had suffered at the dentist's just before his analytic hour, but instead of playing dentist tore up rubber bands, broke pencils, and cut up string—Anna Freud demonstrated that identification with the aggressor may often in fact be identification with the aggression per se (1936a, pp. 111–112), with inevitably diffuse and varied acting out following as one consequence.

The final stage of identification with the aggressor may take the form of some active assault on the external world, and a number of subtle examples are used to illustrate the process of projection. Thus, one young girl condemned her analyst's alleged secretiveness at precisely those moments when she herself was caught suppressing material, thus breaking the fundamental rule of analysis. Foreseeing the analyst's rebuke, the girl herself adopted the active role and "criticised the analyst for the very fault of which she herself was guilty" (A. Freud 1936a, p. 117).

As a response to objective anxiety, Anna Freud considered normal the mechanism of identification with the aggressor (1936a, p. 120). But she considered it abnormal if apparent in the relations, for example, between husband and wife when one partner with an impulse to be unfaithful displaced that impulse onto the other partner, reproached the alleged unfaithfulness, and developed an obsessional jealousy (1936a, p. 120). In this and similar instances, the mechanisms of introjection and projection are probably best conceptualized separately.

This defense process can be applied to studies of prejudice, racial tensions, ethnic minorities, and the like, in addition to individual anxiety situations in the outer world of psychological reality. With her example of the marital couple, Anna Freud introduced an additional psychosocial field in which it could be used, and there are others as well. In her final example, of projection as a defense against homosexual love impulses—when the reversal of love into hate "completes what introjection and projection have begun, and the result is the development of paranoid delusions" (1936a, p. 121)—she touched on a difficult area to which in later years she applied the concepts of negativism, emotional surrender (*Hörigkeit*) (1952d), and passivity (1968g).

The concept of the mechanism of identification with the aggressor is the core of Anna Freud's contribution to the study of defense mechanisms. One commentator noted that she described essentially five defensive mechanisms: denial in fantasy, denial in word and act, restriction of the ego, identification with the aggressor, and a form of altruism (Brown 1961, p. 69). Otto Fenichel also pointed out that the first three processes listed above were the ego's first steps to avoid pain, whereas the remaining two, identification with the aggressor and a form of altruism, were really "two new, that is, new as far as evaluation goes, types of defence" (1938, p. 118). Anna Freud also paid special attention to the defenses peculiar to puberty (1936a, chaps. 11 and 12), and her "new contribution" to defense psychology was as follows:

Defense Mechanism	*Concept Status*
Denial in fantasy Denial in word and act Restriction of the ego	Preliminary stage of defense
Identification with the aggressor A form of altruism	Special form of defense (new)
Asceticism Intellectualization	Defense characteristic of puberty

It is in the descriptive evaluation of these seven mechanisms of defense that *The Ego and the Mechanisms of Defence* is principally renowned, rather than for its list of ten established defenses. Nevertheless, analysts occasionally offer "Anna Freud's mechanisms of defence" (Flugel 1945) without distinguishing the old, such as repression, from the new, such as identification with the aggressor.

With this original contribution to defense theory, plus the systematic ego psychological model in which the specific defenses were enumerated, the ascendancy of the Vienna School of Child Analysis was confirmed.[9] The school now had not only an effective technical method and an active membership but also a potent and elegant theoretical model against which to test its observations and theories. The psychological and scientific apprenticeship of Anna was now complete.

The importance of this most recent aspect of Anna Freud's thinking naturally did not go unrecognized by those closest to her. Lou Andreas-Salomé summed it up correctly when she wrote to Freud regarding Anna's pending lectures to the Vienna Society: "How unremittingly her mind must have been preoccupied with this, despite all her other concerns" (Pfieffer 1972, letter dated January 2, 1935). Freud replied:

> My one source of satisfaction is Anna. It is remarkable how much influence and authority she has gained among the general run of analysts. . . . It is surprising too how sharp, clear and unflinching she is in her mastery of the subject. Moreover, she is truly independent of me; at the most I serve as a catalyst. (Pfieffer 1972, p. 204)

The words "remarkable" and "surprising" in this letter seem to indicate Freud might have had difficulty recognizing that his own daughter had indeed become the commanding professional figure that he described.

Particular importance has been attached to Anna Freud's elaboration of the preliminary stages of defense (Zetzel 1971) and especially to the various forms of denial (Hendrick 1938, p. 482; Shevrin and Toussieng 1965). Several sources illustrated denial in fantasy, namely (1) Freud's classic and pioneering case of Little Hans and his animal phobia, (2) a 7-year-old boy patient who imagined himself taming ferocious wild animals, and (3) stories from folklore and children's literature (A. Freud 1936a, chap. 6). Anna Freud cited Frances Hodgson Burnett's *Little Lord Fauntleroy*

[9]The phrase "Vienna school of child analysis" was used by Anna Freud herself in 1935 in discussing her technical method. The phrase is still used (A. Freud 1935b, 1966e).

and Annie Fellows Johnston's *The Little Colonel* as depicting children who tame or control powerful and bad-tempered adults. In other words, these children reverse, or deny, reality.

So plentiful are the observations in everyday work with children that relate to processes of denial, that they undoubtedly support Anna Freud's view of their essential normalcy. Such a psychological mechanism, aimed at the avoidance of objective danger and discomfort in the real outer world, "does not come under the heading of the psychology of neurosis, but is a normal stage in the development of the ego" (A. Freud 1936a, p. 102). The defenses, in this view, are distinguished as largely unconscious processes resulting in compromise solutions to internal dangers (i.e., part of the psychological inner world reality). An example of such a danger is the instinctual drive seeking gratification in inappropriate circumstances.

Though agreeing that Anna Freud "clearly pointed out that, in general, denial is directed against the outer world," Maurits Katan added that "this does not mean that denial of inner reality does not exist" (1964, p. 237). Katan's caution seems to broaden the potential applications of the denial concept, though it is not clear whether a denial of inner reality would constitute a defense or a preliminary stage—a neurotic or a normal solution.

The following kinds of observation and material may be gathered daily in normal school and play situations, and illustrate denial: Children known to be from less affluent homes, when mixing with friends from more affluent families, may often be heard upgrading their own attributes and possessions so as to include imaginary new cars, exotic trips abroad, and so on. "Keeping up with the Joneses" is clearly a variant of this. When this denial is acted out in the real world, it is thereby reinforced, though at the cost of becoming dangerously close to a rigidly established defensive stereotype in itself:

Two brothers S. and D., aged five and nine years respectively, regularly played the following game when travelling by car. Each took one side of the road as his, and they began to collect objects of value in their joint estimation. Gas stations and candy stores appeared to have special score-point value. Inevitably, as the game progressed, an increasing element of fantasy elaboration became apparent, and with great insistence many scores were claimed with no real existence of the object in the outside world. Attempts to refute the other player's outlandish claims soon regressed to countering efforts by producing even more and greater fabrications of one's own. (Dyer 1980, personal observations)

Games such as this, based largely on denial (in word and act), may be overheard daily on elementary and junior high school playgrounds and typify the developing ego's efforts to reverse, counter, or otherwise avoid any sensed inferiority in the outer world of psychosocial reality. One-upmanship is a variant of the above strategy. This is the continuum for such phenomena proposed by Anna Freud (1936a, p. 90, n. 2):

| *(A)* | *(B)* | *(C)* |

Denial in phantasy ⟶ Impersonation in play ⟶ Denial in word and act

One-upmanship probably fits between (B) and (C), as would the circus clown's game of "Oh yes, it is! Oh no it isn't!" and the children's game of "T'is, t'isn't." To the right of (C) may be placed deliberate lying, which under certain circumstances may be accepted as falling within the normal range of behaviors, and to the extreme right of that may be placed "logical or correct denial," as when a child correctly denies a self-evident untruth or injustice.

Another preliminary defensive process, or *mechanism*, is Anna Freud's concept of ego restriction (*Ich Einschränkung*). In her description of this mechanism, a small child-patient is drawing on a writing pad, notices the parallel productions made by the adult-therapist, judges his own efforts to be inferior, and thereafter refuses to produce any more drawings of his own (1936a, chap. 8; 1937a). There are related accounts of other children, in varying situations, whose egos' efforts at avoiding unpleasurable anxiety are shown to be capable of spreading to include more distantly related activities in the restriction of ego interest and cathexis. The following example is from my own childhood:

At nine years of age R. D. was first introduced to English football when the class teacher organized a game. Immediately recognizing the superior skills of his peers, R. D. showed a total lack of interest in participating and elected to be a mere spectator. The subsequent anathema to the playing of football came to include as its resultants poor knowledge of clubs and their colors, lack of familiarity with famous players, and so forth. Physical sports in general were in some danger of being classed as boring, and the reversal of this undesirable trend required the advent of the powerful forces of puberty, together with an encounter with the quite different skills of rugby.

Other examples exist in the literature (E. Klein 1949, Alpert and Krown 1953), and so graphic and familiar are such observations that it is difficult to avoid concluding that similar phenomena must have been noted many times before by teachers and others involved with youngsters. What differs in Anna Freud's observations is that they were not made in isolation but instead were integrated with a meaningful psychological theory of the ego. What might otherwise have remained a relatively minor piece of information was explained, and the solitary or replicated observation was clarified using important theoretical reference points such as ego, defense stage, and the like. The mutual and beneficial interaction of theory and practice thus began to develop. Discrete data were systematically stored, thus aiding and enhancing their retention and recall, and the theoretical framework (model) was enlarged and its elements corroborated and strengthened. This reciprocal interaction of theory and observation was typical of Anna Freud's approach to child study and the science of psychoanalysis.

The defense theory of the ego, as presented in *The Ego and the Mechanisms of Defence*, has been constructively criticized and modified by Anna Freud's own one-time pupil Erik Homburger Erikson. The basis of Erikson's early training in psychoanalysis is often ignored or missed, perhaps because of his rapid assimilation of the cultural anthropology of Margaret Mead and others in the United States in the years immediately after his emigration from Europe. Instead, Erikson has been widely acclaimed as belonging to a "culture psychology" school.

There are no formal studies on the relationship between Erikson as an ego psychologist and Anna Freud. Pumpian-Mindlin's account is not acceptable in this sense, since it is really two separate accounts in one chapter (1966). Also rejected is Pumpian-Mindlin's view that in regard to Anna Freud and Erik Erikson, "their foci and frames of reference complement each other, but do not overlap in the formal sense, at least at the present time" (1966, p. 519). But this is certainly no longer so. It can demonstrably be said that both Erikson and Anna Freud based their most important work of the past two or three decades on comparable frameworks emphasizing a psychoanalytical-metapsychological and specifically a developmental-genetic standpoint.

Already in 1945, after having carried out fieldwork among the Sioux and Yurok Indians, Erikson questioned the term defense mechanism and sought to relate the implied process to wider areas of personality (1945). He also suggested that besides id content as a determinant of the eventual defense mechanism, as in Anna Freud's view, parental and other adult models and wider communal environmental factors may also act as determinants. The classical-orthodox analytic view, with its emphasis on a psychobiological infantile drive mechanism thus was extended to psychosocial and cultural concepts. A year later Erikson had developed his critique of mechanization in ego theory to the point of seeing such descriptions as reflecting not the ego processes themselves, but more accurately the contemporary historical dilemmas manifest in the discussion of those processes. Clearly, Erikson's approach is relevant to such modern, technologically accelerated tyrannies as "the mechanization of people" and "the dehumanization of industry." His obvious common ground with others such as Erich Fromm should not, however, be taken to imply any undue distance between Erikson's standpoint and that of classical Freudian psychoanalysis. Erikson is here accepted as occupying a conceptual middle ground, halfway between Anna Freud and socially oriented neo-Freudians.

In writing about child rearing, Erikson observed that certain modern trends seem to represent a magic identification with the machine, similar to the identifications of primitive tribes with their principal prey. If modern man's ego seems to crave mechanical adaptation, "then we are not dealing with the nature of the ego, but with one of its historical adaptations, if not . . . dysfunctions" (1946). Erikson also criticized the classical structural model, since to him the id, ego, and superego are not static compartments, but they reflect "three major processes, the relativity of which determines the form of human behavior" (1946).

The key word in the Eriksonian critique is "processes." Charles Rycroft, for example, indicated that "defences are better regarded less as mechanisms than as techniques, manoeuvres, strategies or ploys" (1968, p. 72). All such reformulations of defense theory imply a degree of conscious ego control in the defensive process, whereas orthodox Freudians appear to emphasize the automatic, repetitive nature of the largely unconscious defense mechanisms.[10] This whole question is thus part of the larger field of controversy among the various schools of metapsychology versus personology (Brierley 1951), instinct theory versus object relations theory (Fairbairn 1952), and classic Freudian psychobiology versus an interpersonal relations theory in terms appropriate to humans as persons rather than organisms (Guntrip 1961). (This particular theoretical divergence will be considered in more detail in Chapter 6, when we compare the work of Anna Freud with the radical theoretical revisionism of W. Ronald D. Fairbairn.)

By 1950, in his *Childhood and Society*, Erik Erikson saw his own work as being "a psychoanalytic book on the relation of the ego to society" (1950, *Foreword*). Quickly distancing himself from earlier analytical formulations, however, he reached "beyond the mere defensive aspects of the ego which have been so conclusively formulated in Anna Freud's *The Ego and the Mechanisms of Defence*" (1950, pt. 3, pp. 187–188). The ego to Erikson was here an "inner institution," evolved to safeguard the inner psychological order on which all social order depends. The ego was neither the individual nor his or her individuality, although it was indispensable to the individual.

In April 1950, Anna Freud and Erikson met again during Miss

---

[10]Nevertheless, in Anna Freud's own case illustration of the little girl afraid of meeting ghosts (1936a, pp. 110–111), the manner in which this child discusses the matter with her brother does suggest conscious maneuvering.

Freud's first visit to the United States, in Stockbridge, Massachusetts, where Erikson was a senior staff member of the Austen Riggs Foundation. The occasion did not then arise—indeed the conditions were not yet ripe—for any discussion or rapprochement between the two in regard to defense theory, and it was another 20 years before such an opportunity presented itself.

In 1956 Erikson raised the issue of whether the concept of identity "is essentially a psychosocial one, or deserves to be considered as a legitimate part of the psychoanalytic theory of the ego" (1956, p. 56). In the same paper he agreed with Anna Freud in viewing adolescence as a "normative crisis" rather than some deeper affliction with psychopathological undertones.

More recently, though in no way retracting any part of his own remarkable theoretical initiative, Erikson has looked again and with greater sympathy and insight at the work of his early teacher Anna Freud. One could almost say that his own identity had finally stabilized and coalesced, a move that coincided with his reacceptance of Anna Freud's early standpoint and with yet another, perhaps the final, of his frequent geographical relocations across the United States. Crucial to Erikson's argument is a passage written by Anna Freud in 1945 in her paper "Indications for Child Analysis":

> All through childhood a maturation process is at work which, in the service of an increasing knowledge of and adaptation to reality, aims at perfecting these functions [i.e., ego functions], at rendering them more and more objective and independent of the emotions, until they can become as accurate and reliable as a mechanical apparatus. (1945a, p. 29)

In quoting this same passage, which in his 1946 paper had spurred him to criticize the "mechanization" aspect thereby implied, Erikson now noted that although Anna Freud described:

> . . . a tendency which the ego has in common, in more than one sense, with the nervous system and the brain . . . she certainly does not intend to advocate mechanical adaptation as the goal of human life. In fact, her "mechanisms of defence," while a highly

necessary part of mental life, render the person dominated by them impoverished and stereotyped. (1968, pp. 229–230)

Apparently Erikson has, at least to his own satisfaction, successfully and finally harmonized his own views with those of his early formative analytical training.

Eventually, Anna Freud and Erikson met once more, appropriately enough on a panel discussing "The Ego and the Mechanisms of Defense" (Slap 1974). There Erikson took up the question of the sharing of defenses, and the relationship of that sharing to the inner economy of the individual. In presenting examples of groups of children and others using the same defense mechanism in similar circumstances, Erikson illustrated both his thorough grounding in the psychoanalytic study of the individual and his own particular synthesis of this with group dynamics and wider social forces. On her part Anna Freud stated that at first "she was surprised when she learned that Professor Erikson was going to talk about the social aspect of defense, because it was her feeling that defense mechanisms were highly individual matters" (Slap 1974). On reflection, however, Miss Freud conceded that she could now see that Erikson was correct.

With this memorable rapprochement of two valuable but potentially conflicting viewpoints we shall leave Erikson's critique of Anna Freud's defense theory of the ego. It had, after all, sought not to destroy but to fulfill. At the present time it is not possible to predict the outcome of any future confrontation between the formal studies of individual dynamics and group dynamics. But what is more certain is that Anna Freud's and Erikson's works indicate where much of the vital middle ground lies.

EGO SYNTHETIC FUNCTION AND ADAPTATION

Synthesis usually is understood as an integrative process, quite the opposite of analysis proper. Nunberg defined the synthetic function as involving ego processes such as assimilating internal and external elements, reconstructing conflicting ideas, uniting contrasts, and activating "mental activity" (1932, p. 151). Clearly ego synthetic function is important in mediating internal conflict and psychological processes generally, including shaping the defensive mechanisms (processes) that characterize much of the compromise formation of human personality and experience in one's relations with oneself and with others. This function is not, however, widely associated with Anna Freud's ego defense work, and many academic psychologists and professional therapists might be tempted to look obliquely at such a contention.

Nevertheless, *The Ego and the Mechanisms of Defence* notes the ego synthetic function, along with superego anxiety, objective anxiety, and instinctual anxiety (dread of the strength of the drives), as another motive for instigating a process of "defence against instinct" (A. Freud 1936a, p. 60). Elsewhere in this work this function is referred to as an organizing and unifying process which, for the more mature ego, opposes the defensive use of denial of reality (p. 90).

Despite the importance of such an all-embracing ego function, Anna Freud's attitude toward it was at best neutral, and sometimes negative, from the point of view of defense analysis. In the first chapter of *The Ego and the Mechanisms of Defence*, she showed just how inimical the ego's synthetic function was to the very different process of analysis. During the early stage of a typical analysis the observation of internal psychological conflict is obscured by successful repression but may be made transparent and visible by "the return of the repressed," as frequently happens with much material subsequently provided by neurotics. As Anna Freud then emphasized, however, owing to the ego's quite different function, namely, its tendency toward synthesis, the above condition of affairs "which is particularly favourable for analytic observation, lasts only for a few moments at a time" (1936a, p. 9). A fresh conflict then develops between the drive derivative from the unconscious and the new ego activity, and if the ego activity imposes a successful new defense, then the resultant psychological state once again will be rendered "most unfruitful" for analytic observation.

The salient work of Anna Freud's Vienna phase could, therefore, hardly stress the significance and importance of the ego's synthetic function, since her contribution had the avowed aim of offering a therapeutic and analytic technique—"from the psychic surface inwards"—designed to utilize and outflank the ego's resistances and defensive mechanisms and thereby to illuminate the conflicts and compromise formations in the individual's personality. By underscoring that defense was a broader concept than resistance was, Anna Freud advanced significantly beyond Wilhelm Reich's earlier character analysis and offered a viable alternative to Reich's emphasis on "permanent defence phenomena" (Sterba 1953, Van Der Leeuw 1971).

In French's (1938) review of Anna Freud's defense book, he made the following observations on the apparently antithetical aspects of defense and synthesis in ego functioning. He pictured the ego as a delicately balanced organization that under conditions of great stress could lose its fine adjustment of adaptation via the reality principle. In these latter circumstances a cruder adjustment process could operate, and "the normal synthetic activity of the ego must degenerate into a defense mechanism" (1938, p. 550). According to this viewpoint, a more correct relationship between defense processes and the ego synthetic function would identify the former as a more primitive—in the sense of phylogenetically and ontogenetically earlier—type of the latter. Insofar as the defenses themselves allow for some adjustment and compromise in reality-oriented behavior, they here are termed a subset of the total ego synthetic activity, albeit a rigid and potentially irreversible synthesis once formed.

In the years following the publication of *The Ego and the Mechanisms of Defence*, Anna Freud directed her attention to how the synthetic function of the ego, in attempting to unify and centralize mental processes, "is opposed to the free and easy manner in which the infant lives out his most divergent emotions and instinctual urges" (1945a, p. 30). "Splitting" of the personality, considered a defense mechanism, also damages the ego synthetic function.

By 1950, in modifying her 1936 position, she showed that therapeutically and analytically profitable situations may in fact be produced through this synthetic function, which sometimes brings about "painful opposition between incompatible urges such as love and hate, activity and passivity . . ." (1951a, p. 129). More recently Anna Freud acknowledged Nunberg's work on ego synthetic function (1930) as "an exciting paper which inevitably arouses the envy of many other authors on the subject of ego psychology" (1969k, p. 200), and she considered Nunberg's lucid description second only to her father's. Nunberg described the ego in its relation to both internal and external worlds in the classic simile of "the rider and the horse": at once both helpless and masterful. In the light of Nunberg's comprehensive and powerful advocacy of the synthetic function, "it becomes obvious, of course, why no synthesis needs to be introduced into the technique of psychoanalytic treatment, this being provided automatically by the restored synthetic function of the ego after the analytic process has run its course" (A. Freud 1969k, p. 200).

Anna Freud's further employment of ego synthetic function was almost as comprehensive as the function itself. In a paper on obsessional neurosis she stated that "it is above all the failure of fusion and synthesis which determines the occurrence of an obsessional neurosis" (1966b, p. 246), and she also pointed to functional regression, which includes reduction of the ego synthetic function. The synthetic function itself may become a diagnostic criterion, since with the passing of early childhood, as with the absence of reality testing, the conspicuous absence of the synthetic function indicates that "the borders of neurosis have been overstepped" (1969d, p. 313). In a technical discussion (1968a), she demonstrated how interpretations may lead to the return of repressed material to the ego's synthetic function, and she continued to feature this important ego activity in her work (1965a, 1969a, 1978a).

We believe that the foregoing review of Anna Freud's use of the concept of ego synthetic function indicates that she was above any criticism of having stressed either too narrow or one-sided a view of the ego. The early reviewers of *The Ego and the Mecha-*

nisms of Defence certainly took just such a critical stance (French 1938, Hendrick 1938, Fenichel 1938), but we believe that Hoffer (1946) was more accurate when he pointed out that *The Ego and the Mechanisms of Defence* implicitly accounted for adaptive measures taken by the ego, particularly during puberty. Sperling likewise was correct in observing that Anna Freud's book recognized the ego's prime integrative role, for example, in establishing harmony in the interrelations among id, superego, and external world (1958).

The marked divergence frequently alluded to between Anna Freud's work on defensive ego function and Heinz Hartmann's work on adaptive ego activity (1939) may now be seen in its proper context. Each chose to detail a relatively circumscribed approach to the ego. Such an approach reflects, in fact, a widely accepted strategy in the general pursuit of science, when some degree of isolation and simplification from a more complex totality of phenomena is required before the objects of study become fully amenable to effective scrutiny. In the 1972 Philadelphia panel discussion on "The Ego and the Mechanisms of Defense," Miss Freud recalled that when she gave the first chapters of her defense book to the Vienna Psychoanalytic Society, Hartmann presented his work on the ego's conflict-free sphere. At that time Hartmann said to Anna Freud, "Defense activity is not everything that can be said about the ego" (Slap 1974, p. 39). She, on her part, conceded the truth of his remark and noted for the benefit of the audience that ego theory had taken two different directions, that of defense activity and that of the ego building up its own organization. "Somehow," she observed, "these two trends are apart and are never fully unified. . . . In my talk [1974d] yesterday I tried to find a solution by showing that these two areas of phenomena . . . belong to two different types of psychopathology" (Slap 1974, p. 39). In a more general way one could argue that adaptation, at least to the biologists from whom it was borrowed, must remain the broader concept. Psychologically, any synonymity and permanence in the equation defense $=$ adaptation must appear narrow and counterproductive to the making of relevant observations.

In reviewing the important prewar publications on ego theory of both Anna Freud and Hartmann, Kanzer and Blum concluded that "both were interrelated approaches to the total personality" (1967, p. 94). The specific *raison* behind Freud's preferred approach was almost certainly the technical-therapeutic requirement for improved analytical progress. The special efficacy of that approach is indicated by the observation that no ego function so sensitively reflects the balance between drives and ego as defenses (Alpert, Neubauer, and Weil 1956). Not surprisingly then, the analysis of ego defenses remains essential to many analytical therapies, particularly those associated with the mainstream of orthodox Freudian theory and practice.

In her work published after 1936 Anna Freud frequently returned to clarify and augment her initial statement on ego defenses. Wartime studies of evacuated children provided ample corroborative material: for example, Anne, 6 years old, graphically and poignantly described as attempting to defend herself against anxiety (A. Freud 1973a, pp. 313–323); the many children who defended themselves against aggressive behavior from peers (1944a, pp. 570–571); and children such as Peter, 4 years old, whose father, although killed in an air raid was nevertheless "taking me to the zoo today" (1944a, p. 642). All these and related observations, as Anna Freud noted, indicated the "inevitable defences against the inner feeling of loss and deprivation" (1944a, p. 642). In her postwar work Anna Freud stressed the notion of age-adequate behaviors and was then able to state in regard to the ego's defensive activity, in contrast to the early therapeutic concern with the quantitative factor in repression, that "educators and therapists should now be concerned with the question of whether the methods of defence used by a child's ego are appropriate to his age level, and adequate for dealing with his current problems" (1950a, p. 620).

Anna Freud's other references to and uses of defense concepts are too numerous to catalogue, occurring as they do throughout her published writings. But there was one particularly valuable historical synopsis in 1968, in her discussion of the emergence of ego analysis—also referred to as defense analysis—which integrated

The Ego and the Mechanisms of Defence with the approaches of such contemporary workers as Edward Bibring, Otto Fenichel, and Heinz Hartmann (A. Freud 1969a).

To illustrate aspects of defense theory currently of interest, attention is directed to the question of chronology or the developmental sequence of defenses (Hoffer 1968, W. E. Freud 1975); the applications of Anna Freud's relatively late concept of negativism and the fear of emotional surrender (Valenstein 1973); and the creation of a definitive inventory of defenses with a view to attaining the "optimum scope" of psychoanalytic therapy (Rangell 1975).

THE LATER YEARS IN VIENNA

After 1936 and her major theoretical work of the first half of her life, Anna Freud, then 41 years old, was at the peak of her position and influence in Vienna. That these "golden years" were few can be attributed to the beginning in Europe of violent political and anti-Semitic movements.

Anna Freud continued to be interested in teacher education throughout the late 1930s. No sooner had she published her book on defense than she presented to the Vienna Psychoanalytic Society on June 17, 1936, "A Contribution to the Analysis of Teachers" (Report of the Vienna Psychoanalytic Society 1937), which was apparently not published separately. During this period, with her colleague Willi Hoffer, she gave a course of lectures on the "Development of Psychoanalytic Paedagogy" (Report of the Vienna Psychoanalytic Society 1938), which was presumably the same Viennese Training Course for Psychoanalytic Paedagogues (*Lehrgang für Psychoanalytische Pädagogen*) referred to elsewhere (Ekstein and Motto 1969). Other participants included Dorothy Burlingham, Steff Bornstein, and Editha Sterba. Many years later Anna Freud credited Hoffer with the principal role in this "Vienna Course for Educators" (1966e), which she also noted as including a three-year postgraduate program.

An interesting innovation around this time attributed to Anna Freud was the practice of organizing what Eitingon termed the "conversations" at the Vienna Institute (Report of the 14th I. P. A. Congress 1937). These conversations were regular weekly meetings of some five or six candidates in training with a training analyst. The intention was to induce novices to join more freely into the discussion of ideas and problems in theory and technique, and it seems likely that with this subtle scheme, Anna Freud wished to spare others the long years that she herself had experienced as a silent candidate at larger gatherings, envying the vocal fluency and command of more experienced analysts such as Nunberg (A. Freud 1969k). Anna Freud's broader expertise in training candidates was acknowledged with her appointment as vice-president to the International Training Commission (I. T. C.) of the International Psychoanalytic Association (Report of the 14th I. P. A. Congress 1937).

Liselotte Frankl, a young Viennese postdoctoral student of psychology, first met Anna Freud in 1936, was interviewed by her at the *Lehrinstitut*, and began training with her. Frankl had worked in Charlotte Buhler's academic psychology department at the University of Vienna. Living in a house across from August Aichhorn's, Frankl was first drawn into working with Aichhorn's adolescent patients and their parents, and thence into psychoanalysis (Dyer 1980, letter dated April 6, 1977). She later worked in the Hampstead War Nursery while studying for her medical and psychiatric degrees in London, and she eventually became the first medical director and psychiatrist in charge at the Hampstead Child Therapy Clinic. Perhaps in part influenced by the academic sympathies of colleagues such as Liselotte Frankl, Anna Freud in recent years effected a synthesis between the analytical and academic approaches to the child and appropriately cited works by Buhler and others (A. Freud 1950a, 1963a, 1965a, 1969u).

Another student, the American psychiatrist Edith B. Jackson who had trained in Anna Freud's child analysis seminar, founded and maintained in Vienna during 1937 and 1938 an experimental day nursery. In the "Jackson Nursery," as it was thereafter called, the term *experimental* was applied because "at that time group care for children of that age was unheard of" (A. Freud 1967c, p. 226). The children's ages were between 1 and 2 years; some 20 toddlers from families in the poorest quarter of Vienna were selected; and facilities were rented in a local Montessori school building. The key workers at the Jackson Nursery were, in addition to Anna Freud and Edith Jackson, Josephine Stross as pediatrician, Julia Deming in charge of feeding schedules, Dorothy Burlingham, and a number of both Austrian and American professional and volunteer workers (A. Freud 1978c). The motivation for this venture was the desire

> . . . to gather direct [as opposed to reconstructed] information about still earlier ages, particularly the second year of life, which we deemed all-important for the child's essential advance from primary to secondary process functioning; for the establishment of feeding and sleeping habits; for acquiring the rudiments of superego development and impulse control [and] for the establishment of object ties to peers. (A. Freud 1978c, p. 731)

This nursery was the model for the later Hampstead War Nursery, and even the attention paid to underprivileged groups of children remained a feature of the later work done there, countering the common argument that psychoanalysis is only for the very rich.

It would probably be an error to think of the Jackson Nursery, or indeed any single venture, as representing Anna Freud's principal work and interests. Her own view was that the Vienna nursery was simply one more venture, besides the child guidance clinic for young children directed by Editha Sterba, the similar clinic for adolescents directed by August Aichhorn, and the various teacher training programs in which Willi Hoffer was especially closely involved (A. Freud 1974e, p. ix). All these endeavors—along with the pupils and colleagues who shared them, the child analysis seminars and related training activities, and the pedagogical *Zeitschrift* and similar publications—were merely aspects and logical developments of that Vienna School of Child Analysis, whose single most representative and respected member was Anna Freud. It was part of the character of the subject that she herself did not say this, but pointed instead to the colleagues (Sterba, Aichhorn, Hoffer) whose initiatives she found most worthwhile.

Our assessment of Anna Freud during the late 1930s differs sharply from that of Paul Roazen, who concluded that "during Freud's lifetime Anna Freud was never in her own right a leader in psychoanalysis, but by now she has inherited Freud's throne" (1975, p. 447). Unfortunately Roazen confused two distinct possibilities for Anna Freud, namely, becoming an independent leader in psychoanalysis and eclipsing her father. Although the latter was scarcely feasible during his lifetime, as he continued to work almost to his last days, it by no means follows that the first possibility should be dependent on the latter. By the Vienna of the mid-1930s, Anna Freud had become a highly organized child analysis leader and an enduring force in the world of psychoanalysis generally. This was especially true from the standpoint of the growing ranks of the younger generation of European child analysts, many of whom even 30 years later continued to stand professionally close to Anna Freud.

The new analytical education continued to occupy Anna Freud's time, though her paper, "A Review of Psychoanalytic Paedagogy" given at the second Four Countries Conference in Budapest in May 1937, was unfortunately never published. The available abstract (*Bulletin Report* of the I. P. A., *International Journal of Psychoanalysis* 1938) indicates two parts to the contribution: (1) a historical survey showing the piecemeal emergence of the new education as a continual by-product of psychoanalytic theory, as well as certain instances of contradictions and misconceptions arising from this; and (2) a discussion of child training and masturbation as a special instance.

A new conceptual force was seen forming at the same Budapest Conference which attracted Anna Freud's contribution to the new education. She chaired a symposium on "Early Stages of Development of the Ego: Primary Object Love," in which Michael Balint made an early bid to shift the trend of ego theory into object relations theory. A key analytical figure of that period, Balint was trained initially with Sachs in Berlin before being analyzed by Sandor Ferenczi in Budapest (Sutherland 1972). Balint soon became a daring analytical theorist who, independently of Ronald Fairbairn of Edinburgh, early distinguished between the psychoanalytic theory of personality based on the development of instinctual aims and that based on the development of object relations. Emigrating first to Manchester, then London where be began a long association with the Tavistock Clinic, Balint coined the term *basic fault* to denote important areas of pathology in the early development of the infant-mother relationship (Balint 1962). This concept found immediate support from Anna Freud, who used it on a number of occasions (1962d, 1971f, 1974d). At the 22nd I. P. A. Congress in Edinburgh in 1961, Anna Freud and Balint sat on a panel discussing "The Theory of the Infant-Parent Relationship." Miss Freud's own later work on the early interactions of the first years of life made a veritable quantum jump in theory, advancing a genetic corollary to the dynamic-structuralist model offered in *The Ego and the Mechanisms of Defence*.

Balint's early paper on the ego and primary love was notable also in that it presented an independent criticism of the rival child analysis schools of Vienna and London. (Balint, along with Imre Hermann and Alice Balint, formed a "Budapest group" firmly grounded in the work of Freud and Ferenczi.) Balint saw the London group, typified by Joan Riviere, as overstressing the insatiability of the child's biological nature, as well as the intensity and vehemence of its frustration reactions. Balint criticized the Vienna group, typified by Robert Waelder, for clinging to the hypothesis of primary narcissism, which to Balint had the great drawback of barring the assumption of a relationship with external objects (1937). But in the ensuing years these rival groups came to agree on many points.

An English edition of *Das Ich und die Abwehrmechanism* appeared in 1937, translated by Cecil M. Baines. Two of the chapters were also considered of sufficient importance to merit separate publication in the *Almanach der Psychoanalyse*: Chapter 8 dealing with ego restriction (A. Freud 1937a) and Chapter 12 on the theme of puberty (A. Freud 1937b).

It was at this time too that Sigmund Freud wrote to his old friend Max Eitingon, then in Palestine, to say that the most gratifying thing in his surroundings was "Anna's capacity for work and her consistent achievement" (E. L. Freud 1960, pp. 431–432). Freud undoubtedly saw his daughter's professional field as being the application of psychoanalysis to education and the upbringing (*Erziehung*) of the child. In his *New Introductory Lectures* of 1933 Freud wrote in regard to that theme, "I am at least glad to be able to say that my daughter, Anna Freud, has made this her life-work, and is in this way making good my own neglect of the subject" (1933, lecture 34). Although Anna Freud certainly made good her father's confessed neglect of the subject of education, this was by no means her principal claim to recognition in the literature of psychoanalytic psychology; rather it was her contributions as a developmental psychologist (Chapter 6).

Early in 1938 Nazi Germany put an end to all organized psychoanalytic activity in Austria. Anna Freud was one of the signatories to a document formally suspending the activities of the Vienna Society and Institute.[11] From then on she became involved in urgent efforts to extricate as many analysts and their families as possible from Austria before the inevitable closing of the frontiers. Her own experiences have been described by eyewitnesses in Vienna at the time (Jones 1957, Schur 1972, M. Freud 1957). One of them, Schur, admitted that he never actually asked her about her experiences with the Gestapo. However, he did repeat a story that she many years later authorized him to report. When things seemed hopeless, Anna had asked her father, "Wouldn't it be better if we all killed ourselves?" to which Freud had retorted, "Why? Because they would like us to?" (Schur 1972, p. 499). The rationale for recounting this episode—which on the surface does nothing to enhance Anna Freud's own character—is perhaps to be

[11]On March 20, 1938. The other signatories were Jones, Federn, Marie Bonaparte, Kris, Waelder, Hitschmann, Bibring, Hoffer, and Hartmann on behalf of the Vienna Psychoanalytic Society; Muller-Braunschweig and Beranek from the Berlin Society (Nazified); Berta Steiner and Martin Freud on behalf of the I. P. Verlag; and Anton Sauerwald, the Nazi commissar in Vienna. A facsimile of the document is available in the *International Journal of Psychoanalysis* 1938.

found in her desire to demonstrate her father's defiance and characteristic determination, which few could sustain in those difficult times.

In the month after the annexation of Austria, Freud submitted to the British Consulate in Vienna a list of 16 persons for whom he wished to obtain visas. In the fourth place on the list was *"Tochter Anna, 42 Jährigen,"* preceded by the names of Martha Freud, Minna Bernays, and Sigmund Freud himself. The others were Martin and Esti Freud and their children Walter and Sophie, Ernst Halberstadt, Mathilde and Robert Hollitscher, Max Schur and his wife and two children, and Paula Fichtl, the Freuds' family housekeeper, who 40 years later still was working in Anna Freud's London residence. The complete list of Freud's "family" is given in a footnote to Schur's biography of Freud (1972, p. 501).

Freud's earlier biographer, Ernest Jones, noted that father and daughter passed the difficult waiting days in Vienna by doing translation work together (1957, p. 239). The major work undertaken was Marie Bonaparte's book *Topsy, Chow-Chow au Poil d'Or* (Topsy, the Golden-Haired Chow), which was translated into German.

Anna and her father finally left Vienna by train for Paris on June 4, 1938 (Jones 1957). A close friend, Josephine Stross, accompanied them and acted as Freud's physician during the unavoidable absence of Max Schur. The Vienna phase of Anna Freud's life was now over, though she continued to work for some months to secure the release of others from Austria. It was more than 30 years before she returned to Vienna.

The emigration from Vienna of Anna Freud's circle of professional colleagues is of real significance to the subsequent dispersal pattern of senior analysts in Britain and the United States. England initially received, in addition to Freud's party, Edward and Grete Bibring, Dorothy Burlingham, Ludwig Eidelberg, Eduard Hitschmann, Willi and Hedwig Hoffer, Otto Isakower, Ernst and Marianne Kris, Maxim Steiner, Erwin Stengel, and a number of students who became better known in later years. Most of the other prominent analysts and child analysts went to the United States, including Berta Bornstein, Edith Buxbaum, Gustav Bychowski,

Felix and Helen Deutsch, Beate Rank, Annie Reich, Richard and Editha Sterba, Heinz Hartmann, Fritz Redl, Otto Sperling, Maurits and Anny Katan, Margaret Mahler, Robert and Jenny Waelder, Ludwig Jekels, Paul Federn, Herman Nunberg, and Anna Maenchen (*Bulletin Reports* of the I. P. A. 1939 and 1948). The initial group in America was soon joined by a second wave from England, including Ernst and Marianne Kris, Max Schur, Eidelberg, the Bibrings, Hitschmann, and Isakower.

Anna Freud's good friend and colleague August Aichhorn remained in Vienna throughout the Nazi period, "in solitude and obscurity" (A. Freud 1951k), as she later observed. Aichhorn engineered the postwar reemergence of the Vienna Psychoanalytic Society,[12] thereby holding open the prospect of Freud's daughter eventually returning to visit an analytically aware Vienna.

---

[12]Aichhorn's solitide was not as complete as Anna Freud infers. Alfred Winterstein also remained in Vienna throughout the war, later becoming president of the revived Vienna Psychoanalytic Society. Similarly, in Budapest, Imre Hermann, Istvan Hollos, and Endre Almasy survived the holocaust and later revived the study of, and training in, psychoanalysis.

CHAPTER FOUR

Emigration and War Work

Sigmund Freud, his wife Martha, and daughter Anna arrived in London on June 6, 1938, aboard the train from Dover. They were met by the faithful and tireless Ernest Jones, his wife Katherine, and certain members of the Freud family who had managed to leave Vienna earlier. Jones then drove them to the house at 39 Elsworthy Road adjoining Primrose Hill in North London, where Ernst Freud had rented temporary quarters for the family. Here they stayed until September of that year. What was for Freud's biographer a final chapter and ending (Jones 1957) is, for us, the start of a long and comprehensive phase in the life and work of Freud's daughter, the child analyst Anna Freud.

Forty years later the house on Elsworthy Road is still there, large and pleasant, and the view to the top of Primrose Hill cannot have changed much from prewar days. The old-fashioned lamp posts still survive, and the original dark-tiled street signs are still in place. Only from the brow of the park has the scenery changed, with a much altered London skyline in the distance. Interestingly, a number of Anna Freud's colleagues and associates moved in later years into houses along Elsworthy Road (for example, Ruth Thomas and Alex and Elisabeth Holder).

Eva Rosenfeld visited Anna Freud and her father almost daily at the temporary dwelling. "I went, naturally, as a close friend" she observed (Dyer 1980, interview). At this time too Eva told Freud and Anna of her desire to undergo a further analysis, this time with Melanie Klein, whose work she had become interested in during the years since 1936 and from attending the meetings of the British Psychoanalytic Society. Roazen (1975, p. 441) offered a most misleading portrayal of these events, even suggesting a final rift between Anna Freud and Eva Rosenfeld at that time. Rosenfeld's recent verbal testimony is therefore given here:

Dr. Paula Heimann, a student of Mrs. Klein's, first introduced me to her work. By 1938 I had developed the desire to approach Mrs. Klein, to find out more and to have a further analysis. I wrote to Professor Freud about it first. He felt he ought to keep out of it. I went to see them and discussed it. . . . With Anna, yes. She was very understanding. She knew I had only had a year or so of analysis with Professor Freud. I was in analysis with Mrs. Klein from June 1938 to September 1939. It was interrupted by the outbreak of war, when Mrs. Klein left for Scotland. (Dyer 1980, interview)

Paula Heimann, a venerable figure among the British Psychoanalytical Society's middle generation, is of some interest here. Though initially a student of Klein's, Heimann has in more recent years moved closer professionally to Anna Freud, while managing to preserve an eclectic and essentially independent standpoint. Perhaps her friend Eva Rosenfeld's wide sympathies were partly responsible. Heimann (1968) has duly acknowledged the "original and unprecedented" nature of a recommendation by Anna Freud (1966f) to the effect that psychiatrists would benefit by learning not just isolated aspects of psychoanalysis, but rather the whole language and metapsychology. On another occasion, Heimann and others enthusiastically acknowledged Anna Freud's lucidity and ability to clarify difficult themes at congresses (Heimann and Valenstein 1972). For her part, Anna Freud (1969a, p. 151) pointed to Heimann's "foremost contribution" to the topic of countertransference.

Ernest Jones listed a number of important visitors who were received by Freud, and presumably by his daughter Anna, in the first few weeks in London. These included H. G. Wells, Salvador Dali, Stefan Zweig, and the anthropologist Bronislaw Malinowski. Toward the end of June three secretaries of the Royal Society stopped by with their charter book for the old psychoanalyst to sign. Thirty years later Herman Nunberg (1969) recorded his own impressions of seeing Freud in these last months and was deeply shocked to find his old mentor so enfeebled and suffering. Nunberg had left for the United States in 1933 and saw Freud only briefly again in 1936. For a long time after 1938, Nunberg wrote, he remained under the shadow of that last visit to London (1969). If any such spiritual denouement impressed Anna Freud, she did not show it, and her adjustment to and acceptance of the inevitable seem to be clearly implied by the unremitting work obligations that she took on almost immediately after her arrival in England.

The London County Council Inspector of Schools, J. C. Hill, first met Anna Freud in the summer of 1938 and immediately enlisted her help in presenting a series of lectures on psychoanalytic psychology to teachers and educators in London. Hill had, for 15 years or more, been personally interested in Freud's psychology and its application to education and teaching. He initially had hoped to persuade Freud himself to give a lecture, though he was clearly unaware of Freud's physical condition. Ernst Freud answered Hill's letter and suggested that his sister Anna might help with the lectures to teachers. In due course Hill was invited to discuss the matter with Anna Freud, and she thereupon agreed to a series of three lectures. Many years later Hill recalled that he did not impose any conditions on the speaker's material and that she had "a free hand" to develop her theme (Dyer 1980, letter dated February 24, 1977).

According to a specimen ticket to these lectures (Ekstein and Motto 1969), they were simply entitled "Psychology by Miss A. Freud." They are especially noteworthy as being Anna Freud's first public lectures in England, and in the absence of any known copies, we may perhaps assume for them a certain similarity to their author's earlier Vienna lectures to teachers. The London series extended into 1939,[1] and Hill indicated that they were very well attended and enthusiastically received.

The 15th International Psychoanalytic Congress took place in Paris in August 1939. Anna attended only a part of the congress, owing to her father's illness, but she nevertheless presided as joint vice-president and was reelected to the International Executive Committee and also to the International Training Commission

---

[1]The first lecture was given on Thursday, October 27, 1938, at the Central School of Arts and Crafts, London.

(Report of the 15th I. P. A. Congress 1939). Together with Federn she chaired a symposium on "Ego Strength and Ego Weakness," and although she gave no scientific paper, she did read in German her absent father's paper "The Progress in Spirituality."

Training matters continued to exercise a controversial sway that summer, and it appears that sharp differences arose over the question of lay analysis (Jones 1957), which was discussed at the Paris meeting. There Anna Freud presented her views on the difficulties and advantages of what were termed "after-analyses" (Report of the 15th I. P. A. Congress 1939), and the same summer she presented a report on the *Probleme der Lehranalyse* (1950b) to the International Education Commission in Paris. Though not published for about 12 years, the report stated rather fully Anna Freud's views on many aspects of the psychoanalytic training of candidates. Although she had taken an active interest in training matters since at least 1925, it may well have been that by 1938 her concern in that direction had been sharpened by the sudden exodus of analysts from continental Europe. One eyewitness in particular recorded that the whole of the Paris Congress was overshadowed by the mood of political events, and almost all of the participants were refugees who did not know which way to turn (Nunberg 1969). Though Nunberg's account of the feeling of despair and disorientation may have been valid for the majority of displaced European psychoanalysts, Anna Freud apparently did not have such feelings. This possibly may be due to the Freuds' greater security of status as citizens in their new homeland, which to some extent distinguished the Freuds from others less fortunate. Even more certainly, though, was their identification with the wider purpose and *Weltanschauung* of psychoanalysis, which inspired Anna Freud possibly more than any other individual, except her father. In other words, Anna Freud's principal *raison d'être* did not alter or suffer with her displacement from Vienna to London, and this undoubtedly sustained her through the difficulties of those troubled times.

Anna and her father moved into their permanent London home, at 20 Maresfield Gardens, Hampstead, on September 27, 1938, a week after Martha Freud and the maid Paula Fichtl had gotten it ready for them.[2] "Tante Minna" soon joined them there, though the brothers Ernst and Martin Freud each had houses of their own in North London. Dorothy Burlingham, who in Vienna had occupied the apartment directly above the Freuds' apartment, initially settled in London at 2 Maresfield Gardens and in later years lived at the same address as Anna Freud did.

The involvement of the newly arrived Viennese in the internal and business affairs of the British Psychoanalytic Society was automatic and immediate, and as early as June 1938 Anna Freud was on the influential training committee of the British Institute, together with Melanie Klein and Ella F. Sharpe (Report of the British Psychoanalytic Society 1939). The institute's premises at that time were in what was referred to as "the old building," and the third-floor meetings there between the continental émigrés and the more enthusiastic students and members of the British Society's non-Kleinian group were described by Elizabeth Zetzel (1969). Then known as Elizabeth Rosenberg, in later years Zetzel became a sympathetic ally to the Viennese in their professional resettlement.

Some of the warmest interest in and support for Anna Freud in her early days in London came from two young continental analysts who had arrived some years previously, Barbara Lantos and Kate Friedlander. Elizabeth Rosenberg Zetzel noted "happy contacts" between the Vienna newcomers and many of the younger members of the London Institute, and she also viewed this personal rapport as being significant in efforts to understand prevailing theoretical differences. By the late thirties these theoretical differences had resulted in the tendentious "Kleinian controversy," and the arrival of Anna Freud in London was to a British Psychoanalytic Institute largely dominated by Klein and her followers. The various groupings of the British Society before, during, and after the Second World War were outlined by Glover (1966), who was closely involved in the controversy and who himself at different times variously belonged to the pro-Klein group, the pro-Anna Freud or orthodox group, and the nonaligned or independent group.

[2] At the time of her death, Miss Freud had lived there for 44 years, two years longer than at the Berggasse apartment.

An intriguing figure in the internal difficulties of the British Society at this time was Melitta Schmideberg, the daughter of Melanie Klein. According to one eyewitness, theoretical discussions at the London Psychoanalytic Institute's meetings in the late thirties often found Schmideberg, supported by Edward Glover, ranged against Klein, supported by Ernest Jones (Dyer 1980, interview with Eva Rosenfeld). In the opinion of the late Eva Rosenfeld, Schmideberg was probably more anxious to rebel against a powerful mother figure than to champion the work of the Vienna School against the Kleinian viewpoint. (But Schmideberg contributed little to our information about Anna Freud, just an isolated review article [Schmideberg 1935]. In return, Anna Freud occasionally cited Schmideberg's early work on the connection between eating inhibitions and inhibitions of intellectual activities [1946a, p. 40].) Other notable Britishers of the emigration period were Ella F. Sharpe and Helen Sheehan-Dare, both of whom were sufficiently independent to accord a sympathetic hearing to Anna Freud and her colleagues and both of whom gave constructive reviews of Anna Freud's work a few years later (Sharpe 1946, Sheehan-Dare 1945).

At the time of her resettlement in London, Anna Freud's motto was "We are guests in this country and were not brought here to create trouble" (Lantos 1966, citing Anna Freud verbatim). Sigmund Freud himself had set just such a tone before leaving Vienna, and in a letter to Jones he remarked, "I hope that in England [Anna] will also be able to do much for analysis, but she will not intrude" (E. L. Freud 1960, letter dated May 15, 1938). Despite the approach of wartime emergency conditions, which caused Melanie Klein to leave London for the far north of the British Isles, there was no respite for Anna Freud from the internal frictions that threatened to embroil the British analysts in verbal internecine warfare of their own. The available evidence suggests that Anna Freud sought to adopt her father's conciliatory advice and only reluctantly defended her continuing theoretical divergencies with the Kleinians.

Anna Freud began her professional work at the London Institute almost at once. Practical seminars on the child were held regularly throughout the winter of 1938–1939 (Report of the British Psycho-analytic Society 1940), and a year later the seminars of both Anna Freud and Grete Bibring attracted, among other interested persons, Elizabeth Rosenberg. Many years later Rosenberg attributed her own interest to the earlier informal contacts with the Viennese almost from the moment of their arrival (Zetzel 1969).

Of Anna Freud's students in this period, Elisabeth Geleerd is of particular interest. The Dutch-born Geleerd had begun her analyti-cal training in Vienna in 1936 and then continued it with Anna Freud in London. She then went to the United States around 1942, becoming Elisabeth Geleerd Loewenstein a few years after (Tartakoff 1970). An independent thinker, Geleerd presented her views forcefully and capably, even when the area for discussion centered on such professionally awkward topics as the technical efficacy of Klein's methods versus Anna Freud's (Geleerd 1963). Geleerd's contributions to adolescence were briefly cited by her early teacher in some of Anna Freud's most significant publications (1958b, 1965a).

Sigmund Freud's cancer continued to cause concern, and a new consultant was invited to give an opinion. This man, Wilfred Trotter, had had a long association with psychoanalytic ideas. As early as 1903 it was he who first urged the young neurologist Ernest Jones to read an early English review of Freud's work in the celebrated journal *Brain* (Jones 1957). Trotter's eminence, however, failed to dazzle Freud's daughter. Right or wrong, she and Max Schur disagreed with the consultant's conclusions and in February 1939 carried on with their own regime of care. During these months Anna Freud's daily routine involved seeing patients of her own, training candidates, organizing the exodus of the remaining analysts from continental Europe, and being on more or less 24-hour duty as her father's nurse.

One of Freud's favorite pupils, Heinz Hartmann, visited the London house early in 1939 before leaving for his own new home in New York. The Freuds' old friend Marie Bonaparte also visited several times from Paris. In the summer of 1939 the British and French Psychoanalytic Societies held a joint meeting at which Anna Freud, on June 30, read a paper on "Sublimation and

Sexualisation." The same paper was apparently reread at the London Institute in 1940 (Friedlander 1945). It does not appear to have ever been published in its original form, though it may well have been incorporated into a later paper on educational hygiene (A. Freud 1948a).

By July 1939 Sigmund Freud was receiving his last visitors. One of them was Hanns Sachs—"one of the very last" before the old psychoanalyst's death, according to Ernest Jones—and the loyalty of colleagues such as Sachs was not lost on Anna. A decade later she (1948b) contributed a foreword to Sachs's last and posthumously published book. Several pages in length, this was the first prefatory piece she wrote for a colleague, and it inevitably placed the recipient in a unique position.[3] Sachs emphasized the social applications of psychoanalysis as a psychology of normal states. He brought to psychoanalysis his own feeling for *Menschenkenntnis* as a form of artistic-intuitive "knowledge of human beings," and more than for most in this field, "psychoanalytic psychology meant, above all, the means to inquire into the daily behaviour of human beings, into their relations with each other and with their chosen love-objects, as well as in their attitude toward the inevitable problems of life and death" (A. Freud 1948b, p. 9).

THE DEATH OF SIGMUND FREUD

Anna Freud's much revered father died on September 23, 1939. His personal physician Max Schur had moved into the house at 20 Maresfield Gardens during the last days so as to be closer at hand in time of need. Schur was the guardian of one of the few details concerning his patient, which was kept from Anna Freud until the

---

[3]In a wider consideration, one could accept that the daughter was in part doing what Freud would have done, had he lived. The acknowledgment thus places Sachs with Abraham, Ferenczi, and other close colleagues to whom Freud bestowed testimony.

end, namely, Freud's pact with Schur on the question of his eventual release from the physical torment he had endured for so long. Freud's last words, spoken to Schur, were to "tell Anna about this" ("sagen sie es der Anna," Schur 1972).

If the death of her father was the blow to Anna Freud that one might expect of such an event, there was apparently no public show of such. Her father had many times touched on the subject of death in his writings, and no doubt also in his conversations. The appropriate sense of the inevitable is such in Freud's work that one could, with Montaigne (*Essays*, 1580–1588), say of him that "to study philosophy is to learn to die." We have made clear Anna's close identification with both the man and his work, and to this we add the suggestion that, for Anna, her father also possessed all the qualities of a hero figure. Certainly his manner of dying was nothing if not heroic, and the Nietzschean quality of it would not be lost on the daughter who had been compared with Antigone.[4]

Freud was cremated at nearby Golders Green in North London. Stefan Zweig and Ernest Jones read the funeral addresses (Jones 1957), and the Freud family was joined by Marie Bonaparte from Paris, Hans and Jeanne Lampl from the Netherlands, and a great many students and followers from London and elsewhere. Thereafter, on the anniversaries of Freud's birth and death—May 6 and September 23 respectively—a small gathering of close followers would go with Anna Freud to her father's sepulcher. In his later years it seems likely that Freud had increasingly identified himself with the Old Testament Moses, albeit unconsciously, as a solution to a problem of religion that had pursued him all his adult life (Pfieffer 1972, letter dated January 6, 1935). The role of Joshua, who saw the Promised Land that Moses could view only from afar, had many years earlier been attributed to C. G. Jung (Jones 1955, letter dated January 17, 1909), before Jung's quarrel with Freud, and would in any case have almost certainly been unacceptable to Anna Freud. If one had to settle on a biblical parallel appropriate

4"One should die proudly when it is no longer possible to live proudly." F. Nietzsche, *Twilight of the Gods*, 1888, p. 36.

to Freud's daughter, it would perhaps be found in Ruth, with her example of fealty to the aging Naomi (Ruth 1:16–17).[5]

The external Freud had departed, but the internal Freud remained, a focus for memory, object relationship, and exemplary pattern. The work of training and therapy continued virtually unabated, and new colleagues continued to swell the ranks of Anna Freud's nascent London circle. The Australian-born educational psychologist Ruth Thomas met Anna Freud for the first time in 1939 when she applied for training at the Institute of Psychoanalysis and "chose Miss Freud as my analyst" (Dyer 1980, letter dated April 21, 1977). During and after the war years, Ruth Thomas was educational psychologist to the Central Association for Mental Welfare (later the National Council for Mental Health) and was a frequent contributor to the then influential journal *New Era in Home and School.*

By now the non-Kleinian group within the British Psychoanalytic Society, enlarged by the influx of colleagues from Vienna and elsewhere, had begun holding group discussion meetings with a view to "keeping themselves sharp," as one commentator put it (Armytage 1976). The lead in this initiative seems to have stemmed largely from Kate Friedlander, who was also forming close mutual links with Anna Freud. The group meetings soon took on the form of a regular Wednesday seminar, led by Anna Freud at her own home (Lantos 1966). The choice of Wednesday was by no means mere chance, and we are reminded here of Freud's Wednesday Psychological Society in the early part of the century and the subsequent Wednesday evening meetings of the Vienna Psychoanalytical Society.

Eva Rosenfeld was one of those who went to Anna Freud's Wednesday seminar in the early months of the Second World War. We went regularly, she confided, "bombs or no bombs" (Dyer 1980, interview with Rosenfeld) and with a full wartime blackout. Others attending included Barbara Low, the Hoffers, Elizabeth R.

[5]Ruth said, "Entreat me not to leave thee, or to return from following after thee: for whither thou goest, I will go, and where thou lodgest I will lodge. . . . Where thou diest, will I die, and there will I be buried" (A. V. version).

Zetzel, Dorothy Burlingham, Barbara Lantos, and Kate Friedlander. Activities at the London Institute had virtually ceased, and in the absence of formally arranged lectures and similar meetings, the early Hampstead seminars served a valuable and by no means merely parochial role. The special needs of young students in training continued to attract Anna Freud's special concern, and records show that even in the most difficult period of the war, from January 1940 until 1942, she conducted a regular practical seminar for the British Psychoanalytic Society.

In addition to all these ventures and activities, Anna Freud was also busy editing her father's voluminous writings. This eventually resulted in the appearance in London, at the height of the air raids, of Sigmund Freud's *Gesammelte Schriften*, the most complete edition of his collected works then available, albeit only in German. For this particular project Anna Freud collaborated with other editors, namely Marie Bonaparte, Edward Bibring, Willi Hoffer, Ernst Kris, and Otto Isakower.

With the onset of the German Luftwaffe's bombing blitz on London in the autumn of 1940, many people were made homeless, especially in the already underprivileged East End of the city where the docks and military arsenals were located. Many children who, for one reason or another, had not been evacuated in the previous year to safe countryside areas, were made either homeless, parentless, or both, and many mothers engaged in war work sought safer residence for their young ones. In response to this emergency, Anna Freud and a few of her closest associates embarked on what is now widely accepted as a landmark in the story of residential child care and psychoanalytic child study.

THE HAMPSTEAD WAR NURSERY

The first wartime Children's Rest Centre was set up on an *ad hoc* and financially very precarious basis in a house a few minutes' walk from Anna Freud's North London home. Money was donated by friends, the house and equipment by a charitable Swedish Committee, and by October 1940 the new evacuation center was complete with its own basement shelter reinforced against possible bombing. It might have been deemed cramped by later standards, but it nevertheless included a large nursery room "equipped as a complete Montessori nursery school" (A. Freud 1973a, p. 3), a toddlers' room with space for running about, a room for afternoon naps, a babies' room with cribs, a doctor's room with a sun lamp, a hospital room for noninfectious illnesses, a parents' clubroom, a staff meeting room, and four staff bedrooms. The large basement, in addition to the shelter with space to sleep 48 children, also had its own kitchen and dining room, and the house had three bathrooms and four toilets. Though residential, it was not run on institutional lines, a point that Anna Freud reemphasized (A. Freud 1973a, p. xxv), and the only real similarity to institutional life was the absence of family.

The financial insecurity of this desirable venture was soon corrected, thanks to the generosity of American sponsors. By March 1941, the American Foster Parents Plan, Inc. of New York had virtually taken over the monetary situation, and Anna Freud's and Dorothy Burlingham's war nursery became one of 30 to 40 such projects sponsored during the war years by the American charity. The Hampstead Nursery had the distinction of being the largest of these relief colonies, and the first of the required monthly reports was submitted to New York in February 1941 (A. Freud 1973a, pp. 3–10). Eric G. Muggeridge, the organizing director of the Foster Parents Plan in England, was for many years the only individual to have ever contributed a prefatory note to a publication by Anna Freud (Burlingham and Freud 1942, A. Freud 1942a), though in more recent times Dorothy Burlingham also wrote a preface (A. Freud 1973e).

The two women together directed the affairs of the Hampstead Nursery, and their close colleague Josephine Stross acted as pediatrician. Hedwig Schwarz headed a team of young nursery assistants, mostly refugees from all over Europe. One of these was Sara Kut, a nurse from Berlin who even then stood out as "slightly older and more composed" (A. Freud 1973, unpublished) than the majority of 16- to 18-year-olds interviewed by Anna Freud. Many years later, under the name of Mrs. Sara Rosenfeld, she wrote some remarkable studies based on children suffering from otherwise inaccessible borderline illnesses.

Another young trainee, Hannah Engl from Vienna, was drawn into the nursery work by Hedwig Schwarz. Forty years later, as Mrs. H. Kennedy, she joined Anna Freud as one of the codirectors of the modern Hampstead Clinic and is expected to play an important part in future developments there (Dyer 1980, interview with H. Kennedy). Other wartime staff included James Robertson, then a social worker, who made films of childhood in a wartime nursery and was later closely associated with the Tavistock Institute.

Liselotte Frankl, then in training at the London Institute of Psychoanalysis, was assigned volunteer duties such as sorting clothing, but she rejects the idea that she was actually a member of the nursery staff (Dyer 1980, interview). Another senior analyst, Ilse Hellman, first met Anna Freud in December 1940 and related the circumstances as follows:

> There had been a flu outbreak amongst the staff of the Hampstead Nursery, and I received a telephone call to go and help out for the day. I went, and was working on the floor with a small group of infants, when someone came in quietly and stood in the background observing. Later she introduced herself as Anna Freud, and offered me the post of Superintendent of the proposed new nursery. (Dyer 1980, interview with I. Hellman)

The initial suggestion for another house had come from the American Foster Parents charity, which also undertook to support the new premises. The new house, or Babies Rest Centre, catering exclusively to the youngest infants and toddlers up to 2½ years of age, was located in the street next to Anna Freud's home, and it opened in June 1941. A month later 29 infants had been taken in, in addition to 32 at the original Children's Rest Centre, which now became known as the "old house" (A. Freud 1973a, pp. 67–68).

The regimen at the Hampstead War Nurseries depended on fresh air and sunlight for the pale shelter-children sent to them from the blitzed areas of London. The nurseries were run partly on the familiar Montessori pattern and partly as an experimental setting for the collection of objective observations on "artificial war orphans" in residential care. Ilse Hellman (Dyer 1980, interview) and Sara Kut (A. Freud 1973a, pp. 353–364) both noted the careful recording on index cards of all relevant details concerning the nursery's children, and it is clear that Anna Freud encouraged all her staff to make similar records from the very start of their work and training. Many years later Humberto Nagera sought to corroborate his own findings by referring back to the sleep-pattern charts of children at the Hampstead War Nurseries (1966). Typical in many ways of such children was Minna, 4½ years old, who was first visited by Anna Freud on the underground platform of the Regents Park tube station, which for a year had served as her sleeping quarters (A. Freud 1973a, p. 105).

Anna Freud summed up the general child-oriented approach of the Hampstead group: "We try to attain hospital standards as far as cleanliness, hygiene, medical supervision and diet are concerned, and try to combine that with the freedom and educational possibilities of nursery life" (1973a, p. 105). To these ends more staff were hired, and a scientific, though informal, training program was introduced into the houses' work schedule, which by the middle of 1941 had grown to three residential buildings with the opening of the "Country House" outside London in Essex.

Notable additions to the nursery staff were two refugee sisters from Augsburg, Sophie and Gertrud Dann, who were appointed as the heads of the babies and toddlers departments, respectively. Sophie, the older sister and a trained social worker and nurse, had first met Anna Freud on December 31, 1940, when applying at 20 Maresfield Gardens for the position of private nurse to Anna Freud's ailing aunt Minna Bernays. After the war and through her work with concentration-camp children, Sophie Dann joined the small and distinctive group of persons who became Anna Freud's scientific coauthors (1951j). The younger sister, Gertrud, continues to the present day as the librarian at Anna Freud's London clinic, and she is extremely knowledgeable regarding her late employer's publications.

Another refugee, Alice Goldberger, had left Berlin on "the very last train out" (Dyer 1980, letter dated June 22, 1977), and on the outbreak of war in England she was placed in an aliens' internment camp. She had become acquainted with psychoanalytic ideas during seminars taken as part of her kindergarten teacher-training program in Berlin in the early thirties. Now, in the internment camp, Goldberger began her own kindergarten for the internees' children and began to train some of the older girls to help. When this venture was reported in the press and came to Anna Freud's attention, she had the Hampstead Nursery send for Goldberger and hired her as the superintendent of their new country house in Essex. The importance of the country house soon increased with the evacuation to it of all the children from the original Children's Rest Centre house, which was then closed for much-needed repairs.

Student training activities began within a few months of the opening of the War Nursery, and the staff held short, almost daily lunchbreak discussions. The topics covered were observations of children's war games and conversations, thumb sucking and toilet training, toddler aggression and ways of handling it, parental attitudes and war experiences, and individual children and their problems (A. Freud 1973a, pp. 22–23). By October 1941 there were 20 female trainees aged 16 to 21 employed in the various houses of the Hampstead War Nursery, and the decision was taken to start up "a purely private and unofficial training scheme" (A. Freud 1973a, p. 122). The aim of this scheme was to educate the students in the common theoretical basis of their work with children, this basis being, of course, psychoanalytic child psychology.

The course of training offered to the wartime students consisted of an introduction to emotional and instinctual development, followed by regular seminars covering the literature; a course of 30 lectures on physical health and sickness; and a series of 16 lectures on mental development, including sensory and intellectual aspects, play and toys, and individual testing. Also covered in the short courses were house management and cooking and sewing, and practical courses were offered in baby and toddler gymnastics and in the widely affirmed Montessori methods (A. Freud 1973a, pp. 123–125). By most standards of child care and study available in the forties, this was a comprehensive and pragmatic course of study, with the prospect of some insight into the psychoanalytic model of the mind, which then, as now, was one of the more powerful conceptual tools in the arena of psychology.

The intensive and productive teaching methods employed by the Hampstead group in those early days was well demonstrated by the exercise that they set themselves in June, July, and August 1942 (A. Freud 1973a, pp. 274–275). Everyone from the most junior to the most senior staff member was required to answer a set of question papers, and this was then followed up a week later by discussions and summaries. The subjects covered in this interactional approach included instinctual development and disturbances such as feeding and sleeping difficulties; character formation, with the appearance of disgust, boastfulness, and so forth; and nursery education and the role of adults. Staff were also asked to categorize their daily activities according to whether they were viewed as being directed toward the child's bodily development, intellectual development, or transformation of instinctual drives.

In the following war years certain advanced students of the war nursery were invited further afield, for example, into local authority schools. This and similar aspects of the interdepartmental training program caused great difficulty for some of the children, who had to put up with their special nurse being moved around the various training facilities. Thus, Miles, a little boy of 3½ years, complained bitterly at the loss of his favorite nurse. He had unfortunately "changed hands too frequently" and showed the bad effects of such experiences by difficult behavior, failure to adapt to the simple rules and regulations of the nursery, and a general slowing up of the normal process of becoming social (A. Freud 1973a, pp. 444–445). Sixty-six trainees received instruction, varying from one to four years in duration, with 14 students being optimally trained for three or more years (A. Freud 1973a, p. 539). Throughout most of this middle war period there were, on the average, 120 children in care under the directorship of Anna Freud.

With the basic nursery provision established and the enthusiastic staff organized, valuable therapeutic and scientific insights, observations, and material began to flow. Time and again the War Nursery's monthly reports stressed that the real trauma for the younger evacuee children was their abrupt separation from their mother or mother figure. In contrast, the much publicized picture of the so-called bomb-shocked child simply did not bear scrutiny. "We have little knowledge of such states in children," wrote Anna Freud and Dorothy Burlingham (A. Freud 1942a, p. 73) in 1941, at the peak of the London blitz. The children did, however, show all the bad effects attributable to shelter life, to anxious mothers, and to disruption of their family life by being separated from their fathers. These chronic factors of prolonged shelter life and family disruption were likewise ranked as greater in their psychological traumatizing effect than was the actual bombing. Implicit in the low etiological priority ascribed to bombing itself is, of course, the idea that most of these children were emotionally protected by their mothers—"shielded" by an "auxiliary" or "caretaking" ego, as later terminology would have it. Edward Glover's early wartime report, condensed from the Hampstead monthly reports, also underscores the virtually complete absence of traumatic shock in the children, none of whom had suffered actual bodily injury (1942). Clearly indicated is the all-important fact of the mother's and familiar mother substitute's role in protecting the child from emotional damage.

During the worst year of the London blitz, Anna Freud was invited to give a short talk on "The Need of the Small Child to Be Mothered."[6] The paper was not published at the time and indeed did not become available until over 30 years later (A. Freud 1973a, pp. 125–131). In effect it was one of the earliest contributions to what would later be widely known as "the maternal deprivation syndrome."

The question posed in the title of Anna Freud's talk was "one of the main questions around which our nursery work is centred" (A. Freud 1973a, p. 125), and it was therefore reported in full in the original monthly report sent to the New York offices of the Foster Parents Plan, Inc. Whereas all the previous provisions of nursery

[6]On October 29, 1941, to the Conference on Wartime Nurseries, held by the Nursery Schools Association of Great Britain under the chairmanship of Lord Horder.

schooling, free milk, child guidance, and so forth had been merely an extension of the real home, the quite different circumstances of the residential wartime nursery work were the fundamental source of many of the difficulties found in running such ventures. An analogy was drawn with the foster home, and the essential task was to find "a really good substitute for the mother relationship" (A. Freud 1973a, p. 127). However, owing to the staffing and organizational characteristics of the professional nursery, "wherever we base nursery work purely on the personal tie between the individual child and the individual worker, we prepare the way for possible new shocks of separation, i.e., for repeated disappointment" (A. Freud 1973a, p. 128). The ideal from the child's point of view is therefore illusory, and alternative strategies need to be sought. Here again, as with its planned involvement of the real parents and other measures, the Hampstead War Nursery instituted methods later widely accepted.

Anna Freud concluded her short piece with an outline of the mother-child relationship at different ages and the implications that may be thus derived for the practical care of the child. Before the end of the first year of life, for example, because of the infant's relatively simple and primitive needs for bodily care and feeding, "it seems comparatively easy to exchange the person of the mother for another one if this person takes over completely" (A. Freud 1973a, p. 129). The ensuing sequence of emotional development centers increasingly on real relationships with recognized persons in the child's family environment, and the removal of the child from the significant people he or she knows will lead to inevitable processes of mourning and regression, the introversion of the child's love, and the consequent inability of education to influence the child. Anna Freud concluded that educational success in the war nurseries would therefore largely depend on "whether we can succeed in creating or in conserving for the children their proper emotional relationships with the outside world" (1973a, p. 131). The issues touched upon in this brief wartime conference contribution foreshadowed the key elements of Anna Freud's interpretation of the early mother-child relationship. She enlarged the new infant-parent model in her two most important wartime publications (1942a, 1944a), and this proved to be the most enduring and psychologically valuable of all the insights gained from the psychoanalytic care and study of the evacuee children.

INFANT-PARENT RELATIONSHIPS

Of the two major publications that came from the Hampstead War Nursery, the first (1942a) presented an objective and comprehensive account of children under conditions of evacuation and enforced nursery life, and its conclusions were aimed largely at improving the manner in which young children might in the future be better prepared for similar evacuations. Many pertinent psychological data were necessarily included, which gave the book an applicability beyond the confines of World War II. The second major book (1944a) was a much more thoroughgoing comparative treatment of the psychological development of the child's emotional life under two very different sets of conditions, namely, those of normal family life and those of the, at best, imperfect substitute family life found in a residential nursery.

The crucial section of *Young Children in Wartime* (1942a) is entitled "Survey of Psychological Reactions" (pp. 156–207) and examines the effects of war experiences on the psychology of the individual child. This important synthesis of empirical observation and analytical interpretation is arranged under a number of headings, the most important of which are considered here.

Any young child's reaction to destruction was found to be heavily determined by separation from the mothering figure. When there was no separation, incidents peculiar to war became to the child part of the wider world of accidents "in line with other accidents of childhood." Anna Freud quickly dispelled the widespread view that scenes of violence and destruction would in themselves somehow sadden and disturb young children, as she, from the vantage point of child analysis, perceived that outer scenes of a world at war largely paralleled and reflected the infant's and youngster's existing aggressive endopsychic state. Certainly children need to be spared as much as possible the horrors of war, "not because horrors and atrocities are so strange to them, but because we want them at this decisive stage of their development to overcome and estrange themselves from the primitive and atrocious wishes of their own infantile nature" (A. Freud 1942a, p. 163). The war thus reinforced what the child already knew but what society desired him or her to outgrow.

There followed Anna Freud's description of the "Five Types of Air-Raid Anxiety." Three types of anxiety were already well known, which she had described metapsychologically in *The Ego and the Mechanisms of Defence.* Two new types of anxiety were now observed under the extreme conditions of bombing, and the comprehensive range of anxiety reactions was quickly accepted by interested authorities (Glover 1942). Such was Anna Freud's insight and lucidity that it may be useful to review here the various anxiety types, highlighted as they were by the new material provided by the blitz.

"Real anxiety" coincides with events in the actual outer world, and in the child it is quickly replaced with disregard and contempt (denial). The motivation for this latter ploy is not difficult to find, and it permits children to "return apparently undisturbed to the pursuits and interests of their own childish world" (A. Freud 1942a, p. 166).

"Instinctual anxiety" arises from the young child's fear of the same infantile aggressive and destructive impulses that he or she has just barely been taught to view as asocial and bad. Younger children who have not yet met this socialization in full have no fear of the air raids that can be attributed to this inner source. The slightly older child will, however, sense the bombing and destructiveness as endangering not only the real outer world but also the fragile and recently established order and control of his or her own inner world.

"Moral anxiety" arises from the child's use of the air raid as a symbolic reinforcement of his or her own inner conscience. Child analysis offered a deep understanding of the psychological state of the 4- or 5-year-old in forming a core of inner ideas that we call conscience. At this stage in development the child "turns back continually to the figures of the outside world on the one hand, to the imaginations of his own fantasy on the other, and borrows strength from both to reinforce the inner commandments" (A. Freud 1942a, p. 167). Quite apart from wartime, Anna Freud pointed out that children have always shown themselves capable of transferring anxiety to such symbolic substitutes as police officers, gypsies, lions, tigers, earthquakes, thunderstorms, and so forth. Even religious symbols are not immune from this transfer of fear, and by an all too easy process "Hitler and German planes take the place of the devil, of the lions and the tigers" (p. 168). As one who later established many salient diagnostic criteria in development, normal and pathological, Anna Freud here made an interesting prediction when she said that we shall know whenever peace returns, for then "nothing is left for the children to be afraid of except their own former ghosts and bogeymen" (p. 169).

These three types of anxiety correspond to the objective anxiety, id anxiety, and superego anxiety whose earlier metapsychological description aptly indicated their structural-dynamic source in the individual's object world. Moreover, the three processes all rightly belong to the quite normal process of child development before the age of 5 years. Additionally, however, and by some primitive form of identificatory mechanism, young infants and preschool children are prone to sharing the fears of the adults who care for them. This led Anna Freud to a fourth kind of anxiety response.

"Displaced maternal anxiety" was shown in the case of Jim, 5 years old, whose mother developed agoraphobia during the air raids. She would stand at the door trembling and insist that the boy dress and stand next to her holding her hand. Jim developed extreme nervousness and bed wetting, but when separated from his mother at the Children's Rest Centre, he showed no special alarm during either the day or night raids. The etiological factor of prime importance seems clear, and Anna Freud affirmed that "no understanding of their own [i.e., of the danger], no development of inhibitions against primitive aggression, and no guilty conscience are necessary for the onset of this further type of anxiety" (1942a, p. 169). She also cited other case material, for example, Isabel, aged 3½ years, and concluded that the generally quiet and self-controlled manner in which the London population met the blitz contributed to the extremely rare occurrence of overtly traumatized and shocked children.

"Anxiety following loss of the father" was noted in the case of four children whose nursery play showed a particularly forced and uncontrolled gaiety. Further bombing forced these children to relive their former traumatic experiences, and "every bomb which falls is like the one which killed the father, and is feared as such" (A. Freud 1942a, p. 172). As with the fourth type of anxiety, this fifth kind was shown to be related to the mother's emotional state when told of her husband's death. We might add that the observed gaiety in the child's play also suggests an element of the denial and reversal of reality already familiar in children's defense mechanisms.

The crucial mother-child relationship and the traumatic effects of separation from the mother were considered against a genetic-developmental curve that supplements other metapsychological descriptions. It was one of the earliest such accounts, and these and similar "developmental pathway charts" are one of Anna Freud's noted achievements (see Chapter 6). The account in question is also valuable as providing possibly the key initial publication in a heterogeneous and multiauthored series that eventually led to the delineation of the now familiar "maternal deprivation syndrome."[7]

The first phase of Anna Freud's description of the mother-child relationship drew upon earlier psychoanalytic formulations and ideas regarding the narcissistic nature of the newborn infant. For the first few months of life the infant's self-centered material needs predominate, with the mother largely fulfilling the need-satisfying role. With their needs thus met, babies at this stage typically withdraw interest (libidinal cathexis) from the outer world, fall asleep, and remain totally dependent. Although a special milieu of warmth and affection is important, babies in this phase also will, when separated from the mother, readily accept feeding

[7]Particularly by John Bowlby, in his World Health Organization Report of 1951. In mainstream psychological accounts, the maternal deprivation pattern is generally based on the studies of Bowlby (1944), Ribble (1944), Goldfarb (1943), and Spitz (1945) with an undue neglect of Anna Freud's comprehensive contribution.

and care from a substitute mother. In the Hampstead War Nursery, such young babies did show certain short-term irregularities in feeding and sleeping when they were first left, and breast-fed babies suffered the most pronounced effects during such separation. This was attributed to the sudden weaning, which the infants experienced as an additional discomfort (A. Freud 1942a, p. 180). When the real mothers returned after a few days' absence, their infants would often fail to recognize them.

The second phase occupies approximately the second 6 months of life and is seen in the manner by which the infant regularly concentrates on the mother at times other than obvious feeding times, follows the mother with eye movements, responds to the mother's smile, and so forth. The mother is by now a specific and readily recognized part of the infant's outer environment and is appreciated and missed for her own sake in addition to fulfilling the infant's bodily needs. The infant's newly developed need for the mother's affection now becomes "as urgent for his psychological satisfaction as the need to be fed and taken care of is for his bodily comfort" (p. 181). Any separation from the mother during this phase is marked by more serious disturbance of such bodily functions as feeding and sleeping, and the infant's marked friendly interest in the outer world is withdrawn. Smiles and playfulness reappear only after the bodily functions have returned to normal, but the interruption of psychological contact with the external world was found not to be a simple consequence of bodily discomfort.

The third phase occurs during the second year of life. Here the baby's personal attachment to the mother is fully developed, and "it can now be safely said that he loves her" (p. 182). Children separated from the mother or substitute mother during this phase are subject to marked grief and distress, perhaps in the form of refusal to sleep or eat or be comforted by others. Such children when distressed will cling to a blanket, toy, or other object that provides a memory of the mother's presence. Alternatively, as in the case of Carol, 1 year and 7 months old, she continually repeated a significant utterance, mm, mum, mum, for three or more days (A. Freud 1942a, p. 183). Despite this marked appearance of early infantile grief, it is essentially short lived in its outward forms and, on the average, runs its course in two or three days. Adult grief, by contrast, may last a year or more. Anna Freud and Dorothy Burlingham found that this difference largely explained why many observers are misled in their judgment as to the depth and severity of the small child's grief. In offering their own early account of the true depth of the child's response to separation from the mother, they based their theoretical views on the established pleasure-pain principle of psychoanalytic theory, which predicts for the child a need for the more or less immediate gratification of emotional requirements—"promises of pleasure do not aid him." The infant at this stage "will, therefore, after a short while, turn away from the mother image in his mind and, though at first unwillingly, will accept the comfort which is offered" (p. 184). Again in the case of Carol, she would allow herself to be held by an unseen person, would turn her own face away, and would cry when she caught sight of the actual face of her new substitute mother. Anna Freud reconciled and rationalized these somewhat confusing and conflicting behavioral characteristics in her psychoanalytic model. Thus, Carol would "enjoy the familiar sensation of being held, and probably add to it in her own mind the imaginary picture of her own mother" (p. 184). Clearly, when the child was forced to perceive the actual face of the person comforting her, its reality refuted the child's fantasy elaboration, and loss and pain were experienced.

The greater permanency of the adult's object representations in inner-world terms was contrasted with the infant's situation, though perhaps not to the extent of evolving a full-fledged object relations theory. This aspect of Anna Freud's theorizing will be discussed more fully in Chapter 6.

In "The Mother Relationship of the Child Between 3 and 5 Years," Anna Freud touched on the wider social complications of family life, for example, in what classically was referred to as the oedipal relations of children with parents; the differences that now emerge between boys and girls; and the twin forces that now increasingly oppress the child's drive-endowed nature, namely, "disappointment in early love and the pressure of education" (1942a, p. 188). The child's ambivalence and guilt were clearly shown, as with Billie, aged 3½ years, who on hearing that his mother had gone to the hospital with a bad leg, "began to remember a time when he had kicked her and began to wonder whether her illness was his fault" (p. 189).

A section entitled "Further Fate of the Child-Parent Relationship" centered on the problems associated with return of the child's real mother, whether for brief visits or more permanent relations. After 3 years of age, even when "the relationship with the parents persists in fantasy, the real affections of the children slowly leave the parents . . . [and] . . . the child of this age lives mainly in the present" (p. 191). The case of Jane, aged 3¼ years, was cited as an example, and Anna Freud noted the tentative and early nature of her own conclusions and evidence and reminded the reader that more material should become available after another year of their evacuation and war-work studies. It now seems clear that Anna Freud did, at an unprecedented early date, present an accurate and psychoanalytically based description of the infant's response to separation and loss of the mother.

In assessing Anna Freud's wartime contribution to the question of the child-parent relationship and the subsequently conceptualized maternal deprivation syndrome, it is useful to take a wider view of the trends of theory in this multidisciplinary area.

Already in England in the decades between the world wars, H. Crichton-Miller's Tavistock Clinic had produced practitioners and theorists of the caliber of J. A. Hadfield and Ian D. Suttie. Though adding much that was new to their eclectic theory, they were nonetheless much indebted to Freud whom they widely acknowledged even in their criticisms. Suttie, in particular, was unhappy with Freud's patriarchal superego theory and early introduced concepts of the primacy of the mother-infant interaction (1935). Suttie believed orthodox psychoanalytic teaching to be altogether too harsh, leading to a misplaced "taboo on tenderness." In his view, theory and therapy should be less intellectually detached and passive, and we recognize here a fellow traveler of Sandor Ferenczi.

In the United States also, the social-psychological climate had long supported the constructive application of personal-interactional frameworks, with authorities such as C. H. Cooley and

George Herbert Mead providing much of the groundwork. The Gestalt group, led by Kurt Lewin, further indicated the primacy of "field interactional" and related approaches of study, and these trends were enriched and supported by existing psychoanalytic ideas and formulations. This was most apparent in the work of the early émigrés Erich Fromm and Karen Horney, together with Harry Stack Sullivan whose highly original psychiatric writings first gave us the term *interpersonal relationship*.

By the thirties, the allied disciplines of pediatrics and obstetrics had also begun to shift their emphasis, a change that had been germinating either independently or in close association with psychoanalytical ideas on infant care and development. In Britain during the twenties and thirties, a dominant stream of thought, associated with Sir Frederick Truby King,[8] stressed the organic hygiene aspects of infant care, to the detriment of psychological and psychosocial development. In criticizing these regimes, Anna Freud later pointed to the Truby King method in particular as an extreme example of a regime doing violence to the innate laws of infant development (1965a, p. 143). Similarly in the United States, from 1915 to 1940 there had been a shift in childbirth practice to the point that rigid hospital schedules had all but ousted the home confinement (Jackson 1952). Early efforts to alter again the officially established practices came from Joan Erikson in New Haven and Margaret Mead in New York, both of whom, around 1938 and during their own pregnancies and confinements, prevailed on their doctors and obstetricians to allow a much sooner and closer contact with the newborn baby. From these beginnings, prompted by knowledgeable mothers-to-be themselves, there came the self-demand feeding schedules and rooming-in movements currently associated with authorities such as Arnold Gesell and Edith B. Jackson.

In England during the height of the wartime blitz there was a study made of the nursing couple of mother and baby. Its author, Merell P. Middlemore, was by training a doctor and obstetrician.

[8]In 1918, King, a New Zealand pediatrician, introduced the advanced infant hygiene programs associated with the Babies of the Empire and Plunkett Society campaigns and the London Mothercraft Training Society.

According to Edward Glover's introduction, however, she was primarily a psychoanalyst. In her book Middlemore drew attention to the newborn's sensitive oral-vascular structures which differed markedly from the mouth of even a 6- to 7-month old (1941). Unfortunately, Middlemore did not live to see her work published, and the manuscript passed into the care of Ella F. Sharpe and Joan Malleson.

The evacuation to the countryside in 1939–1940 of large numbers of the urban British child population was the most significant, though by no means the only one, of the events that signaled the various phenomena of distressed and disrupted emotional and psychological development contingent on severing the bond between parent and young child. Child analysts and others concerned with the psychological welfare of children and their families had been aware for some time of a number of potential and actual traumatic results of institutional and other forms of unsatisfactory mothering. What the wartime evacuees and their professional guardian agencies elicited was wider sympathy and recognition for the individual consequences of abrupt separation, and the local education authorities and their officers in particular were "rapidly converted by the bedwetters, sleepwalkers and delinquents among the evacuees" (Armytage 1976, p. 95).

In addition to Anna Freud and her close colleagues, a number of other analysts and child students offered professional help and guidance to the evacuee children and their hosts. John Bowlby had trained at the London Institute of Psychoanalysis in the late thirties and had published early studies of abnormally aggressive children. Bowlby's mobile child guidance clinics were based in Cambridge and took problem children from the North London areas of Tottenham and Islington. From Bowlby's experiences came his wartime publication on juvenile delinquents (1944), a work now definitely overshadowed and all but lost behind his postwar contribution to the maternal deprivation question.

Also working in Cambridge during the war years was Susan Isaacs, in many respects the doyenne of British child analysts and certainly the most academically respectable in the wider world of child care and study at that time. An independent and gifted child

psychologist with pioneering observations made in her famous
Malting House School in the twenties, Isaacs then fell under the
sway of Melanie Klein and Nina Searl, both of whom she acknowledged as leaders in child psychoanalysis. Isaac's own prewar study
of emotional and social development (1933) was dedicated to
another Kleinian, Joan Riviere, the personal analyst who "taught
me to understand my own childhood" (1933, *Frontis*).

Similar work was carried on in Oxford, where Eva Rosenfeld
(Dyer 1980, interview) shared her time between there and London,
and where she met and joined Clare Britton, who was working
with the man she would later marry, D. W. Winnicott. With his
solid foundation in pediatrics, plus his wide sympathies and knowledge of the various psychoanalytic techniques,[9] Winnicott used his
own work with the evacuee children to arrive at important conclusions regarding the study of mother, child, and facilitating environment. Other innovators of the wartime period were Michael Balint
and his second wife Edna, working in Manchester.

All the published or existing wartime studies of the child evacuees
were reviewed by Katharine Wolf, whose bibliography ran to 229
entries (1945). Wolf drew particular attention to Freud's and
Burlingham's Hampstead War Nursery studies but was critical of
much else because the data were collected hurriedly and under
adverse conditions. Methodologically and statistically there was
little homogeneity among the various studies, but despite this, two
striking results were apparent in the overall evacuee material:
(1) there was a relatively low percentage of neurosis formation;
and (2) enuresis was throughout the dominant symptom in the
"evacuation neurosis syndrome." A stable relationship with the
original parents was sufficient to explain the first result in most
cases, where the adaptive mechanism consisted in a modification
of the images of the parents which occurred throughout the evacuation experience (Wolf 1945). She considered only two studies as

[9]In 1923 Winnicott had gone as assistant physician to the famous Paddington
Green Children's Hospital in London. At the suggestion of Ernest Jones, he had
also begun a personal analysis, with James Strachey, which lasted for some ten
years. Strachey directed the curious Winnicott to Joan Riviere, from whom he
gained a knowledge of the Kleinian method, though he remained an "independent" (Winnicott 1962).

fully illuminating this point, that of Anna Freud and her associates (1942a) and "The Cambridge Survey" edited by Susan Isaacs.

Many may assume at first glance that the practical conclusions based on the work described in *Young Children in Wartime* are relevant only to the worldwide emergency situation in which the work was carried out. But quite the reverse is true. With the end of the Second World War and the acceleration of social as well as technological changes, many children at increasingly youthful ages are being subjected to psychological trauma and separation which in essence match the personal experiences of the wartime evacuees. In the United Kingdom alone at the time of writing, it is estimated that 1.6 million children live in 0.9 million one-parent families, and though in many of these families the parent is the mother, custody of children in divorce proceedings is not always or automatically awarded to her. The abruptness and acrimony of many marital breakdowns is greatly to be regretted from the young child's point of view and makes even more pertinent the following advice by the authors of the foremost wartime study of mother-child relationships.

As Anna Freud asserted, it is not so much the separation itself that adversely affects the child as the form in which the separation has taken place (1942a, p. 208). Her recommendations were largely aimed at easing the abruptness of the separation (1) by making it a slow process, (2) by introducing the child to its substitute mother beforehand, and (3) by having the real mother reappear several times to see her child while weaning the infant from one mother figure to another. It is true, Anna Freud admitted, that the child's apparent distress may appear greater and more protracted by this means—the pain of separation would be repeated—but even more importantly, "there would be no empty period in which the feelings of the child are turned completely inward" (p. 209). The danger of such a deeply regressive psychodynamic trend is shown in the examples of Georgie, aged 3¾ years, who said, "I don't like you, I don't like anybody, I only like myself"; and John, aged five years, who said, "I am nobody's nothing."[10]

[10]The gradual method of separation was recommended as early as February 1941 (A. Freud 1973a, p. 10) and supported by the case of Billie (pp. 19–22) and others.

In the modern postwar world and at all times in the relational affairs of parents and young children, there may be situations in which the child is placed at risk with regard to the abruptness, if not quite the finality, of separation from the mother or mothering person. The hospitalization of either partner in the relationship, the breakdown of the parent's marriage, and the numerous other reasons conducive to the short- and long-term fostering of children will continue to ensure that Anna Freud's wartime nursery work remain an enduring contribution to social psychology and community and family affairs, especially to the dynamics and prophylaxis of the mother-child relationship.

Anna Freud's other major wartime publication, *Infants Without Families: The Case for and Against Residential Nurseries* (1944a), was published simultaneously in London and New York. Basing her views partly on the earlier material collected by August Aichhorn and partly on the large numbers of observations made in the Jackson nursery in Vienna and the war nurseries, Anna Freud confirmed that differences in the two sets or populations of children, that is, between institutionalized and noninstitutionalized children, effectively amount to a typological difference, especially in regard to character development. Despite the general advantage of boarding out and fostering over large-scale institutions and the preference of most authorities for the former, Anna Freud nevertheless accepted the continuing need for some form of institutional care. Hence this was the motivation for her wartime publication and for our brief consideration, which in no way does justice to the wealth of empirical and observational material in the original.

These differences by no means favor children who grow up in their own family home entirely. Institutional children, for example, gain socially and adaptationally whenever their emotional needs are not too close to the surface. But whenever the emotional bond with the mother and family group is crucial—as in toilet training and speech development—then the institutionalized infant fares less well than his or her counterpart in a more intimate and personal home setting. The range of social behaviors open to the infant in an organized care setting is certainly wide and is everywhere "precociously stimulated and developed" (A. Freud 1944a,

p. 560), even in some respects coming close to matching adult expressions of love and affection. But much remains dormant and unexpressed, "ready to leap into action the moment the slightest opportunity for attachment is offered" (p. 586). In their use of artificial families centered on individual nurses, the Hampstead Nursery staff opened up a wide range of emotional problems and outbursts in the children in their care, as well as the pain of repeated separation. In keeping with their wartime report of two years earlier, however, they believed that the evil of broken and interrupted attachments was preferable to that of emotional barrenness, since the latter offered less prospect for normal character development. The blind spots of the nursery workers engaged in this process were also mentioned, with the recommendation that such workers require a degree of self-awareness and insight regarding themselves, a theme that continued to attract Anna Freud's concern in later years.[11]

A wealth of data followed on the nursery behaviors engaged in by young infants as a means of coping with instinctual satisfaction and frustration in the general absence of intimate bodily contact with the mother or adequate mother substitute (A. Freud 1944a, pp. 559–634). Autoerotic habits such as thumb sucking, rocking, head banging, and masturbation; infantile exhibitionism; and curiosity all are dealt with at length and through many examples. The rarer question of the role of fathers in residential institutions centers on the issue of the father's impact as an arbiter of social mores and moral commandments, as well as his absence as a rival for the mother's love. One would expect profound differences here with respect to young girls and young boys, as one would with later phases of identification and the emergence of self-concepts. Anna Freud concluded that "far from being of minor importance, the father, where he is present, is . . . one of the main determining influences in the child's life" (1944a, p. 641). The work goes on to consider children and their relationships with dead fathers—a

---

[11]Anna Freud noted the need for some form of analysis and personal insight in regard to teachers and others working nonanalytically with children (1929a; 1930a, lecture 4), and she reiterated it over 20 years later (1952b).

preponderance of forms of denial, as with Susan, aged 4½ years, who said "My father is deaded . . . he will come back, much later when I am quite big" (p. 641)—and relationships with merely absent fathers and fantasy fathers.

The balance of care and therapy, together with ongoing scientific research and the development or corroboration of theoretical models, should never be forgotten or underestimated in Anna Freud's and her colleagues' work. In *Infants Without Families* they, as child analysts, rightly stress the great scientific opportunities in the residential venture for prolonged longitudinal observation and comparison of children, especially in the crucial period from birth to 5 years and in the absence of such factors as the regular family constellation and oedipal situation of normal home life. One of the hallmarks of Anna Freud's wartime work as a child analyst and scientist was her ability to balance the practical and applied aspects of care and therapy with the empirical-experimental testing of selected areas of theory and the corroboration or necessary modification of her psychological model. The work of the wartime period shows this particularly well, and Anna Freud's epistemological rigor continued to be evident in later years (see Lustman 1967).

In addition to her active directorship of the Hampstead War Nursery project, she also conducted a weekly practical seminar for the London Institute of Psychoanalysis and was included on its influential training committee.[12] At a meeting of the British Society she also presented, on March 18, 1942, her "Excerpts from an Annual Report on Work in a Wartime Nursery," which appeared to have relied heavily on the major publication discussed above (1942a). Throughout the forties, Anna Freud was closely linked with the Nursery Schools Association of Great Britain and attended most of their wartime summer schools. Many years later, when responding to their request to lecture, she recalled those strenuous years when she served as "an active member of the Executive, and repeatedly a speaker at the summer schools" (1960b, p. 315).

[12]Other committee members for 1942–1943 were Edward Glover, John Rickman, James Strachey, Sylvia Payne, Marjorie Brierley, Ella F. Sharpe, and Melanie Klein (Report of the British Psychoanalytic Society 1944), though the last was presumably "in absentia" only.

New associates continued to enter Anna Freud's circle. Anneliese Schnurmann, working as a wartime nurse for the Women's Voluntary Service, was one, and she was soon involved in the war nursery work (Dyer 1980, letter dated July 22, 1977). Also in 1942, Ruth Thomas finally began her own training analysis with Anna Freud, having first been interviewed for her candidacy the year war broke out (Dyer 1980). Ilse Hellman, having worked in the Hampstead Nursery for a year, at Anna Freud's prompting applied for formal psychoanalytic training. Her training analyst at the London Institute was Dorothy Burlingham (Dyer 1980).

THE KLEINIAN CONTROVERSY

By 1943 the controversial theoretical differences that for over a decade had divided the British Psychoanalytic Society once more came to the surface and now involved Anna Freud who had previously sought to remain out of the internal divisiveness. But now, however, she took the lead in attempting to place the discussions on a rational and amicable basis, in contrast to the earlier heated sessions that had plagued the British Society in the thirties.

An eyewitness, Barbara Lantos, recorded that in a bid to take any personal element out of the divergencies, Anna Freud had during the midwar period proposed that the earlier haphazard and emotive discussions be replaced by systematic discussion centered on various prepared papers (Lantos 1966). This suggestion was quickly adopted, and the meetings continued over the following three years. These discussions have recently been made available (British Psychoanalytic Society 1967), and we shall make no attempt to review them here.

The wartime Kleinian controversy began on January 27, 1943, with a prepared contribution by Susan Isaacs on "The Nature and Function of Phantasy," to which Anna Freud and others contributed the discussion. In her comments Anna Freud noted that although the speaker had attempted to demonstrate an apparent orthodox allegiance to Sigmund Freud by citing his earlier writings, she had nonetheless implicitly rejected that work. As an example, Miss Freud used the Kleinian definition of unconscious fantasy. This had now come to include a wide range of mental processes, regardless of whether or not they were instinctual derivatives, whereas other aspects of the accepted primary process were apparently denied in the Kleinian interpretation of the child's fantasy.

Anna Freud's critique was later used by Edward Glover in a caustic attack of his own on Klein's system of psychoanalysis, and he accepted Anna Freud's assertion that the Kleinian concept of fantasy involved secondary-process thinking in the dynamic unconscious (1945). The attempts by Klein and her supporters to justify their theoretical views by referring to Freud came to naught when pitted against Anna Freud's critical faculties, for none knew her father's writings better than she did. In another sense, too, Klein's champion was no match for Anna Freud. By 1943 Susan Isaacs was in the last years of her celebrated life, whereas Anna Freud was not yet 50 and had reached almost the height of her powers.

Glover's position at this time is a most interesting one, and he himself has gone to some lengths to explain his various shifts of thought and allegiance (1945, 1966). During the twenties, Glover had enthusiastically accepted Klein's teaching, having assumed all her material to be clinically valid and tested. By the thirties, however, he came to realize the extent of speculation in Klein's thought, and his critical review of her *Psychoanalysis of Children* sharply contrasted with his critique of Anna Freud's technical lectures, which in 1927 he had delivered to the Critical Symposium on Child Analysis. Glover has noted a general lack of originality in the British group of analysts in the twenties, and this he sees as influencing the ready acceptance of Klein's views as an alternative to being simply the mirror for the Freudian concepts emanating from Vienna. Having himself broken many a lance against Klein's followers in the heated British debates of the thirties, and after the exodus of the Viennese analysts to England, Glover tended increasingly to support Anna Freud and her more rigorously empirical psychoanalytic theorizing. As the supposedly nonemotive wartime controversial discussions began in their turn to fail to settle differences rationally, Glover apparently attempted to persuade Anna Freud to form a separate breakaway society or group within the British analysts, but this she declined to do (Dyer 1980, interview with I. Hellman). Glover subsequently resigned all his positions in the British Society, having, as he himself later acknowledged, greatly overestimated the strength of the Kleinian "apostasy," with the concomitant underestimation of the powerful middle group of eclectics or independents (1966).

By the closing stages of the Second World War, the newly revived Kleinian controversy had once more reached the proportions of an internal crisis in the British Psychoanalytic Society, and Sylvia Payne was called forward as a leading "independent" to preside over some form of settlement of the affair. But settlement did not come until the immediate postwar years. Meanwhile, Anna Freud was excluded from the training committee of the London Institute for a number of years.[13]

Apart from the controversial discussion meetings, the last years of the wartime period appear to have been a professionally trying time for Anna Freud. Consider, for example, the difficulties she encountered in publishing a new English translation of her technical lectures of the late twenties. Initially, as she stated, the book was "rejected when offered to the International Psychoanalytical Library for publication, and the matter lapsed, so far as England was concerned" (1946d, *Preface*). In her new and somewhat caustic preface to this work, Anna Freud assured her readers that it was not her fault that the material was appearing before the English reader at such a late date.

The new book itself was a composite of several pieces by the time it appeared. Based on the original *Einführung in die Technik der Kinderanalyse*, her four lectures were accompanied by a short paper of the same period—*Zur Theorie der Kinderanalyse*—and by a more recent, similar contribution.

---

[13]In 1944–1945 the influential training committee consisted of Bowlby, Balint, Strachey, Scott, Payne, Isaacs, and Klein, an apparent preponderance of independents and Kleinians. In 1945–1946 the elected members consisted of Bowlby, Scott, Rickman, Payne, Isaacs, Klein, and Adrian Stephen, with a marked absence of Anna Freud or her closest supporters (Report of the British Psychoanalytic Society 1946).

This new contribution, which formed the third and final part of Anna Freud's eventual English edition[14] of her technical lectures, was in fact an important and innovative initiative, well deserving of its date of publication at the watershed between war and peace (1945a, 1946d). In more recent years this same seminal paper gave its title to the appropriate volume of Anna Freud's collected writings (1968h).

In her "Indications for Child Analysis" (1945a), Anna Freud attempted to shift the diagnostic burden in childhood disorders away from neurotic symptomatology and psychopathological categorization. The new approach that she now recommended undertook to assess the degree of interference and retardation in the normal sequence of the child's maturational development. As Anna Freud herself observed, the emphasis "is shifted thereby from the purely clinical aspects of a case to the developmental aspect" (1945d, p. 37). With this important outcome of her own practical and clinical studies of childhood, Anna Freud pointed to the future direction of child psychoanalysis as a true developmental psychology and a powerful instrument for the study of normality in childhood (see Chapter 6).

At the height of the wartime Kleinian controversy, Anna Freud apparently arranged for the private printing of a small book detailing the theoretical views underlying her work at the Hampstead War Nurseries (A. Freud and Burlingham 1941–1945). Michael Balint presumably owned or read a copy and described it as sharply critical of the ideas of Melanie Klein and others (1945). To the best of my knowledge, Anna Freud herself nowhere made reference to this work. The critical preface added to the expanded English edition of her republished technical lectures (1946d) is also omitted from her later *Collected Writings*, and we must conclude that perhaps she wished to withdraw any inflammatory or unduly strong views regarding her differences with Klein.

---

[14]An English translation had, of course, appeared in New York and Washington, D.C., in 1928. What is implied above is an eventual "in England" publication, which required the assistance of the recently established Imago Publishing Company in London.

Certainly, in her later publications, Anna Freud made significant points of contact and rapprochement with Klein's work as, for example, with Klein's important concept of the "good" and "bad" mother objects in the child's early psychological development (A. Freud 1954a).

Despite these professional wrangles, made more onerous by the renewed enemy rocket attacks on London, which at the end of the war necessitated the evacuation of most of the Hampstead War Nursery's children and staff to the safety of their country house, Anna Freud continued to launch important new projects. The old maxim "If you want something done, send it to a busy person" was certainly true in Anna Freud's case, and now she became involved in organizing a new child analysis journal and publishing venture.

The journal was the *Psychoanalytic Study of the Child*, which was a quarto-sized annual published simultaneously in New York and in London (volume I appeared in 1945). The title page of the opening issue showed Anna Freud as coeditor in a most distinguished company of psychoanalytical and childhood authorities. In their preface the editors stated that their intention was to emphasize contributions that would "centre on psychoanalytic hypotheses. . . . It is hoped that from this centre contacts with neighbouring fields will be established" (1945, *Frontis*). The success of this initial aim is today duly attested by over 30 annual volumes, which together comprise and document much of the best postwar work in child analysis, as well as such cognate areas as education, pediatrics, genetic psychology, child psychiatry, and the like.

The Anglo-American origins of this important organ of child analysis were outlined 30 years later in a special historical note by the then editors Ruth Eissler, Anna Freud, Marianne Kris, and Albert J. Solnit. There the outcome was noted as "a remarkable feat" for a period when communications between the two countries were slow or even completely disrupted. Another problem was finding a willing publisher for such a new venture, and A. S. Kagan of International Universities Press was gratefully acknowledged (R. Eissler et al. 1975). In an editorial insertion written by Anna Freud, Ruth Eissler, Marianne Kris, Seymour Lustman, and Lottie M. Newman, it was stated that Heinz Hartmann "founded

the *Psychoanalytic Study of the Child,* together with Anna Freud
and Ernst Kris in 1945" (A. Freud et al. 1970).

Despite the authoritativeness of these editorial remarks, the
general picture they present varies slightly from the detailed information from another reliable source. In his account of psychoanalysis in New York since 1925, Sandor Lorand observed that at
the close of World War II he was approached by Josef Rifkin,
founder of the International Universities Press (Lorand 1969).
Rifkin asked Lorand if he would organize two new publications, a
Yearbook of Psychoanalysis and a corresponding *Yearbook of
Child Analysis.* Lorand agreed to undertake the former, but for the
child analysis project he directed Rifkin to Ernst Kris and Rene
Spitz. Spitz appears to have played the lesser part, though he was a
coeditor of the new publication until his death almost 30 years
later. Kris presumably drew Heinz Hartmann and Anna Freud
into the new project and may well have coined the present title as
an alternative to the proposed *Yearbook.* No doubt at some future
date the correspondence between Anna Freud and her New York
colleagues will shed more light on this most interesting episode.
Meanwhile, there is, after all, no real dissonance between the two
accounts of the origin of the *Psychoanalytic Study of the Child,* and
the apparent discrepancies may be dealt with in terms of the
relative incompleteness of both accounts. Certainly, and for many
years now, the title pages of the journal have carried the subhead
"Founding Editors," under which are placed the names Anna
Freud, Heinz Hartmann, and Ernst Kris. When, 25 years later,
Anna Freud and her coeditors wrote the obituary note for Heinz
Hartmann, it no doubt seemed natural to emphasize his contributions and to place his name before their own.

Anna Freud's own contribution to the first issue of the new
annual was based on the prophetic and equally new "Indications
for Child Analysis" which, more perhaps than any other single
piece, directed the general course of childhood diagnosis and assessment in the field from then until the present and well into the
foreseeable future. Gone were the labels and categories of the
psychopathology of Kraepelin's era, and gone were the hasty
typologies of Kretschmer. Gone too, for all but those with a vested

interest or mathematical bias, were the static trait listings and factorial compilations of Spearman, Burt, Terman, Allport, Cattell, and others who, while gathering their multitudinous and disparate data, somehow lost the essential integration and synthesis of the individual person's object-filled and goal-directed behavior which exists at a given moment at a particular developmental level that may or may not be age adequate and that may progress both forward and backward to other levels of adaptation and relationship. Although psychoanalysis, especially as led by Anna Freud, has never eschewed other psychologies nor attempted to usurp their prerogatives in assessing cognitive and related abilities, it is regrettable that some psychologies and their academic leaders fail to acknowledge, still less utilize, the immense contribution that psychoanalysis and, in particular, experimental child analysis has made. In the postwar decades that contribution, in the hands of Anna Freud and a number of others, was gradually shaped into a powerful psychological model (see Chapter 6), capable of comparison with any other psychology in its conceptual rigor and depth, experimental validation and clinically applied efficacy, and therapeutic outcome.

WARTIME EMPIRICISM

Even during the early forties, if not before in Vienna, Anna Freud's synthesis of psychoanalytic theory with observation in an experimental nursery matched the empirical rigor of an elegant academic discipline such as learning theory (e.g., the work of J. B. Watson, E. L. Thorndike, and O. H. Mowrer). Learning theory explains many items of infant behavior, for example, coitus play, with reference to concepts such as imitation; whereas child analysis in addition refers to biologically innate instinctual drives. In the war nursery setting children could be observed in the absence of their parents, and it was precisely in regard to the intimacies of parental intercourse that nursery life was most atypical (A. Freud 1944a, p. 626). A prime behavioral experiment thus existed, with the possibility of imitative experiences neatly controlled. One outcome was the collection of many data supporting the psychoanalytic model's biological drive theory, though imitation and other concepts of learning theory were not ignored. In a postwar contribution to child development presented in Stockbridge, Massachusetts, Anna Freud noted the observations on infant coitus play as "the most intriguing data of the nurseries" (A. Freud 1951b, p. 160) and agreed that in the absence of the controlled conditions every analyst would have invoked the concept of imitation of coitus observed in the parental bedroom.

Other puzzling phenomena reported in the wartime book *Infants Without Families* (A. Freud 1944a) concerned the oedipal reactions of small boys in the absence of real oedipal experiences. During the transition from the anal to the phallic phase, the boys' behavior to their substitute mothers altered markedly, and "they developed masculine qualities and a protective, often overbearing, sometimes indulgently affectionate attitude" (A. Freud 1951b, p. 160-161), despite the absence of either the father and/or the prospect of identification with him directly. Anna Freud suggested that these phenomena were the "behavioural manifestation of the phallic trends" (p. 161), implying an innate basis without excluding the boys' outside observation of the stimulation by other men. Other data were discussed in regard to the assumption that there are innate attitudes in the child that are stimulated and developed by later life experiences.

CHAPTER FIVE

International Recognition

The postwar years saw Anna Freud once again as the general secretary to the International Psychoanalytic Association. Her wartime predecessor had been Edward Glover, now withdrawn from all active office following the internal crisis in the British Institute. As editor of the first peacetime I. P. A. Bulletin—a position she held until 1949 when Grete Bibring replaced her as secretary— Anna Freud noted that after a long break in relations, "the first reports of psychoanalytic activity in German-occupied territory have arrived from the French Psychoanalytic Society" (Bulletin Report of the *I. P. A. International Journal of Psychoanalysis* 1945, p. 84).

Also arriving from liberated Europe were the children who had survived the notorious concentration camps. Six in particular, all 3-year-olds born of Jewish parents in Vienna or Berlin, found their way into the caring hands of Anna Freud's close associates. These children had been liberated from the so-called model ghetto camp at Theresienstadt (Tereszin) in Czechoslovakia, from which they were supposed to join a children's transport to "an unknown destination in the East," almost certainly Auschwitz-Birkenau, Poland (see Gilbert 1981). The adults' rate of turnover and deportation was more rapid than the children's, with the result that the children had had a great deal of unsatisfactory, short-term, substitute mothering. Moreover, the mothering persons available in the special Ward for Motherless Children at Theresienstadt simply did not have time to play with the children (A. Freud 1951j), and so they were prepared for a significant retardation and pathology in development.

The concentration-camp children, as they are now both academically and popularly referred to, were flown to England a month or so after the hostilities in Europe ended, and reception quarters were provided at Lake Windermere by Alice Goldberger and Oscar

Friedman (see also Paneth 1946). With the provision of a large house, Bulldogs Bank in Sussex, and the financial support of the same New York charity that had sponsored the wartime Hampstead Nursery, it was possible for the six 3-year-old children to be kept together in their original group. The daily supervision of the Bulldogs Bank nursery was managed by Gertrud and Sophie Dann, previously of the Hampstead War Nursery. The new nursery opened in the autumn of 1945 and was initially intended to operate for one year.

On arrival at the new nursery the children were "wild, restless and uncontrollably noisy . . . they destroyed all the toys and damaged much of the furniture. . . . In anger, they would hit the adults, bite or spit. Above all, they would shout, scream, and use bad language" (A. Freud 1951j, p. 168). Their negative attitude toward adults was matched by the children's positive attitude toward one another, as shown by many examples of behavior. While out one day, the children were approached by a dog that terrified them all. Ruth, "though badly frightened herself, walks bravely to Peter who is screaming and gives him her toy rabbit to comfort him. She comforts John next by lending him her necklace" (A. Freud 1951j, p. 177). Aggression toward one another among these children was almost entirely confined to verbal arguments, although against others they used weapons such as biting (a developmental retardation of around 12 to 18 months for a 3-year-old), spitting, and urinating. Within a short while these primitive methods were replaced by hitting, and a few months later this gave way to "the usual verbal aggressions used by children between three and four years" (p. 186).[1]

It was five or six years before the observations on the concentration-camp children were published (A. Freud [with S. Dann] 1951j). The rapid rate of developmental progress in these children must have been heartening to those involved with them and boded well for the authors' concluding hope that future contacts would illuminate the subsequent developmental phases of the oedipus complex, adolescence, and adult life. Anna Freud and her associates

[1]Therapy was conceptualized around the "fusion of drives," which is discussed below in relation to Anna Freud's postwar contributions on aggression.

continued to examine the long-term question of the concentration-camp orphans, and Edith L. Gyomroi published an important study from the analysis of one child at 17 years of age. More recently, Gertrud Dann reported (letter dated November 12, 1981) that two of the Bulldogs Bank children, now grown up with families of their own, were reintroduced to her after many years. Both families seemed to be settled and very happy.

In the years immediately following the return to peace in Europe, the long series of controversial discussions of the British Psychoanalytic Society came to an end. This was marked by a historic extraordinary meeting, on June 26, 1946, and at that time resolutions were passed to the effect that (1) all schools of analytic thought acceptable to a substantive part of the society should be represented in the training curriculum and (2) a committee of six people would be formed to discuss training matters. Of these six, two each were nominated by Sylvia Payne (independent), Anna Freud, and Melanie Klein (Report of the British Psychoanalytic Society 1946). With this compromise, the Kleinian controversy was effectively over.

Anna Freud was not slow to demonstrate the conciliatory implications of these resolutions. Already in 1946, in her survey of infantile feeding disturbances (1946a), she had included Melanie Klein's study on aggression and had observed the use of Klein's theoretical ideas in the systematic study of earliest infancy by Merrell Middlemore (1941). Thereafter, even after Klein's death in 1960, Anna Freud never in her published writings criticized Klein and her views, but rather introduced her and her work in a neutral-to-positive fashion. References to Klein and her work in Anna Freud's publications may be generally grouped into two phases, a phase of critical comments (1927–1945) and a longer phase of positive noncriticism. (Klein's work is cited or discussed in A. Freud 1927a, 1928a, 1935b, 1936a, 1945a, 1946a, 1949a, 1949g, 1950a, 1952a, 1952e, 1954a, 1954b, 1955b, 1956a, 1958a, 1963a, 1965a, 1966e, 1967b, 1969a, 1971b, 1974d, 1974e, 1974f, 1975c, and 1979b.)

Something of Anna Freud's motivation and rationale for so rigorously maintaining this conciliatory approach to Klein's work may be seen in her remarks in "A Short History of Child Analysis"

(1966e). They also show Anna Freud's ability to judge scientific priorities and her distaste for such unproductive argument as had plagued the long years of controversy. She lamented that "it was not to the advantage of the development of child analysis that from the outset it proceeded on two lines distinct from one another" (1966e, p. 51). After briefly reviewing in this same neutral tone the main ideas of both her own standpoint and that of Klein, she mentioned "one point, nevertheless, on which the two schools were in full agreement" (p. 53). This was the form in which each of the rival groups offered instruction to candidates, and the value of this to Anna Freud, intent as she was on maintaining the validity and rigor of psychoanalysis as a science, was that "we had seen too much of the danger of 'wild analysts' in the adult field to wish to produce a similar breed for the treatment of children" (p. 53). Clearly, Klein and her followers were not classed as wild analysts, but as child analysts who had a differing technique and theoretical background superimposed on a basically common technique and theoretical background. In the later phase of her own approach to the Kleinian question, we see Anna Freud at her best as a lucid scientific-rationalist thinker. She tried to avoid merely controversial problems and worked in an integrative-synthetic fashion. Finally, when she could neither accept nor refute, she presented the differing viewpoints impartially. No scientific *Weltanschauung* can hope for completeness without adhering to these principles.

In later years the controversy over the Klein versus orthodox theoretical divergences continued to surface occasionally in public, though brought up by people other than Anna Freud, for example the argumentative mêlée that developed at the I. P. A. Congress held in Edinburgh in 1961 when the Kleinian presentation of Esther Bick (1962) was contested by Elisabeth Geleerd (1962) and Ilse Hellman (1962). And critiques of Klein and her views continue to emerge even today from close associates of Anna Freud and the London group in Hampstead (Yorke 1971).

By the late forties, two obstacles to Anna Freud's wider recognition and productivity had been effectively removed, i.e., the cessation of wartime hostilities and the resolution of the British Society's internal disputes. Anna Freud was once again elected to the important training committee of the British Psychoanalytic Society,[2] and she also conducted a seminar course for first- and second-year candidates, as well as a lecture course on the "Principles of Psychoanalysis." Her closest colleagues at the London Institute were Willi Hoffer, Kate Friedlander, Barbara Lantos, and Hedwig Hoffer, and her formal activities at the official training institute in London continued into the mid-1950s. By then, most of her energies had become absorbed in an exciting independent venture almost without parallel in the field, which in later years inspired a number of "Anna Freud centers" throughout the world.

International recognition slowly came to Anna Freud in the postwar period and was based initially on acknowledgment of her immense contribution derived from wartime work with the evacuees. Thus, under the new auspices of the nascent UNESCO program Miss Freud was invited to the University of the Sorbonne in Paris to deliver a lecture entitled *"Problèmes d'adaptation posés par l'éducation des enfants qui ont souffert de la guerre"* (1946c). To the best of my knowledge this has never been translated.

In her UNESCO paper Anna Freud acknowledged that it was because of her father that the adult-centered child education of the early part of the century had begun to give way to the proper pedagogical study of the child. But although university teachers had introduced the study of adolescence into their curriculum, the study of early childhood still merited little respect. In arguing for the incorporation of psychoanalysis into more child-centered education, Anna Freud noted the First World War as having witnessed the beginnings of the acceptance of psychoanalytic ideas, whereas the Second World War *"fut d'un grand profit au monde pédagogique"* (1946c, p. 184), if only people would learn the lesson. After briefly presenting the psychoanalytical scheme of early emotional development, she then spoke of the significance for early schooling of the formation of stable groups around artificial mothers. Of all

[2]The full committee for 1946–1947 was Sylvia Payne (chairman), Anna Freud, Melanie Klein, Bowlby, Gillespie, Rickman, and Adrian Stephen (Report of the London Institute of Psychoanalysis 1946–1947).

the lessons from the wartime studies of evacuees in residential nurseries, this was probably the most valuable and the most readily translated into common educational practice.

The following year saw Anna Freud in Amsterdam to attend a meeting of European analysts where she gave a paper on the "Transformation of Instinct in Early Childhood" (1947b) in which she summarized the young child's defensive strategies for coping with instinctual drive forces. In the final published version of this paper, she added sections on the development of object love as well (see Chapter 6).

Anna Freud again went to Amsterdam in 1947, to open on October 25 the new buildings of the Dutch Psychoanalytic Society and Institute. At the opening session Miss Freud read "a very interesting lecture on the connection between the theory and technique of psychoanalysis" (Report of the Dutch Psychoanalytic Society 1947, p. 209).

Back in London she gave another paper on December 9 to the Symposium on Aggression held by the Section of Psychiatry of the Royal Society of Medicine. In this paper, "Aggression in Relation to Emotional Development: Normal and Pathological" (1949f), she stated that her intention was "to outline in general the contribution made by Freudian psychoanalysis to the subject" (p. 489), that is, to achieve a psychological model and framework that would include both the general process of character formation and the distortions of personality seen in neurosis and severer forms of mental illness. According to this model, instinctual shaping of personality leads to a "never-ending series of inner conflicts [which] serves as a constant stimulus toward higher development of mental functioning" (p. 491). Psychoanalytic theory had kept abreast of recent movements in the 20th century's social and political upheaval, and by the forties, "aggression, destruction, their expressions and their development are as much in the center of interest of dynamic psychology now as the development of the sexual function was at the beginning of the century" (p. 493). Basing her views on her own wartime observations and those of Hoffer, Anna Freud offered some insight into the pathological aggressiveness seen in the concentration-camp children as well as in contemporary urban children. On close observation, Anna Freud stated, the center of pathology was found to reside not in the aggressive drives themselves, "but in a lack of fusion between them and libidinal [erotic] urges" (1949f, p. 496). Disruption in the child's love life, through the family's breakdown, exposure to a noncaring environment, and too frequent changes in object relations can lead to an inner psychological state in which "the aggressive urges are not brought into fusion and thereby bound and partially neutralised, but remain free and seek expression in life in the form of pure, unadulterated, independent destructiveness" (p. 497). She then gave her therapeutic recommendations, discouraging force and other coercive measures aimed at the child's destructiveness. "The appropriate therapy," she insisted, "has to be directed to the neglected, defective side, i.e. the emotional libidinal development" (p. 497). A further implication of this is the need for small-scale fostering out and similar corrective care programs for such children, since the necessary emotional contact will almost certainly not be achieved in larger institutional settings.

An International Congress on Mental Health was held in London in August 1948, with most of the participants talking on the theme of aggression. Anna Freud noted that the war had in fact "taught us nothing about aggression which might not have been learned before" (1949g, p. 61) and that the study of human relationships and child development has "at all times" provided the material necessary for observation of aggressive behavior. With this she reiterated her view of two years earlier in Paris, when contrary to much popular opinion she asserted that "*la guerre ne fut d'aucun profit aux enfants*" (1946c, p. 184).

According to Anna Freud, the mechanisms available to the child for the transformation of aggression are basically those mechanisms of defense listed earlier and described in relation to the erotic-libidinal drives (Chapter 3). Attitudes such as suspicion and intolerance she held to be caused by the projection and displacement of aggression away from the key (parental) figures in the developing person's object world of inner emotions. As such they were not reversible by exposure to experience, since "they are not rooted in a real assessment of the hated persons, but arise from the necessity to prevent the hate reactions from reverting to the original, ambivalently loved objects" (1949g, p. 72). She used the term *sublimation* for the fusion of erotic and destructive impulses that relieves the aggressive urge of its destructiveness and leads to a contribution to the "purposes of life."

In 1949 Anna Freud was once again in Paris for a UNESCO conference that had as its theme mental attitudes affecting international understanding. Her paper examined instinct-driven human behavior (1953d) and was first published five years later as part of a commemorative *Festschrift* volume for Marie Bonaparte.[3] The material highlighted the social development of the human being, from the asocial infant dominated by the drive forces of sexuality and aggression through the adaptations achieved through emotional dependence on the parents and fear of losing the parent's love. Although believing that frustrations in early childhood are part of the psychoanalytic picture of socialization, she reaffirmed that psychoanalysis was an instinct theory, in contrast to those psychologies that "regard aggression merely as the product of environmental influences, i.e. as the individual's answer to the frustration of his early emotional wishes" (1953d, p. 502). Ambivalence, displacement, projection of hostile impulses, and the persistence of these largely unconscious processes formed the core of the psychoanalytic explanation of tension and mistrust in human relationships, and in 1949 Anna Freud was apparently still some years away from accepting a more complete object relations model in which to couch her description.[4]

Anna Freud's second UNESCO presentation also pointed out that education by suppression of instinctual behavior was far from satisfactory, whereas education through peer-group influence was restricted to limited gains, and the individual children did not

[3]Other close colleagues thus honored by a *Festschrift* contribution from Anna Freud were Max Eitingon, August Aichhorn, Jeanne Lampl-de Groot, and Heinz Hartmann.

[4]By 1954 Anna Freud had partly accepted Klein's "good" and "bad" mother objects (1954a), which provided an alternative scheme for the discussion of ambivalence and interrelational prejudice.

basically alter their mode of impulse transformation. Only by establishing the parent relationship—and in the war nursery setting this had been achieved with the "artificial families" based on a favorite nurse—did emotionally disturbed children release their pent-up libidinal needs and begin once again to progress toward normal socialization. The observations made by Anna Freud and her associates, particularly those relating to the war nursery and to similar residential ventures, were "a most impressive demonstration of one of the principles of psychoanalytic psychology: that it is the libidinal attachment to the parents (or their substitutes) which, by way of imitation of them and identification with them, finally makes the next generation amenable to the cultural demands which every civilized society imposes on its members" (1953d, pp. 522–523).

By the late forties, with the return of the complete *Bulletin of the International Psychoanalytic Association* listing all members and component societies, it was clear that during the intervening interval Anna Freud had gained international recognition of a different sort. The bulletin for 1948—the first complete one since 1939 and once more edited by Anna Freud—showed that the societies of Detroit and Paris and the Swiss Psychoanalytic Society had given her honorary membership. Many similar acknowledgments of her growing eminence throughout the analytical world followed in later years, including honorary membership in the American Psychoanalytic Association and the Philadelphia Association for Psychoanalysis in 1950; the New York Psychoanalytic Society in 1955; and, more recently, the societies in Boston, Chicago, Cleveland, San Francisco, Western New England, Vienna, Germany, and Sweden.

Accompanied by Kate Friedlander, Anna Freud traveled to Geneva in 1948 (a busy year of travel) to lecture in a postgraduate course organized by Philippe Bovet. August Aichhorn also came from Vienna. Tragically, within the space of about a year, both of these close colleagues of Anna had died—Aichhorn at age 71 in October 1949, and Kate Friedlander at the early age of 47, having just begun with Anna Freud the Hampstead Child Therapy Training

Course (discussed below). Friedlander had recently reviewed the *Psychoanalytical Treatment of Children* and had regretted, as had Anna Freud, the long delay in its publication in England (Friedlander 1947). The technical recommendations in this volume were fundamental to Friedlander's analytical thought and practice, as shown in her major work on child guidance (Friedlander 1945).

The 16th International Psychoanalytic Congress, the first of the postwar era, was held in Zurich from August 15 to 19, 1949. Anna Freud attended as general secretary and edited the now extensive and valuable congress report (1949h). She also presented a scientific paper and clinical contribution of her own, the theme being male homosexuality (1949b). In the next years Anna Freud devoted much time to this topic, and she eventually arrived at a concept of complete emotional surrender (*Hörigkeit*) and its antithesis as found in states of negativism (1951c, 1952d, 1968g). She also provided the congress with a commentary during the showing of Willi Hoffer's wartime films of infant feeding behavior in the Hampstead Nursery, and was asked to store at her home old I. P. A. records, as she had throughout the war years stored in her cellar bundles of her father's letters. Finally, Anna Freud was elected a member of council with Marie Bonaparte, Jeanne Lampl-de Groot, and Heinz Hartmann. In thanking Ernest Jones as retiring president of the International Association, she reminded the members of Jones's efforts during the struggle to rescue the continental analysts, including her own father, from the Nazis. From her own experience Anna Freud was also able to describe the difficulties of holding office in the I. P. A., and she duly acknowledged Jones's help. Thirty years later Anna Freud wrote a far more detailed and personal account of her dealings with Jones over the years (1979b), and there she corrected the erroneous idea (Roazen 1975, p. 38) that she had closely supervised and vetted Jones's biography of her father. No one ever directed Ernest Jones, she later asserted, "It was always the other way round." Jones was his own master in writing his biography of Freud. "He used to appear at our house emptyhanded and depart with armfuls of documents, letters, handwritten notes, etc.," and Anna Freud added "It made little difference whether we were always willing to part with them" (1979b, p. 353).

In addition to Anna Freud's clinical contribution to the Zurich Congress, her other publications that year included a paper on social maladjustment for the Aichhorn *Festschrift* (1949a); a foreword (1949c) to a book on childhood by Edith Buxbaum, who had emigrated to the United States; a cautionary paper on nursery school education in which Anna Freud advised the school to extend or supplement the home but not attempt to duplicate it, though when therapy was required then the child groups must be kept small, since "no woman can assume the role of mother substitute for more than a very limited number of infants or young children" (1949d, pp. 558–559); and a paper, for many years available only in German, on preadolescents' relations with their parents (1949e). (A list of all of Anna Freud's known publications is included in the Appendix.)

THE HAMPSTEAD CHILD THERAPY TRAINING COURSE

In terms of its practical influence throughout the Western Hemisphere, it would be difficult to find any single project that has advanced Anna Freud's name and standing more than the Hampstead Child Therapy Training Course did. In the 35 or so years of its existence, it has produced well over 100 qualified analytical child therapists who have established "little Anna Freud centers" in Europe and the United States.

This training course began in 1947, though there are earlier links, in both personnel and method, with the wartime Hampstead Nursery. Despite Anna Freud's participation in all of the developments associated with child analysis in Hampstead, in this instance the initial stimulus came instead from a source close to her.

The training prospectus of the Hampstead course notes that "Miss Anna Freud founded the Hampstead Child Therapy Course in co-operation with the late Dr. Kate Friedlander" (p. 5). Other contemporary authorities have confirmed that Friedlander's success in establishing the West Sussex Child Guidance Service in the closing years of the Second World War was instrumental in encouraging the postwar Hampstead venture (Jacobs 1949, Glover 1966, Lantos 1966). Ilse Hellman also described Friedlander as "a friend of Miss Freud's" who had suggested the continuation of the teaching and training program begun earlier in the war nursery. The present Hampstead course and clinic had begun gradually, and Anna Freud "continued to be influenced" by Friedlander up to the time of Friedlander's death (Dyer 1980, interview). Barbara Lantos, a close associate of both Friedlander and Anna Freud, disclosed that after "some initial hesitation" Anna Freud took up the plan and went on to establish the course for trainees (1966).

Another important factor in the immediate postwar period was the persistent pressure by previous trainees and unqualified assistants of the Hampstead War Nursery for a training course. Some of these people, of whom the young Sara Kut (later Rosenfeld) and Hanna Engl (later Kennedy) were probably typical, approached several senior analysts in their efforts to secure further adequate grounding in analytical child therapy (Sandler and Novick 1969). This new interest by the war nursery assistants, together with Friedlander's organizing genius and drive, was given a place of honor by Anna Freud herself as the means by which the Hampstead Child Therapy Training Course came into being (A. Freud 1975b). On another occasion, Anna Freud singled out Friedlander as "the real initiator of our training course" (tribute to Sara Rosenfeld, October 3, 1973).

In addition to the two founding analysts, the senior workers joining the venture included Dorothy Burlingham and Hedwig and Willi Hoffer, and the lecturers and seminar tutors included Barbara Lantos, Margarete Ruben, Hedwig Schwarz, Liselotte Frankl, Ruth Thomas, and Ilse Hellman. Most of them maintained a close association with Anna Freud up to the time of her death. In 1947 the Hampstead Training Course had only a single rival in the field of child-therapy training and practice: the course offered by the Institute of Child Psychology founded in London in 1933 by

Margaret Lowenfeld. This provided an eclectic training of several years duration, with an emphasis on clinical observation, play techniques, and their dynamics.

The first group of trainee child therapists in Hampstead consisted of six students who had worked in the Hampstead War Nursery: Joanna Kohler, now Joanna Benkendorf of Cleveland, Ohio; Alice Wallentin, now Alice Rolnick of Cleveland; Sara Kut, later Sara Rosenfeld of London; Hanna Engl, now Hansi Kennedy of London; Alice Goldberger; and Anneliese Schnurmann; as well as a seventh member, Lily Neurath, who had been closely associated with the International Psychoanalytical Press (I. P. Verlag) in prewar Vienna and was extremely knowledgeable regarding Sigmund Freud's publications. These seven early students were later joined by an Australian psychologist, Ivy Bennett (later Ivy Gwynne-Thomas of Kansas City, Missouri), who had trained in adult analysis at the London Institute. Goldberger had taken her training analysis with Anna Freud, Anneliese Schnurmann with Kate Friedlander, and Lily Neurath with Willi Hoffer. Other training analysts included Hedwig Hoffer, Barbara Lantos, and Dorothy Burlingham.

During their training the students worked with child cases of their own in either of the two existing child guidance clinics where several of them had worked after leaving the Hampstead War Nursery at the end of the war. These two clinics were the West Sussex Child Guidance Clinic directed by Kate Friedlander and the East London Child Guidance Clinic directed by Augusta Bonnard. Seminars and lectures took place in the homes of actual training analysts, and the first books owned by the Hampstead Child Therapy Training Center were simply kept on a shelf in Anna Freud's house. The intervention of American friends who financed the purchase of proper premises was still in the future.

Because of their previous experience, the members of the first-year group in training were allowed to begin at the second year of the course, and most were fully qualified by the summer of 1949. The child therapists from this and later years were spread almost equally between the United Kingdom and the United States, though whether by chance or other design is not known. In 1949 the Association of Child Psychotherapists (non-medical) was established in Britain, largely through the efforts of Jess Guthrie, John Bowlby, and Kenneth Soddy. The Hampstead course was quickly accepted by the new association, as was the longer-standing Institute of Child Psychology course and a new course associated with the London Tavistock Clinic.[5]

In addition to those workers already mentioned, the following centers welcomed these Hampstead graduates: in New York, M. Caplan, E. Furst, E. Landauer, T. W. Lopez, K. Rees; in Cleveland, E. Daunton, Erna Furman, E. Koch; in Ann Arbor, Michigan, A. Gehr, C. Kearney, C. Legg, S. Lundberg, S. Mason, I. Sherrick; in Washington, D.C., Dale Meers; in Los Angeles, K. Gilbert, Christoph Heinicke, Randi Markowitz, W. Wheeler; in Stanford, California, I. Paret; in Malibu, California, L. Leibman; in Baltimore, R. Oppenheimer; and at other centers around the United States, M. Bradley, A. M. Bry, A. Colonna, C. Corrie, E. Dansky, M. Flumerfelt, and B. Rosenblatt. In London, at Hampstead itself and elsewhere, were recently Arthur Barron, M. Berger, M. Burgner, P. Cohen, Rose Edgecumbe, I. Elkan, Irene Freud, Audrey Gavshon, Bianca Gordon, Alex Holder, Ann Hurry, R. Joffe, E. M. Mason, E. Model, J. Novick, Renate Putzel, Patricia Radford, Ann-Marie Sandler, Marjorie Sprince, P. Tyson, P. Wilson, and Dora Wills. Other graduate therapists have settled in Sweden, Montreal, Berlin, New Zealand, and Western Australia, and still the list is not complete.

Within two or three years after the inaugural class completed its training, there emerged the Hampstead Child Therapy Training Course and Clinic, which represents, custodianlike, Anna Freud's monumental contribution to the field of psychoanalysis and child study.

[5]At the time of this writing, other organizations in the United Kingdom offering accepted training are the Society of Analytical Psychology (Jungian) and the British Association of Psychotherapists (Freudian and Jungian). For the United States, see the American Association of Child Psychoanalysis, now the international Association for Child Psychoanalysis.

THE HAMPSTEAD CHILD
THERAPY CLINIC

With the loss of Kate Friedlander the task of organizing the Hampstead Clinic was taken up by Anna Freud, in association with Dorothy Burlingham, Josephine Stross, and Ruth Thomas. Financial support was once again forthcoming from private American trusts and friends, and Miss Freud recently singled out Helen Ross and Maxwell Hahn of the New York Field Foundation as being "the true founders of the clinic and the donors of our first house" (1975b, p. vii). She also listed Helen Ross, Muriel Gardiner, and Kurt Eissler as "establishing, housing and tirelessly assisting" the organization of the clinic (1965a, *Acknowledgments*). Another early staff member was Anneliese Schnurmann (1977, personal communication). Liselotte Frankl acted as the new clinic's psychiatrist in charge, and various medically qualified senior analysts were named as honorary consultants, among them Augusta Bonnard, Willi Hoffer, and Josephine Stross (Sandler and Novick 1969).

Around this time, Anna Freud, now in her fifties, relinquished the task of analyzing child cases herself, as noted by her close colleague Hedwig Schwarz (1974). This move by the clinic's director, coupled with her continued presence as training analyst, supervisor, and consultant, was probably to the advantage of the students and therapists around her. They could now present their own first clinical cases and benefit from her comments without being compared with her. From Anna Freud's own point of view the daily work with children had all but served its purpose after over a quarter of a century, and her vast theoretical and practical knowledge enabled her to experience vicariously in the regular report sessions the analytical sequence between trainee-therapist and child patient.

In many ways the new situation was ideally suited to the needs of the clinic and its work, as judged by the clinical and scientific results. Material illustrating its potential for clinical and scientific collaboration is evident in an early paper by one Hampstead-trained worker. Read initially at a general meeting of the clinic, the paper cited unpublished discussion comments by Anna Freud and related the author's own clinical material to the broad corpus of Anna Freud's published writings (Harries 1952). In the 30 years of the Hampstead Clinic's existence many child therapists and other clinicians have documented similar evidence of the value of this liaison with Anna Freud to their clinical or research activities.[6]

For the celebration in May 1956 of the Sigmund Freud Centenary, the Hampstead Clinic held special scientific meetings with invited guest speakers of international reputation and long-standing association with Anna Freud and psychoanalysis. Following the centenary events, large amounts of money were donated to the Hampstead Clinic, particularly from friends and trusts in the United States. In addition to the Hampstead Clinic's centenary events, the British Psychoanalytic Society and the International Psychoanalytic Association also held special events in London for the Sigmund Freud Centenary. Anna Freud's home at 20 Maresfield Gardens became a natural focus for much of this activity, and the London County Council placed a commemorative plaque on the house. After the ceremony, Anna Freud hosted a reception at which Ernest Jones gave an address (I. P. A. announcement 1955).

At the Hampstead Clinic itself, the centenary lectures were begun by Elisabeth Geleerd with her "Clinical Contributions to the Problem of the Early Mother-Child Relationship," and the next day Heinz Hartmann gave his paper "Notes on the Reality Principle." Following these activities, the Hampstead Clinic received generous funds from the Freud Centenary Fund (England), the Grant Foundation (New York), and the Wolfson Foundation (England). In this centenary year the New-Land Foundation of New York donated the building at 21 Maresfield Gardens as the clinic's second house. Eleven years later, the Lita Hazen Charitable Trust of California similarly donated the clinic's third house, at 14

[6]Bergen 1958, Sandler 1960, Nagera 1963, Rosenfeld and Sprince 1965, Thomas 1966, Colonna 1968, Novick and Kelly 1970, Sprince 1971, Hayman 1972, Radford 1973, Holder 1975, Sandler, Kennedy, and Tyson 1975.

Marsefield Gardens. Thus, all three major premises of the Hampstead Child Therapy Clinic stand in the same thoroughfare, all within a short distance of Anna Freud's own home.

In the years immediately following the Sigmund Freud Centenary, the Hampstead Clinic was extended to include a well baby clinic, directed by the analytical pediatrician Josephine Stross, and a nursery school unit, headed by Manna Friedmann. For research into more specialized areas of theory and technique, a number of special study groups were formed, prominent among them being the "Group for the Study of Borderline Children" which, under the leadership of Sara Rosenfeld, outlasted many of its contemporary projects. These projects illustrate the range of the Hampstead approach at this early stage, which included the Adolescent Project (Hellman), the Motherless Children Project, the Blind Children Study Group (Burlingham), the Identical Twins Study (Burlingham), the Pooling of Case Material Project (de Monchaux), the Simultaneous Analysis of Mother and Child, Comparisons of Observational and Analytical Data, and Diagnostic Interviewing (A. Freud 1969h, pp. 13–21).

In the late fifties Anna Freud directed one of her pupils, Bianca Gordon, into a close and valuable cooperation with the Woolwich group of hospitals in London, thus beginning "the Woolwich experiment" in pediatrics and maternity nursing, published 13 years later as part of the Hampstead Clinic's contribution to preventive mental health work in the community (A. Freud 1970b). These applied aspects of the clinic's work complemented three other roles, those of research, therapy, and training. The Hampstead Clinic thus had "a four-fold aim: to learn, to treat, to teach and to apply psychoanalytic knowledge to educational and preventive purposes" (A. Freud 1975b, p. ix). Others have described the clinic as having only three goals, namely "training, service and research" (Kennedy 1978, p. 8). However, the term *service* is imprecise; indeed, virtually all of the clinic's various activities could be defined under such a comprehensive heading. There are two major service areas which need to be distinguished: treatment and therapy, and preventive measures in the form of educational and similar applications.

Two areas of concern to the Hampstead group were the "Hampstead Psychoanalytic Index" and the "Assessment of Childhood Pathology."[7] The latter project is now better known as the Developmental Profile. Together, the Hampstead Index and the Developmental Profile were the most fruitful and far-reaching initiatives, not merely for the analytical child therapy organization associated with Anna Freud, but also for the whole field of developmental child psychology. The index is discussed in some detail below, and the profile, which is more closely linked to Anna Freud's published writings, is considered separately in Chapter 6.

The Hampstead Index made its public début on May 13, 1958, before the Section of Psychiatry of the Royal Society of Medicine in London, with Erwin Stengel presiding. At that meeting Anna Freud noted an ongoing methodological research project involving the pooling of analytical case material. In discussing the planned retrieval system for the project's data, the term *subject index* was introduced (A. Freud 1958d).

For the same audience Cecily de Monchaux elaborated on the index topic, indicating that it had been Dorothy Burlingham around 1954 who had first suggested indexing as a means of facilitating the accessibility to the Hampstead Clinic's rapidly accumulating case material. A pilot scheme had collated the differing index categories used by individual therapists in 50 case reports. From these initial indications was derived a set of common categories for subsequent use on a wider scale. We should add here that with this attention to the difficult problem of categorization when dealing with much material, the Hampstead child analysts were some decades ahead of those psychologists researching and refining the difficult field of creativity and divergent thinking. This latter field was not similarly organized until the early seventies (Dyer 1974).

At its simplest the Hampstead Index offers a set of categories for, say, symptoms. Under each symptom category is then filed a

[7]This title headed a series of applications made by Anna Freud to the National Institute of Mental Health, Washington, D.C., during 1962–1966 (1969j; chap. 3 [I–III]).

series of cards indicating in which particular clinical case histories that symptom occurs. But, since analytic data are typically over-determined and capable of conceptual many-sidedness, a multi-dimensional classification is also used. With this, any unit of observation may be variously followed up according to any of the several viewpoints of psychoanalytic metapsychology. These view-points are generally recognized as having five conceptual frame-works in all. Freud's classic three—the dynamic, structural, and economic—as well as the genetic and, following later theorists such as Hartmann, Rapaport, and Gill, the adaptational. In the earlier accounts of the Hampstead Index material three such dimensions predominate, the dynamic, structural, and genetic-developmental. De Monchaux attempted to add object relations as a fourth dimension, though in this she was somewhat at variance with more orthodox Freudian analysts and soon after ceased to be associated with the index or other Hampstead projects.

Cross-indexing is an important feature of the Hampstead ap-paratus, and several conceptual pathways are thereby offered for search and exploration before a particular behavioral-symptomatic action can be adequately explained. In her preface to the Hampstead Psychoanalytic Index (Bolland and Sandler 1965) Anna Freud described the project as a "laborious method" by which it is hoped to produce something akin to "a collective analytic memory" (A. Freud, 1965c, p. 484), which will then be at the disposal of any individual worker, researcher, or therapist. Although the concept may be applauded as brilliant and enduring, the laborious method-ology thus far employed should eventually be superseded by pro-gramming and computerization of the retrieval-classification system, a logical next step in streamlining and improving the viability of such a reference tool. A centralized "collective analytical memory" or data bank could then feed and support innumerable telephone-linked computer terminals in clinical and research establishments throughout the academic and treatment worlds. Difficulties such as confidentiality are discussed below.

The index itself soon began to generate new questions, problem areas, and avenues of further research. Some of the special study groups evolved by the Hampstead team to resolve these new problems included the Metapsychology Study Group, Classification of Superego Material Group, Fantasy Research Group, Diagnostic Research Group, Clinical Concept Research Group, Depression Research Group, and a group revising an Object Relations Manual.

Prominent in much of this work was Joseph Sandler, who for many years has directed the Hampstead Index Project (Sandler 1962). His coworkers for the classification of the superego material publication were Maria Kawenoka, Lily Neurath, Bernard Rosenblatt, Anneliese Schnurmann, and John Sigal; and for a subsequent study of the concepts of ego ideal and real self Sandler was joined by Alex Holder and Dale Meers. It is typical of the policy associated with Anna Freud's style of work and research that everyone associated with the Hampstead Clinic, from the most inexperienced student to the most senior analyst, is drawn into these research and study groups. The group researching fantasy was particularly comprehensive and representative of the different levels of student and staff, and it included Irvin Janis, Max Goldblatt, Hansi Kennedy, E. First, S. Baker, Anneliese Schnurmann, and Lily Neurath, as well as its principal authors Joseph Sandler, Humberto Nagera, Dale Meers, Alex Holder, and others. When one considers all of the available expertise in the Hampstead Clinic that the groups may call upon, including that of Anna Freud until her recent death in 1982, then the range of input assumes impressively large proportions.

The fantasy research paper emerging from the above group's work contained an actual card from the Hampstead Index. The reader was thus able to see a particular case categorized under "Fantasies: Manifest Theme—Vegetarianism," with the subhead "Latent Theme: Oral Incorporation." Three paragraphs of material then follow, with reference to a second card of the index under the heading of "Latent Theme." There also are other cards, headed "Characteristics," which contain statements by various therapists on the frequency of this fantasy, its form, and so forth (Sandler and Nagera 1963).

By the early sixties, the Depression Research Group of the Hampstead Psychoanalytic Index had reached a point in their studies where they came to acknowledge the various important formulations of Klein, Winnicott, and Bowlby. In particular was an aspect of the concept of individuation that Sandler and Joffe described in their paper (1965), which had a relation to the process which Klein has called "working through the depressive position," as well as to Winnicott's studies of the development of "concern for the object." Clearly, with the approach thus described and its wide eclecticism, the Hampstead Index workers and their clinical and scientific contributions went far toward establishing a comprehensive repository of psychoanalytic findings.

For the topic of transference, the work of the particular metapsychology research group was undoubtedly much indebted to Anna Freud's own extensive deliberations in that area. In Chapter 2 we saw how the special constraints of child analysis prompted her to a radical reappraisal of transference, which she initially viewed as playing a less complete part in the child setting than in the adult setting. But her views were by no means fixed, as they were based on her own technique of observation and experience in the actual analysis of children. As she modified her technique she also altered her assessment of the role of the child's transference reactions, though not to the point of accepting that "what is called transference neurosis with children equals the adult variety in every respect" (1965a, pp. 38–39). After more than 30 years of experience with child analytic technique and its conceptualization, Anna Freud continued to review the adult concept of transference and offered insight via (1) the analyst's role as auxiliary ego and object for externalization, and (2) externalization as a subspecies of transference and best conceptualized separately during interpretation (1965a, pp. 43–44).

In dealing with the clinical and theoretical aspects of transference, the Hampstead research group[8] accepted Hoffer's maxim that the analytic situation is merely a variant of all human transference relationships. Nunberg's earlier clarification was also used, as was Anna Freud's definition of transference in terms of the special analytic situation:

[8] J. Sandler, A. Holder, M. Kawenoka, H. Kennedy, and L. Neurath (Sandler, Holder, et al. 1969).

By transference we mean all those impulses experienced by the patient in his relation with the analyst which are not newly created by the objective analytic situation but have their source in early—indeed, the very earliest—object relations and are now merely revived under the influence of the repetition-compulsion. (1936a, p. 18)

For many analysts in recent decades, transference phenomena have been interpreted from the start of an analysis; they "crowd out most other sources of material" and become "the royal road to the unconscious," a title that had in the past been reserved for dreams (1965a, p. 39). The Hampstead group has been a little more reserved on this issue, and Anna Freud warned against becoming so involved with transference phenomena as to forget that "transference is a means to an end, not a therapeutic measure in itself" (1965a, p. 39). Though this view is described as orthodox —that is, the treatment situation as starting from a real relationship, becoming increasingly distorted through transference manifestations, and ultimately returning to the dominance of a real relationship—such a description is also well suited to other, more interpersonal and object relations oriented theories and models, as well as to common human experience. In most human situations, including at least the milder forms of mental illness, the everyday coping ego is rarely, if ever, completely obliterated in the waking state, and some aspect of a real relationship may well be expected to manifest itself throughout all but the severest of regressive episodes. The question of the real relationship between patient and therapist has become part of what, in modern parlance, is termed the "widening scope of indications" for psychoanalysis.

Eventually the Hampstead researchers came to realize that developments in the technique of child analysis at the Hampstead Child Therapy Clinic had not been documented adequately (Sandler, Kennedy, and Tyson 1975), and in the late sixties they began a series of weekly meetings in which Anna Freud actively participated. They focused on transference, its treatment situation and technique, and they named "treatment situation and technique" as one of the ten sections into which the then current Hampstead

Index was divided. Each section has its own manual, which provides appropriate headings and definitions to assist workers and therapists in indexing their case material. From the relevant manual for treatment situation and technique the researchers listed 46 subheadings under which differing aspects of the treatment situation may be indexed and cross-referenced. This refinement and definition emerged only gradually, and at some effort and cost. The continuing problem of defining basic psychoanalytic terms and concepts was one of the earliest that the project tackled, since the indexers had to agree on both a common use for terms and a common theoretical model.

A series of important monographs is now available,[9] edited by Humberto Nagera, an expatriate Cuban who worked and published in Hampstead during the early sixties before moving to Ann Arbor, Michigan. Each monograph offers a definition and use of basic psychoanalytic concepts and describes the changes that have taken place in the same, especially in reference to Sigmund Freud's ideas. The first volume covered libido theory, and in her foreword (1969b), Anna Freud commented that psychoanalytic concepts have changed throughout the various technical, clinical, and theoretical writings. Later volumes treated the concepts of the theory of dreams, the theory of instincts, metapsychology, conflicts, and anxiety. The Hampstead Psychoanalytic Index systematically collects clinical material in keeping with a theoretical orientation (Holder 1977), the theoretical orientation being classical-orthodox psychoanalysis as developed and exemplified by Anna Freud and her close associates.

The Hampstead Index has not gone uncriticized as a research instrument, even by interested and enthusiastic analysts themselves. Seymour Lustman, then a research psychoanalyst at the Yale Child Study Center, considered that the index was not yet able to handle successfully large masses of analytical material (1963), and he envisioned problems of compressibility, fragmentation, and loss of meaning when the material was taken out of context. Sula

[9]*The Hampstead Clinic Psychoanalytic Library Series.* London: Allen and Unwin, 1969, and New York: Basic Books, 1969.

Wolff concluded that the Hampstead Clinic's unique data may even yet not have been collected in an analyzable (i.e., sufficiently preplanned and systematic) form. The data thus "may never lend themselves to the kind of presentation envisaged by the Clinic's founder" (1976, p. 412). Drawbacks of the index noted by Wolff are its lack of definitive conclusions and research findings and its imprecise scientific style.

It now seems extraordinary that over 50 years of intensive clinical and technical work should have passed before a rigorous indexing project was begun. Many early psychoanalytic propositions were vague and based on few or insufficient cases, with little regard for wider cultural, situational, and individual parameters. The index and related procedures now established at Anna Freud's Hampstead Clinic will undoubtedly continue in the forefront of assessment and revision of psychoanalytic theory and recommendations. A problem still to be solved by the index is its availability. It is clear to any visitor who is shown around the premises of the Hampstead Clinic that the index is something of a shibboleth, whose high altar is the index room which is invariably kept locked. The innocent visitor could also perhaps be forgiven for carrying away the impression that to be one of the few keyholders to this inner sanctum has in some ways much of the symbolic significance of the rings or intaglios that Sigmund Freud gave to those whose loyalty was unquestioned.

The personal nature of much clinical material inevitably complicates any move to make the material more widely available to close scrutiny, whereas the scientific value of an accumulated store of knowledge, as represented by the index, doubtless sharpens the desire to safeguard its integrity from theft, arson, or other dangers. But apart from these circumstances, it is difficult to find other valid reasons that could explain such close restriction of its contents.

In regard to the above difficulties, clinicians have already begun making case material available while preserving their patients' right of anonymity. It may well be that with a system of coding and the deletion of the more personal data, much could be opened to academic scrutiny. And as for the problem of easy availability, much could be done with modern duplication and computer software. Only by making information widely available does it become inherently indestructible.

In 1962, Helen Ross of New York[10] visited Hampstead for a six-week stay. She collected data on the number of cases in analysis, the methods and research orientation used, the special projects and study groups, and the problems of adapting the Hampstead Clinic's type of organization to American needs. On her return to the United States Ross presented a report, in December 1962, to the American Psychoanalytic Association, in which she described the close interaction between research and training and the way in which even beginning students were placed on the various research and study panels (1963). In 1965 the editors—Ruth Eissler, Anna Freud, Marianne Kris, and Ilse Hartmann—of the *Psychoanalytic Study of the Child* announced their new monograph series, the first volumes of which were to be on the "various phases of the research work done at the Hampstead Child Therapy Course and Clinic in London by Anna Freud and her collaborators" (1965, editorial, p. 3). The first monograph dealt with the Hampstead Psychoanalytic Index and with the case of Andy as an example of its clinical application (Bolland and Sandler 1965).

VISITING THE UNITED STATES

With the deaths of both August Aichhorn and Kate Friedlander in one year, it is perhaps no mere coincidence that within the next year Anna Freud had accepted an invitation to her first American lecture tour and thereafter visited the United States every other year or so over the next two decades. This is not to suggest that with the continued association of colleagues such as Aichhorn and Friedlander Anna Freud would not have eventually found her way to the United States, nor is there any suggestion that she would have encouraged a "European school" in contrast to an "American school" of psychoanalysis. On the contrary, the evidence of the

[10]Now of Washington, D.C. In the 1930s Ross had been a member of Anna Freud's Vienna child analysis seminar and undergone training in Vienna.

Kleinian controversy and its aftermath had already shown how nondivisive she was in her professional politics. But in different circumstances America may have beckoned longer or, in the long term, have received less attention.

These considerations aside, it seems likely that the historic nature of Anna Freud's first invitation, following as it did the style and occasion of her father's historic visit 40 years earlier, would not have been ignored. Anna Freud's first appearance in the United States was marked by the conferment upon her of the degree of Doctor of Laws (LLD) *honoris causa*, in a ceremony on April 22, 1950, at Clark University, Worcester, Massachusetts. The citation was presented by Heinz Werner of Clark's psychology department, who spoke of the earlier visit of Sigmund Freud who received the identical degree, and added that "it is eminently fitting that on the occasion of the sixtieth anniversity of Clark University, we should honor Anna Freud, eminent psychologist, who has creatively extended her father's work in psychoanalysis" (*International Journal of Psychoanalysis* 1950, *News and Notes*). By 1950 that extension included her technical method of child analysis; her theoretical contribution to ego defensive activity; and her initiatives stemming from the residential war work with evacuee children, including the crucial mother-child relationship. As with her father before her, the Clark University degree was the beginning of three decades of continuing international recognition of the increasing stature and scientific eminence of a remarkable psychologist.

At the New York Psychoanalytic Society and Institute, Anna Freud's opening presentation, on April 17, 1950, was on male homosexuality. The core of her presentation was essentially her paper on the same topic given to the 16th I.P.A. Congress in Zurich the year before (1949b). There she had criticized as merely descriptive the usual classification of homosexuals as either active or passive and had argued instead for the basis of classification to be not the overt practice carried out with the partner but the fantasy that accompanied the act (identification with either the active or passive partner). This radical new nosological attitude was not helped by the fact that the patient's identification with the active or passive partner could change during his encounters. In extending her work beyond the point reached in the Zurich paper, Anna Freud's New York lecture was especially concerned with "those phases of treatment after the potency of the patient has been restored and a heterosexual object chosen" (1951c, pp. 117–118). Using illustrative clinical material of her own, she demonstrated that even at this late stage in treatment such patients are egoistic, with a diminished ability to love, and are likely to be dominated by phallic narcissism.

In contrast, Anna Freud's paper given two days later to Radcliffe College and Harvard University was on problems of citizenship and parenthood. Although available only in abstract (1951d), the lecture is of interest to teachers, parents, play workers, and others who daily handle normal infants and young persons. Despite the trend away from typologies in modern psychology, Anna Freud's three main parental types are a valuable classification. The proposed types are as follows: (1) those who have repressed their own conflicts and permit little individual happiness to the child, (2) those who remain conscious of their conflicts and permit the child to be happy at the expense of citizenship, and (3) those who possess some analytic knowledge and dread the pathological consequences of repression. In identifying the fallacies inherent in all of these attitudes toward the child, Anna Freud suggested that the way to better parenthood rests rather in the exploration by parents of their own childhood experiences. To that end psychoanalysis offers an efficacious method, though we do not imply that all parents should undergo a formal analysis, either for therapeutic or didactic purposes.

A Symposium on Genetic Psychology was held at Clark University during the visit, and the contributors were Anna Freud, K. L. Frank, and R. R. Sears. Anna Freud's paper was entitled "The Contributions of Psychoanalysis to Genetic Psychology" (1951a). She discussed previous efforts to join psychoanalysis and academic psychologies, including those by de Saussure and Bernfeld who had during the 1930s sought to link Freud's developmental libido theory with the complementary psychological theories of Piaget and Kurt Lewin. Other workers noted, particularly from the academic and nonanalytical psychologies, were O. H. Mowrer, Clyde Kluckhohn, Henry Murray, and Robert Sears. She also named the psychoanalytic experimental research activities of D. Levy, M. Ribble, M. Fries, R. Spitz, and J. Bowlby, and she encouraged Hartmann, Kris, Lowenstein, and David Rapaport in their efforts to reformulate psychoanalysis and genetic psychology.[11]

Anna Freud pointed out, following Lawrence Frank, that both psychoanalysis and genetic psychology tried to explain the present in terms of the past. They differed, however, in their method-ologies, with genetic psychology favoring pure research and psy-choanalysis aligning itself with action research. Thus the nature of the subjects (persons) chosen by each discipline also differs, with the academic psychologists being free to choose as they wish and invariably selecting normal subjects, whereas psychoanalytic re-search is generally an outcome of the analyst's clinical work and centers on abnormal manifestations. Other distinctions drawn by Anna Freud were between "the artificial laboratory setting of the academic workers and the life situation between analyst and patient" (1951a, pp. 119–120), for which she gave the following illustration: whereas the academic psychologist may study frustra-tion in childhood, such as occurs with the withholding of a toy, the psychoanalyst is more likely to encounter the quantitatively and qualitatively different phenomenon of frustration based on the early loss of the mother. Moreover, "clinical evidence shows that the child's ego has different means at its disposal when dealing with major events than when dealing with events of comparatively small importance" (p. 120). Anna Freud also spoke of the ease with which psychologists of other persuasions confused or distorted specific psychoanalytical technical meanings, such as the erroneous view of one researcher who expected sublimation to be linked to

[11]A notable omission in Anna Freud's review was Gardner Murphy's early "biosocial theory of personality" (1947). Those who integrate psychoanalysis into their own fields include the ethologist R. A. Hinde, the neurophysiologist K. H. Pribram, the educationalist W. H. G. Armytage, the philosopher R. S. Peters, and psychologists such as Ben Morris and Peter McKellar in England and G. Lindzey, Lois B. Murphy, D. McClelland, and U. Bronfenbrenner in the United States.

agenitality and therefore proceeded to observe the incidence of masturbation in aesthetically gifted adult males.

In her summary of psychoanalysis as genetic psychology, Anna Freud refused to eschew the distinctiveness of the methods and techniques peculiar to psychoanalysis, for it is on these and their particular strengths that hunches, intuitions, findings, theories, and hypotheses have been and will continue to be based, with benefits for many of the social and psychological sciences. In fact, child analysis itself has become an interdisciplinary method, no longer restricted to the clinical analytical setting. From the increasingly systematic observational studies undertaken by analytically trained workers there were by the late forties and early fifties important insights into the controversial preverbal phases of infancy. Although the Hampstead War Nursery studies were mentioned in this connection, so also was Ernst Kris for his advancing the integration of observational-experimental and clinical-reconstructive analytical data (A. Freud 1951).

The day after the Symposium on Genetic Psychology Anna Freud presented the second of her papers to Clark University's psychology department. This paper was on child psychiatry and is available only in abstract (*Bulletin of the American Psychoanalytic Association* 1951). Here Anna Freud suggested that most of what then passed for child psychiatry was "to the largest extent a by-product of psychoanalysis," though what had received the most systematic application had been taken from the area of instinctual drives, as opposed to ego and superego development. In making recommendations for future progress in this field, she pressed further the radical new initiative she had first made public in her 1945 paper on "Indications for Child Analysis" and, rejecting older and obsolete views, argued that current quantitative approaches that tried to determine how much frustration and how much gratification to permit the child should be replaced by a qualitative orientation. In this latter approach, each component instinctual urge and drive derivative would be treated on its merits, that is, according to whether it could find room for direct or aim-inhibited satisfaction in adult life.

Within a year or two of this first United States lecture tour
Lauretta Bender, a child psychiatrist, declared (1952) Anna Freud's
work and views as being more realistic since her war work with
evacuee children. By the end of the decade the World Health
Organization (WHO) also confirmed Anna Freud's view that
dynamic psychology based on psychoanalytic technique and theory
might be considered as the basis of diagnosis and therapy in child
guidance centers throughout the world, and "Anna Freud's observations on the conditions under which the child is brought to the
psychiatrist certainly remain entirely valid" (Buckle and Lebovici
1960, p. 71).

In the same day as she read her child psychiatry paper, Anna
Freud also visited the Worcester Child Guidance Center, there
reading a paper on "Infantile Disturbances of Feeding and Sleeping," based on her earlier postwar study of similar title (1946a) and
giving further emphasis to the work of her colleague Edith B.
Jackson.

After she left Clark University, Anna Freud went to Stockbridge,
Massachusetts to attend a Symposium on Problems of Child Development at the Austen Riggs Foundation on April 23–24, 1950.
The Stockbridge discussion, as the event has become known, was
chaired by Robert P. Knight, and Ernst Kris opened with some
incisive remarks on psychoanalytic child psychology. Other partici-
pants in the discussion—all former colleagues of Anna Freud's or
child analysts and psychiatrists specially invited—were Grete
Bibring, Berta Bornstein, Helene Deutsch, Erik Erikson, Elisabeth
Geleerd, Phyllis Greenacre, Heinz Hartmann, Mary O'Neill Hawkins, Bertram D. Lewin, Rudolph Loewenstein, Margaret Mahler,
Marion C. Putnam, Beata Rank, Melitta Sperling, Rene Spitz,
Emmy Sylvester, and Robert Waelder. Anna Freud's paper for the
Stockbridge symposium, entitled "Observations on Child Development" (1951b), consolidated her new views on child analysis and
experimental work as developed during the period of wartime
work with evacuees. She cited many wartime nursery findings and
related them to current theoretical issues such as reconstruction,
developmental chronology, and discrepancies between theory and
observation. In stating that her observational results "helped to

swell the body of existing analytic knowledge, even though . . . they did not break new ground" (1951b, p. 145), she overlooked the fact that this corroborative method was itself largely a new approach, as was the systematic study and training in such methods for analysts. Also in 1950, Ernst Kris began at Yale his experimental laboratory along psychoanalytical lines.

Psychoanalytic hypotheses and findings corroborated by the observational-experimental work carried on during the forties period included the phases of libido development now seen reflected in the child's direct behavior as opposed to reconstruction from adult clinical material; evidence for the primary process, demonstrated in the behavior of 12- to 18-month-old infants, as opposed to the dream material of patients in analysis; and the fusion of libidinal and aggressive drives, seen in a particular technique of therapy used by the Hampstead group during wartime. This last is particularly interesting as an experimentally planned intercession and for its value for child rearing and social development in the latter part of the 20th century. Since many of the disturbed children in the wartime nursery were known to lack a proper mother relationship, their abnormal aggressiveness was assumed to result not from an abnormally strong aggressive drive but from a lack of fusion of the aggressive with the libidinal drive. Anna Freud described the outcome as follows:

> To test our diagnosis, we ceased any attempts to combat the children's aggression directly, and concentrated our efforts instead on stimulating the emotional side which had lagged behind. The results confirmed that, with the development of good object relationships, aggression became bound and its manifestations reduced to normal quantities. It proved possible, as it were, to effect therapeutic results by bringing about the necessary fusion of the two drives. (1951b, pp. 153–154)

In addition to these corroborative evidences she also touched on certain discrepancies between analytic assumptions and behavioral observations. These discrepancies were phenomena of regression, the telescoping of events in reconstruction, and the chronology of the appearance in development of disgust, shame, and the like.

Another problem area was a parallel to autoerotism in the form of "autoaggression" such as head knocking, and, as noted in Chapter 4, the most intriguing data from the war nurseries concerned the phenomena of coitus play without observation of the primal scene and oedipus reactions without oedipal experiences.

Miss Freud then went to Cleveland, where on April 25 she gave a paper to the members of the Detroit and Cleveland Psychoanalytic Society, on "Variations of Psychoanalytic Technique" (1951h), a theme to which she returned in later visits. Generally, she believed that the individual analyst's modifications in technique were justified insofar as they maintained the modifications in theory.

At the medical school of Western Reserve University on April 26, 1950, an audience of analysts, psychiatrists, and psychologists was joined by medical students and faculty staff to hear her speak on "The Role of Sickness and Hospitalisation in the Life of the Child" (1951g). The interrelations of pediatrics and child analysis always interested Anna Freud (1952a, 1953a, 1956a, 1961a, 1965e, 1975f, 1976d). She saw the child's problem in hospital as twofold, as coping with the psychological consequences of the illness itself and simultaneously with the separation from the home and important mothering persons.

The next day she closed her lectures with "Present Problems of Child Analysis" (1951i), delivered at the Detroit meeting of the American Psychoanalytic Association. She found the multitude of problem areas not surprising, since child analysis had been applied to so many cognate fields and disciplines, and the mixture of therapeutic and educational aims had been matched by the confusion of child analysis techniques with child guidance, counseling, and so forth. Such difficulties could, Anna Freud suggested, be solved by evaluating the etiology of childhood disturbances and specifying the types of therapy indicated for particular developmental interferences. With hindsight we should note that even at this early stage Anna Freud's subsequent reclassification of childhood disorders and indications for analysis was clearly already in her mind as a future goal and endeavor.

The year of Anna Freud's American début coincided with the appearance of the first volume of Sigmund Freud's published correspondence, the German edition of the letters of Freud and Wilhelm Fliess. The editors were Marie Bonaparte, Anna Freud, and Ernst Kris. The foreword states that Anna Freud selected the letters, and Kris wrote the introduction and notes (S. Freud 1950). An English translation by Eric Mosbacher and James Strachey came out a few years later.

The International Congress of Psychiatry met in Paris from September 18 to 27, 1950. Present on this occasion were Marie Bonaparte, Raymond de Saussure, and Melanie Klein. At a discussion group led by Franz Alexander, Anna Freud read "The Significance of the Evolution of Psychoanalytic Child Psychology" (1950a). In conjunction with Anna Freud's lecture on psychoanalysis and genetic psychology at the Clark University meeting, plus her Stockbridge contribution on problems of child development, the Paris contribution of the same year rounded off the description of the scientific basis which from now on would be a hallmark of observational child analysis.

The evolution of psychoanalytic child psychology from 1908 to 1950 can be shown by comparing the number of data sources used at the beginning and the end of this period. We discussed in Chapter 1 how Sigmund Freud had supplemented his essentially reconstructive methodology with two other sources of data, the direct observation of what children say and do and the conscious recollections of adults. By the time Anna Freud outlined her own approach to child analytical investigation, this three-stranded methodological approach had broadened into five, which were, she commented, "of unequal validity" (1950a, p. 615). First in order, from the viewpoint of a psychoanalyst, was the reconstructive method, to which Freud added the interpretation of the dreams of normal adults. The third method was direct observations made during the analytic treatment of neurotic children. Both of the remaining two approaches—though she implied that the list was not exhaustive—concern the collection of developmental data from increasingly systematic studies of childhood, from analyzed parents during the upbringing of their own children, and from professional analytically oriented workers in education, child guidance, and similar vocations.

Hand in hand with an improved technical method and scientific range of approach were the inevitable reformulations of psychoanalytic theory. Here Anna Freud attributed great importance to "Three Modifications of Theory Introduced by Freud Between 1920 and 1926" (1950a, p. 616). These were the now celebrated abandonment of the concept of aggression as an ego instinct and its proper biological definition as an innate drive; the reformulation of the difficult problem of anxiety; and the revival of the concept of defense, which in particular Anna Freud had developed, though by no means to the exclusion of the other strands of theory. On the basis of these advances in theory and with a central viewpoint securely grounded in the ego as an everyday coping organization within the personality, she classified, more concisely than she did in *The Ego and the Mechanisms of Defence*, "the different interferences with gratification which finally lead to the essential transformations of instinct taking place in the first five years of life" (1950a, p. 620). These interferences, as is well known, are held to proceed from three operative sources, the external outer world environment, the internal superego as representative of certain external factors, and the inner world of instinctual drive forces. In stressing the desirability of some forms of experimental testing of these psychoanalytic views, Anna Freud did not seek or advocate a "controlled laboratory situation." Rather, along with Hartmann and Kris among others, she pointed to "involuntary and accidental experiments, provided by fate" (p. 623), and her wartime experiences with children had of course offered just such situations. With this level of corroborative thinking Anna Freud secured for child analysis a high degree of psychological relevance and realism.[12]

[12]Similar attention is evident in the work of Ben Morris, who was able to discriminate from many psychologies those with greater relevance in interpersonal terms (1966). A gifted eclectic who bridged general psychology and psychoanalysis, Morris did psychometric work at the National Foundation for Educational Research, met and listened to Anna Freud during his analytical training, and formally examined my own dissertation on which this book is based.

By the early 1950s Anna Freud's professional life was established in four major areas of interest, all of which were closely inter-related:

1. A private practice of some five analytical hours daily, now only with adult patients and candidates in training.
2. High office and involvement in both the business and scientific affairs of the International Psychoanalytic Association and the biannual I. P. A. Congress.
3. Expanding interest in the United States, with lecture visits biannually or more frequently.
4. Gradual expansion and refinement of the clinical, research, and training interests of the Hampstead Child Therapy Clinic.

As well, there were the additional tasks of writing and scientific and clinical editing for each of these activities, plus the large private correspondence burden that her increasing recognition required.

Almost inevitably Anna Freud's direct involvement with the British Psychoanalytic Society waned in the early fifties. She held no formal office or council positions after 1951–1952, though her lectures and seminars continued until 1955 when she offered a single regular seminar as part of Course B to third-year candidates (Bulletin Reports of the British Psychoanalytic Society 1950–1955). After that time Anna Freud's name no longer appears in the daily organized activities of the British Society, although there were occasional news notices of her other activities, honors, and so forth, which showed her to be regarded still as an esteemed and active member of the British group of analysts.

If Anna Freud's international recognition as a preeminent psychoanalytical and child study expert was ever in doubt, then the postwar Americans quickly dispelled that doubt. So many have expended such warmth, enthusiasm, and effort to acknowledge Anna Freud's leadership in her chosen field (Ross 1963, Lustman 1967, D. Kaplan 1968, L. Kaplan 1971, Greenson 1972) that it is scarcely possible to avoid the conclusion that like her father before her, Anna Freud is more highly regarded abroad than in the country of her birth or later residence. From April 1950 to April

1970 she visited the United States no fewer than 17 times, many being prolonged stays of several weeks or even months.

Cleveland is of particular interest as having one of the leading centers for child analysis outside London. Child analysis began in Cleveland in 1947 with the arrival of Anny Katan, who was appointed professor of child psychoanalysis at Western Reserve University's School of Medicine. Over the following decades there were many exchanges and cross-fertilizations between Cleveland and Anna Freud's group in London. Among those training in Hampstead with Freud and then moving to Cleveland were Joanna Benkendorf, Alice Rolnick, Erna Furman, Elisabeth Daunton, and Ehud Koch. When the Cleveland Center for Research in Child Development came into being in 1966, largely through the efforts of Anny Katan and Robert Furman, Anna Freud and Heinz Hartmann were made honorary trustees. Not surprisingly, the Cleveland center follows a pattern of work and training similar to that found in the Hampstead Child Therapy Clinic (Tenth Anniversary Report 1976).

In May 1954 Anna Freud went to New York, Philadelphia, and Atlantic City, New Jersey. In the Freud Anniversary Lecture to the New York Academy of Medicine, Miss Freud linked analytic child psychology, which she viewed as the most important by-product of psychoanalytic investigation, with education and child upbringing as well as with research into the causation and prevention of neurosis (1954a). The thesis of her lecture was to probe for the causes of neurosis in earliest childhood. She rejected the "rejecting mother" concept as a too-facile, all-embracing cause of neurosis and instead turned to the "need satisfying phase" of anaclitic relationship which precedes even the earliest object relationship with the mother. "The concept of the anaclitic relationship," she asserted, "has never been fully utilised in analytic writings" (1954a, p. 321). She believed that experiences in this early pleasure-pain dominated phase of life influenced the subsequent phase of object relations proper, producing what Melanie Klein termed the *good* and *bad* mother images and what Anna Freud termed the *positive* and *negative* attitudes toward the mother image. The emergent ego structure of the first six months of life is influenced by these same anaclitic relations. Anna Freud was less certain whether "somatic compliance" and the choice of symptom formation also is present in this phase. She closed her talk with comments regarding the causation and fate of neurosis. She did not believe "that even the most revolutionary changes in infant care can do away with the tendancy to ambivalence or with the division of the human personality into an id and an ego with conflicting aims" (1954a, p. 326). The emergence of neurotic conflicts, she concluded, must be regarded as the price paid for the complexity of the human personality.[13]

Following the Freud Anniversary Lecture, Anna Freud took part in the Arden House Symposium on Problems of Infantile Neurosis, held at the New York Psychoanalytic Society and Institute on May 8, 1954. Ernst Kris chaired the meeting, and many prominent analytical workers attended, including Grace Abbate, Anita Bell, Gustav Bychowski, Charles Davison, Sibylle Escalona, Phyllis Greenacre, Heinz Hartmann, Mary O'Neil Hawkins, Edith Jacobson, Judith Kestenberg, Marianne Kris, Bertram D. Lewin, R. M. Lowenstein, Margaret Mahler, Bela Mittelmann, Rene Spitz, and Robert Waelder. In her own remarks, which were linked closely to her Freud Anniversary Lecture, Anna Freud (1954b) singled out Greenacre's work, finding many points of congruence between their two approaches. She enlarged her earlier discussion of the "rejecting mother" with clinical examples of "seducing mothers," in which the child's resultant development was chaotic and grossly distorted. In defending her views in regard to the phase of anaclitic relationship, she did not deny the importance of early object relations and agreed with Klein, Jacobson, and others on the matter of early, primitive "part objects," but she reiterated her own belief that "the first attachment to the mother follows a pattern which has originated elsewhere" (1954b, p. 343). In contrasting her own view of the earliest phase of extrauterine life with those who leaned more toward an object relations orientation,

[13] Anna Freud's fundamental belief here is akin to that of W. R. D. Fairbairn and other object relations theorists, who assert the inevitability of ego splitting in early human development (see Chapter 6 for further discussion of Anna Freud and Fairbairn).

Anna Freud remarked that "what leaves me dissatisfied with these formulations is the fact that in their very terminology they stress the importance of the object, whereas the child is dominated by the need" (1954b, p. 344). In her terminology, the young baby libidinally cathects the moment of blissful satiation rather than the object that provides the satiation.

Another symposium held by the New York Psychoanalytic Society during Anna Freud's 1954 visit dealt with "The Widening Scope of Indications for Psychoanalysis." Both Leo Stone and Edith Jacobson read papers, and Anna Freud participated in the opening discussion (1954c). Technical matters beyond the immediate requirements of child analysis had always attracted Anna Freud's attention, from the early Vienna days when she had watched the modifications of the orthodox technique made by Aichhorn, Federn, Rank, Ferenczi, and Reich. She also named an "experimental technical seminar" instituted in Vienna many years before, at which analysts of equal seniority, theoretical persuasion, and with cases of similar diagnosis found much the same wide variations in technical procedure among them as had been noted by Stone in his symposium remarks. The causes of such variations had not yet been identified, but were determined more by the individual analyst's interest and orientation than by differences in the clinical material.

Included in her discussion of the technical matters arising from "the widening scope of indications for analysis" were the patient's belief in the analyst's magical omnipotence and the question of a real relationship between patient and therapist.

In their symposium papers, both Jacobson and Stone referred to the illusory, magical quality of the patient's transference feelings and the need for the therapist to be omniscient and godlike. Often this was not immediately recognized and could be a danger to the analysis if not interpreted. Anna Freud gave examples from her own practice; one was a civil servant who believed that the analyst could exert influence at the highest level of the civil service on his behalf. Another patient believed that Anna Freud had influence over Hitler's war machine, but that belief was destroyed when the analyst was careless enough to permit the Luftwaffe to drop a bomb at the end of her street!

It is tempting to see in such transference phenomena the universal childhood need for a protective parent, especially a father figure. The dissolution of such fantasized omnipotence is usually accompanied by outbreaks of intolerable anxiety by the patient, again reminiscent of the preschool child's response to the realization that the parent is missing. Anna Freud believed that this anxiety testified to the urgent need to retain the particular transference defense (1954c, p. 371).

Other studies have attained a new significance in the light of the above. Barchilon (1964), for example, collected drawings and other clinical material from a 4½-year-old girl around the time of President John F. Kennedy's assassination, finding a revival of earlier "return to the womb" drawings as one expression of the child's reaction to the threat of loss of love and annihilation that the assassination symbolized. Fairbairn (1936) collected detailed clinical observations from three adults in treatment at the time of the death of King George V. Even at this early time Fairbairn's later theoretical predilection for object relations as a conceptual vehicle is evident, and he concluded his paper with Klein's view that every experience that suggests the loss of the real loved object also stimulates the dread of losing the internalized object.

Anna Freud herself noted that when Hitler rose to power in Europe, many patients lost their magical transference feeling for the analyst. The analysts themselves were victims of the new regime, and not suited therefore to omnipotence (1954c, p. 371). In other words, the analyst was killed as a dynamic object, in much the way that the king and the president had ceased to exist. One of the earliest studies on this subject was by Sigmund Freud (1921c), who discussed the dissolution of groups and the effects on individuals and cited the earlier study of Federn (1919) on the abolition of sovereign authority by revolution. One wonders how often in history, and at what psychosocial cost, the human race has been jarred by events of similar psychological significance and magnitude.

In regard to the question of a real personal relation between therapist and patient and the status of this when compared with the true transference reactions, Anna Freud accepted Stone's discrimination between the two kinds of relationships as it coincided with her own views. Thus, while retaining a belief in "the necessary strictest handling and interpretation of the transference" (1954c, p. 373), she nevertheless still felt that "somewhere we should leave room for the realisation that analyst and patient are also two real people, of equal adult status, in a real personal relationship to each other" (p. 373). But she did not, on this occasion, allow herself to follow this line of thinking too far, since her new ideas were "technically subversive" and needed to be carefully thought out. Two decades later Stone again brought up the themes stemming from this symposium, finding technical "heresy" (as with the question of the real relationship) either latent or manifest and widely pervasive among analysts (1975).

Ralph Greenson of Los Angeles, a pupil of Otto Fenichel and in recent years a sympathetic ally of Anna Freud, has perhaps most cogently distinguished transference relations, real relations, and "the working alliance" (1971). Greenson cited Stone and Fairbairn as the most outspoken advocates of the view that the total object relations between patient and analyst must be considered, and he added that Anna Freud, Gitelson, Knight, Winnicott, Loewald, and Erikson, among others, have also pointed in the same direction. The problem of the real relationship and who will inherit it when the analysis is terminated was taken up by another Los Angeles group closely allied with Anna Freud (Van Dam, Heinicke, and Shane 1975).

By a fortunate coincidence, the theme of the real relationship figured prominently in the discussion following the main presentation at a Wednesday Open Case Conference of the Hampstead Clinic a few years ago,[14] which enables us to bring up to date Anna Freud's views on this controversial topic. The afternoon's paper was entitled "The Demand for a Real Relation in the Analysis of

---

[14]Wednesday, June 1, 1977. The presenter was Arthur Couch, an American student of Anna Freud, who had trained at the London Institute of Psychoanalysis. Others present included Dorothy Burlingham, Hedwig Schwarz, Anneliese Schnurmann, J. C. Hill, Alice Goldberger, Liselotte Frankl, Hansi Kennedy, Clifford Yorke, Sidney Blatt, other members of the Hampstead Clinic, several exchange students from Hahnemann Medical College, Philadelphia, and myself.

an Adolescent," the patient being a girl of above-average intelligence who included psychoanalytical literature in her reading. In her introductory remarks Anna Freud warned that the case had been an especially difficult one from the point of view of therapy, and it soon became apparent that the therapist had endured very many silent sessions, interspersed with the girl's demands for a more real relationship. She had, for example, at one stage suggested that she and the analyst "write a joint paper" on her case.

In opening the discussion of this case, Anna Freud stated that she did not believe that this girl was demanding a real relationship but, rather, was trying to fulfill a fantasy-idealized relationship. Fulfilling the girl's main demand would not have led to a treatment alliance. For the first time the audience's attention was drawn to the importance of the patient's maturational development —from 15 to 19 years of age—and its influence on the final analysis undertaken after a break in treatment. This patient, concluded Anna Freud, was seeking an object that would not leave her, disappoint her, or die. But all objects eventually do one of these things. Comments were then invited from the floor, with Hedwig Schwarz, Dorothy Burlingham, and Hansi Kennedy responding.

Couch had conveniently cited Anna Freud's remarks on the real relationship that she had made following Stone's paper to the 1954 New York symposium. Anna Freud now took up this matter, insisting that on the earlier occasion she had been referring to a "real real relationship," whereas what was now before the gathering was a "fantasized real relationship" in pursuit of a lasting object. "Yes," objected Hedwig Schwarz from the floor, "but is that not what we are all really seeking?" "Oh, yes," countered Anna Freud, "but most of us know when to accept something less and face reality." In summary, she reiterated that no real relationship (i.e., a real real relationship) could hope to fulfill this particular girl's demands, which were for complete identity and reciprocity.

We should note that the conceptual subtlety evident in the above formulations may well prove difficult to apply in practice. Such delicate distinctions may in themselves even become counterproductive and in the hands of those with a differing theoretical persuasion could lead to concept assassination. In the absence of

universally accepted criteria for the finer distinctions of real and
unreal relationships, it is logically impossible to refute further
elaboration and reversal of any conceptual status quo.

As a teacher working with mostly normal pupils between the
ages of 5 and 11 years, I am aware that the child presents aspects of
a real relationship as well as aspects of a usually mild transference
relation. The relevance to the teaching situation of the psychoanalytic drives-ego-superego model, in which the teacher views the
child "not as a unified being but as a being consisting of several
parts" (A. Freud 1952b, p. 565), is here unquestioned and of daily
efficacy in many situations. Nevertheless there is a danger in the
phrase "consisting of several parts," namely that the teacher may,
through ignorance, overenthusiasm, or a personal "blind spot,"
actually relate to just such a circumscribed "part child" and thereby
risk losing or never experiencing the real child. The problem
would seem to be analogous to that of the clinician, who may relate
predominantly or even entirely to the patient's transference aspect
and thus risk losing the real relationship and perhaps also the real
patient-person.

In asserting that the schoolchild is a real person, we enter the
realm of educational philosophy, though in this instance that
realm would appear to receive much suggestive support from child
analysis. The view maintained here is quite possibly incompatible
with the model of classical-orthodox psychoanalysis and leans
toward the spirit of Martin Buber's *I and Thou* (1937) and the total
object relations views of Ronald Fairbairn and Harry Guntrip
(1961), rather than toward the letter of Freud's drives-ego-
superego. The educator is the exponent of an art form rather than
a strict science and may use a wider range of theoretical models and
hypothetical leads in the pursuit of particular professional goals. A
real relationship approach will tend to reduce the interpersonal
distance between teacher and taught. One outcome may be to
increase the risk of emotional conflicts and social difficulties, and
teachers must therefore look carefully at their own emotional and
social vulnerability.

In addition to her many visits to the United States, Anna Freud
continued to attend the biannual congresses of the International

Psychoanalytic Association, presenting several scientific papers in Amsterdam, Paris, and London in the 1950s.

Returning to Worcester, Massachusetts, in September 1957, she gave a paper for the 35th Anniversary of the Worcester Youth Guidance Center. For this, she chose to invoke once again "the subject of adolescence after an interval of twenty years" (1958b, p. 136). Despite the contributions of those intervening years to the theory of adolescence, many of them from Americans—one thinks of Fritz Redl, Erik Erikson, Peter Blos, and Leo Spiegel, among the analytical workers, and Havighurst, Jersild, and Stone and Church among the general psychologists—to Anna Freud, adolescence was still "a stepchild in psychoanalytic theory" (p. 141). That such a state of affairs was regrettable and that adolescence merited more attention from psychoanalysis were corollaries of Anna Freud's account of how adolescent manifestations "come close to symptom formation of the neurotic, psychotic or dissocial order and merge almost imperceptibly into borderline states, initial frustrated or full-fledged forms of almost all the mental illnesses" (1958b, p. 153). In enlarging her earlier (1936) description of defensive ego processes in adolescence, she now included specific defense activities directed against the oedipal and preoedipal relations, and with her acceptance of disharmony as the norm for this phase of development, she devised a "concept of normality in adolescence" which presaged much of her writings and thought in the ensuing years. Beyond the 1950s, in large measure because of Anna Freud, the theme of normality as opposed to pathology became more important to the theory and applied aspects of psychoanalytic child psychology, bringing in its wake the prospect of an even wider academic recognition of child analysis.

PREDICTING DEVELOPMENT AND PATHOLOGY

The death of Ernst Kris was the occasion that brought Anna Freud, on September 2, 1957, to a memorial meeting held jointly by the psychoanalytical societies and institutes of New York and western New England. The meeting was held at the New York Academy of Medicine, and Miss Freud delivered a paper entitled "Child Observation and Prediction of Development" (1958a).

As her starting point she took Kris's earlier initiative in regard to the legitimacy of direct child observation in psychoanalytic investigation, which had resulted in the important Stockbridge symposium of April 1950. On that occasion Anna Freud had acknowledged that it was Kris who had "set up the framework within which an interchange of ideas about current problems in psychoanalytic child psychology may prove fruitful" (1951b, p. 143), though at that time, as she later admitted, she had taken the somewhat pessimistic view that observational studies would not break new ground (1958a, p. 104) and would merely provide corroboration for reconstructive hypotheses. It was, and remained, the view of Ernst Kris, however, that when used properly, observational data would be methodologically comparable to other data sources of importance to analysts. The resultant "double method approach," as Anna Freud (1958a) pointed out, is precisely why the Yale Child Study Center under Kris's directorship had become justly famous.

One aspect of Kris's work that was slower in gaining general acceptance among his colleagues, including Anna Freud herself, was his use of the term *prediction* in relation to the diagnostic dilemma of the earlier recognition of pathological development. But once Anna Freud overcame her initial anathema to vague theoretical speculation concerning future outcomes, she realized that what Kris implied was that analysts should learn to recognize the course of symptomatology before it became manifest. Such recognition should follow from a close observation and understanding of the child's behavior as well as changes in the circumstances of the family unit and detailed knowledge of the history of the mother, the child, and so on. Such predictions would naturally be uncertain, and Anna Freud listed three factors that would make predictive clinical foresight even more uncertain: (1) variations in the respective rates of maturation of ego development and drive development, (2) lack of a suitable method of quantifying drive development, and (3) the uncertain nature of events in the child's environment.

From her own clinical experience Anna Freud selected the case of a 6-year-old boy with a tic, in order to demonstrate the principles that she now advocated. As she observed, the next step should be "to a state of affairs which places therapeutic intervention even earlier, namely, at a time before symptom formation has been resorted to at all" (1958a, pp. 112–113).

This particular child's life history was well known to Anna Freud, since he was one of the former war children whose "family fortunes and misfortunes" had been closely followed. This gave rise to what Anna Freud referred to as a fortunate "additional 'longitudinal' observation," and the child's predisposing conditions included intimacy with his mother in infancy, hostility to the father who returned from the war injured, immense jealousy at the birth of a sibling, and "complete lack of manifest anxiety when his mother fell ill and died in connection with her next pregnancy" (p. 113). A year after his mother died the boy developed the tic after he had had a slight nosebleed.

By combining past and present information, the therapist was able to act in the belief that the tic represented "the culmination and attempted solution of many conflicts of his past history" (p. 113), among which were fear of bodily injury, death wishes against father and sibling, fear of his unconscious striving for femininity, resentment at the mother's rejection of him, and so forth. This boy, because of his threefold disappointment in the mother (the return of the father, the birth of a sibling, the mother's death), had withdrawn libido from the outer world, cathected his own body instead, and ultimately manifested a symptomatic tic which "represented a pathological way of playing mother-and-child with his own body; he took over the role of the mother in a comforting and reassuring capacity, while his body represented himself in the role of the frightened and suffering child" (1958a, p. 114).

The analyst's intervention was entirely satisfactory in this case, and the child's tic dissolved immediately after explaining to the boy its symbolic content and meaning. Anna Freud did not stop there however. Following her colleague Ernst Kris's line of reasoning, she asked whether it was really necessary to let this child wait for help until there was an actual outbreak of pathological symptom formation. Was this not one of those typical sequences that, because of the known life history, was bound to lead to a pathological outcome? Could not the pathology have been detected before it became manifest, by examining the behavior of child and family, the history of mother and child, and the traumatic circumstances surrounding the mother's death?

It is difficult to overestimate the great potential advance in preventive psychotherapy of the neuroses that Anna Freud described here. It had taken a little over half a century since Sigmund Freud, in 1896, had introduced the term *psychoanalysis* for his new method of therapy that was so effective in treating the symbolic content of the psychoneuroses. Now it was largely left to his daughter to make a "quantum jump" for psychoanalytic child psychology in its clinical and applied aspects. The clearest evidence for the new level attained by psychoanalysis after about 1960 can be found in the *Metapsychological Developmental Profile* of Anna Freud.

After the New York memorial meeting for Ernst Kris, Anna Freud's visits to the United States attracted even more attention and spread farther afield. Two years later she visited Los Angeles and San Francisco. She presented many important new ideas and initiatives on these visits, and at the end of the fifties formulated new ideas regarding diagnosis, assessment, and normality. In their early phase these ideas were not widely published, though Anna Freud's lecture on the concept of normality (1959a), given at the University of California School of Medicine, is available in mimeo form.

In addition to the influence of Ernst Kris in this period, Anna Freud supported Hartmann's work on ego psychology and showed that his influence on her ranked with that of Kris (A. Freud 1966a). She acknowledged Hartmann's role in elevating psychoanalysis from a depth psychology to a general theory of mind (1965g) and rejected any suggestion that she was Hartmann's "silent critic" (1966a). In tribute to Hartmann's 75th birthday, Anna Freud noted that the psychoanalytic community had "elected him keeper of our scientific conscience, the personification of a symbolic superego, concerned not with morality but with questions of psychoanalytic theory" (1969s, p. 721).

CHAPTER SIX

The Developmental
Psychologist

Recognizing the imminent decline in preeminence of ego defense theory, Anna Freud stated on May 4, 1977 that her specialist child analysis field should take as its specific goal "the vicissitudes of forward development and exploration of the ego's synthetic function" (1978a, p. 12). This, she asserted, was now the "principal task" for child analysis.

With this emphatic statement Anna Freud reiterated the conclusion she had presented at the 49th Maudsley Lecture on November 21, 1975, to the Royal College of Psychiatrists in London (1976c). She acknowledged there that reconstructive work with adults was largely responsible for the psychoanalytic view of psychopathology, whereas what characterized child analytic observation and study was the ability to account for the normal as opposed to the abnormal course of development. The "chart of normal personality development" to which Anna Freud alluded on that occasion holds enormous significance for teachers, educators, pediatricians, parents, and clinicians and child psychologists generally. And so it is to this key developmental model we shall now turn.

Anna Freud's principal contribution to the developmental model was her presentation of the psychoanalytic concept of "lines of development." This notion had, of course, long existed in psychoanalysis and elsewhere, but it was Anna Freud who first advocated and formulated the systematic study of the range of developmental lines. This she first publicly demonstrated in her celebrated series of four lectures presented in New York in the early fall of 1960.

Developmental considerations had occupied her since her first scientific contribution of 1922, in which she detailed—albeit at that time through largely reconstructive methods—the progression of a daydreamer's fantasy from age 5 or 6 to 15 (1922a). As early as 1905 Sigmund Freud had published a sequence, line, or chart of early development, later extended and enlarged by his colleague Karl Abraham, which centered on the well-known oral, anal, and genital phases of maturation. In her own early work Anna Freud took up this general scheme, presenting it, for example, in her little-known chapter in Carl Murchison's *Handbook of Child Psychology* (1931a). At the height of the prewar Vienna period Anna Freud then extended the psychoanalytic developmental scheme with her own contribution to adolescence (1936a, chaps. 11 and 12) before turning to more powerful methodological approaches, including analytically directed child observation, in the Jackson Nursery in Vienna and then in the Hampstead War Nursery.

The classic libidinal sequence of orthodox psychoanalysis continued to be followed in some of her publications throughout the war years (1944b, c), though even here, she had begun to devise new frameworks. Consider, for example, her description of a developmental sequence for the mother-child relationship, beginning with material need satisfactions and progressing to a genuine personal love relationship (1942a). Although the effects of separation from the mother during the early phases of life inevitably attracted the attention of child analysts and other psychologists during the war years, the later development of the mother-child relationship when the child was 3 to 5 years of age and beyond was also begun, and the whole scheme became a reasonable parallel to the existing oral-anal-genital model.

By 1945, on the basis of her experience with many children and infants in all phases of development, Anna Freud was ready to publish the first of her major diagnostic recommendations on childhood based on developmental considerations. This, published in the opening issue of the new *Psychoanalytic Study of the Child*, introduced a radical new approach to assessing the child's need for analysis (1945a). Such an assessment, Anna Freud argued, should no longer be based on manifest symptoms and suffering but should now be related to the observed disturbances in normal development, its capacities, and tasks. In discussing "the sequence of libidinal development," "the intactness of development," processes

of ego maturation, and other aspects of her thesis, she demonstrated
that her emphasis had thereby shifted "from the purely clinical
aspects of a case to the developmental aspect" (1945a, p. 37). This
paper was a milestone in the field of diagnostic studies, as well as
in Anna Freud's own scientific and clinical thinking. A long series
of diagnostic recommendations and initiatives followed in later
years (1962c, 1963a, 1965a, 1965b, 1968c, 1968h, 1969d, 1969j,
1970a, 1974d, 1976c, 1978a, 1980c), and Anna Freud reaffirmed,
on both personal and scientific grounds, her opposition to "psychiatric name calling" and the crude diagnosis and labeling of
patients merely on the strength of manifest symptomatology
(1970a).

THE NEW YORK "FOUR LECTURES" ON
CHILD PSYCHOANALYSIS

On September 15–18, 1960, Anna Freud was once more in the
United States where, at a series of scientific meetings sponsored
jointly by the psychoanalytical societies of New York, Philadelphia,
and Western New England, she presented her "Four Contributions
to the Psychoanalytic Study of the Child." These contributions
were (1) the assessment of normality, (2) the assessment of
pathology, (3) the therapeutic possibilities, and (4) the status of
child analysis. Although two years elapsed before any of this
material appeared in print, there is no doubt that her later
technically accomplished papers (1962c, 1963a) had their origin in
the talks presented in New York. The importance of the new
direction of Anna Freud's theoretical leaning attracted immediate
comment from her colleagues on both sides of the Atlantic (Katan
1961, Nagera 1963, Neubauer 1967), and in New York two years
later the American Psychoanalytic Association devoted a panel
discussion to Anna Freud's recent initiatives (Ross 1963).

In addition to these important New York lectures, Anna Freud
accepted a long-standing invitation to visit Topeka, Kansas, where
she was Visiting Sloan Professor at the Menninger School of

Psychiatry. In her two Sloan lectures and in her C. F. Menninger Memorial Lecture, she continued to advance her new diagnostic and developmental initiatives to learned American professional audiences (1963b, 1965b), and the *Bulletin of the Menninger Clinic* brought out a special Anna Freud edition (1963). The Topeka Psychoanalytic Society cosponsored her visit in celebration of the 20th anniversary year of the institute's founding. Ishak Ramzy, who had studied in England with both Anna Freud and the academic psychologist Cyril Burt, was president of the Topeka Society. Ramzy and Anna Freud were joined by Marianne Kris, Margaret Mahler, and Helen Ross for a symposium on "Advances in Child Analysis" held the day after the C. F. Menninger Memorial Lecture. On other occasions, including the granting of honorary membership in the Topeka Psychoanalytic Society to Miss Freud, those present included Grete Bibring, Douglas Bond, Leo Rangell, Otto Kernberg, the Menningers, Gardner Murphy, Robert Wallerstein, and many others. Unfortunately at this time, news broke of the death of Marie Bonaparte, for many years one of Anna Freud's closest colleagues and friends.

The early sixties was the final gestation phase of a publication that quickly became one of Anna Freud's most important works, and the verbal presentations in New York and Topeka, together with their publication as short journal papers, were the building blocks of her latest views. This final publication was Anna Freud's *Normality and Pathology in Childhood* (1965a), a work that she herself described in terms that suggest continuity with her earlier theoretical study, *The Ego and the Mechanisms of Defence*, though with more emphasis on "developmental and diagnostic implications" (1966h, p. vi). According to Humberto Nagera, the New York Four Lectures contained the basic elements for the Developmental Profile (1963), which was the heart of *Normality and Pathology in Childhood*. From 1962 onward, in a series of applications for grants for the National Institute of Mental Health in Washington, D.C., Anna Freud asserted that "our long-term aim is a new approach . . . with special regard to the Variations of Normality and the Imbalance of Lines of Development" (1969j,

p. 26). Thus, the main thrust of child analysis study was directed to the developmental aspects of normality as a background against which to assess the phenomena of psychopathology. Child analysis, or more correctly psychoanalytic child psychology, concentrated on developing a theoretical model that would permit the rational handling of both normal and abnormal human experience and behavior.

Throughout this period of intensive scientific productivity, Anna Freud was in great demand in the world of child study. As a guest speaker to the 18th Child Guidance Inter-Clinic Conference, held in London in April 1962 under the chairmanship of A. D. B. Clarke, she read a paper on "Assessments of Normality and Pathology," which was later published under a title taken from the conference proceedings (1962b). In this paper she discussed the various interrelations among the several children's services, argued for a "basic training in childhood" to be undertaken before any specialization was begun, and pointed to the role of child guidance clinics as potential and actual centers for such multidisciplinary coordination. In the same year the Ninth World Assembly of the Organisation Mondiale for Early Childhood Education was held in London, at which Anna Freud also spoke (1962a).

The year before her major publication entitled, *Normality and Pathology in Childhood*, Anna Freud attended the Sixth International Congress of Psychotherapy, also in London, presenting her paper "Some Recent Developments in Child Analysis" (1965i). She identified three advances, in technique, theory, and diagnostic classification. Although she admitted the first two were frequent themes at symposia, the last she noted as being more recent and less well developed than other fields of psychoanalysis. The criteria generally used to diagnose adults, namely, amount of suffering, symptomatology, and degree of disturbance of function, were largely inappropriate to the child analyst, since they emphasized merely descriptive and nondynamic, nondevelopmental concepts. She then called attention to the alternative diagnostic scheme currently in experimental use in the diagnostic service at the Hampstead Child Therapy Clinic. Though duly published in the year following its first presentation, this paper was subsequently excluded from her collected writings, perhaps because she considered her views sufficiently well documented elsewhere.

On June 12, 1964, Anna Freud won another significant academic award, this time an honorary doctorate of science from the Jefferson Medical College in Philadelphia. The toastmaster at her reception was her old Viennese colleague Robert Waelder, then professor of psychoanalysis at Jefferson. The following year, Anna Freud was invited to the White House in Washington to receive the first Dolly Madison Award for Outstanding Service to Children, the occasion being the 150th anniversary of the Hillcrest Children's Center. That was also the year when her major work on childhood was published, to which we now shall turn.

NORMALITY AND PATHOLOGY IN CHILDHOOD

With the appearance of this work on both sides of the Atlantic, Anna Freud offered to academics, parents, teachers, and child therapists a detailed, clear, and comprehensive account of her own new framework for child development. Her model is applicable to both normal and abnormal development for assessment, diagnosis, and recommendations for relevant treatment or general upbringing. This work (1965a) encompassed and epitomized all that Anna Freud had achieved in the two postwar decades, and it is grounded in the new developmental orientation and the rejection of a merely surface descriptive approach.

The chronology of *Normality and Pathology in Childhood* developed in a similar way to the earlier *Ego and the Mechanisms of Defence*, in that Anna Freud first published as short papers the most important sections of the work (1962c, 1963a, 1963b, 1965b). Of particular importance are (1) the "lines of development" for the assessment of normality (chap. 3, II) and (2) the metapsychological diagnostic profile for the assessment of pathology (chap. 4), which together comprise the "new model" for child study used at the Hampstead Clinic in recent decades. Whether labeled "diagnostic" or "developmental," whether used for normal growth or mental illness, or whether the assessment is geared to upbringing and education or therapy and treatment, Anna Freud's profile is a psychologically elegant and metapsychologically comprehensive picture of the child, i.e., "a picture which contains dynamic, genetic, economic, structural and adaptive data" (1965a, p. 119). It is the total view of the child as presented by the complete profile that matters, since "it is basic to analytic thinking that the value of no single item should be judged independently" (1965, p. 119). Bodily malformation, for example, would be weighed against the child's environmental circumstances and overall mental capacity, whereas the occurrence of anxiety would be assessed against the ability of the ego to cope and defend itself.[1]

It is undoubtedly true that psychologists and educators in general have for some considerable time been interested in social and cognitive-academic "profiles" for school-based and related assessment work. In regard to formal assessment, Binet and Henri (1895–1896), working on behalf of the Paris school authorities in the 1890s, may be said to have introduced the standardized profile of intellectual abilities. G. M. Whipple's later *Mental Tests Manual* showed how the range of tested abilities had widened by the First World War period, and a particularly good instrument (test battery) for general intellectual and developmental-behavioral abilities appears to have existed in Vienna in the twenties and thirties, in the form of the Buhler-Hetzer Profile. However, despite much subsequent work of often great mathematical sophistication—for example, in the cognitive-factorial domain (Spearman, Terman, Burt), the personality field (Allport, Vernon, Cattell, Eysenck), divergent thinking (Guilford, Torrance, Hudson), concept development (Piaget, Peel, Lovell), and so forth—a truly comprehensive individual profile nevertheless proved an elusive if not indeed an

---

[1]The same attention to comprehensiveness was included in Anna Freud's advice given at the 20th Reunion of the Menninger School of Psychiatry in Topeka on April 2, 1966, when she exhorted psychiatrists to utilize not only isolated clinical aspects but also the whole language and metapsychology of psychoanalysis (1966f). And in Zurich that year, lecturing in honor of Rene Spitz, she and Spitz both disavowed any overriding theory or view, whether it be based on drives, ego, or object relations (1967a).

illusory goal to psychology in general. Only the detailed profile that emerged from the Hampstead Clinic appears to offer the required insight into and conceptual coordination of the individual's drive behaviors, ego behaviors, and moral tendencies, as well as their genetic-adaptational and social progression through the various phases of development, both normal and psychopathological.

Anna Freud's early interest in normalcy as opposed to psychopathology is evident in her publications, and it was always available as a background against which to assess pathological phenomena. She believed that the child analysts associated with her were by no means the first to attach such importance to the study of normality and instead extended their interest gradually from abnormal to normal psychology in line with "developments in adult analysis . . . as Melanie Klein, D. W. Winnicott and their followers had done from the outset" (1966e, p. 57). But one of her admirers perhaps overstated the case when she wrote that Anna Freud had paved the way "without doubt" (*eindeutig*) to a psychology of normality (Newman 1975). Anna Freud, Kris, Hartmann, Spitz, and Winnicott are here accepted as having made the greatest contribution to a psychoanalytic model suitable for both normal and abnormal phenomena of human development in the psychosocial domain. (Erikson is also of merit here.)

The concept of developmental lines is crucial to Anna Freud's thesis in *Normality and Pathology in Childhood*. Previous workers worked with only isolated and circumscribed sequences of development, e.g., for libidinal-sexual drive development (oral, anal, phallic, latency, preadolescent, adolescent genital phases), aggressive drive development (oral devouring behaviors, anal sadism, phallic domineering, adolescent acting out), and ego development (emergence of reality sense, chronological sequence of defense activity, growth of moral sense). With these trends Anna Freud (1965a, p. 59) compared, and similarly criticized as unduly circumscribed, the age-related scales by which other psychologists have measured intellectual functions.

What is now required, she asserted, are all of "the basic interactions between id and ego and their various developmental levels, and also age-related sequences of them which, in importance, frequency and regularity, are comparable to the maturational sequence of libidinal stages or the gradual unfolding of the ego functions" (1965a, p. 59). This goal may seem distant to many, but much of the groundwork had been carried out and was now restated by Anna Freud. She used object relationships as her first example, no doubt surprisingly to the many who considered her, if not an id or drive psychologist, then an ego psychologist with relatively little to say about interpersonal object relations.

A predominant stream of object relations theory is closely associated with Melanie Klein's initiative in the 1930s and with Fairbairn's theoretical revisionism in the 1940s and later. It would not be entirely inappropriate to characterize Klein and Fairbairn as reflecting a predominant orientation to and interest in endopsychic structure and function, in other words, to "inner world" reality as opposed to "outer world" reality. One consequence of such an inward-looking bias is that the resultant theoretical edifice is more suited to the needs of psychopathology than to the study of normality. External constructs (objects) with continued significance for the mediational processes of the child's internal psychological milieu are inevitably underrated. The parent-teacher-other merits relatively little attention in such a theory.[2]

As an analyst-educator, Anna Freud always recognized the importance in theory and practice of both the internal psychological object representation and the external (real) object or person. In her early technical lectures of 1927 she used the example of infant bowel training to illustrate the relative effects and importance of internal and external influences on the child. The child was viewed as becoming "clean" under the pressure exerted by the surrounding adult world, and observation has shown that the separation of the child at too early an age from the person who toilet trained him or her can lead to regression. The comple-

[2]Similar considerations apparently prompted Hoffer to state that "the educational implications of the Kleinian concept are almost entirely negative" (1945, p. 297). Later object relations theorists such as Ben Morris nevertheless successfully used this conceptual model in teaching (1966). See also the "dyadic" object relations model employed by Henry Dicks and others in marriage counseling.

mentary relationship between the internal and external psychological situation and object representation is clear, since "the impression that the child demanded cleanliness of himself was not altogether deceptive. The inner prompting exists, but it is valued by the child only for as long as the person responsible for the establishment of the demands is actually present in reality" (A. Freud 1927a, p. 55). She later pursued further these ideas based on the positive educational significance of the superego concept (1930a, lectures 3 and 4).

The elaboration of the developmental aspect of object relations theory occupied much of Anna Freud's wartime and postwar writings, though she nowhere cited or referred to Fairbairn. Fairbairn's work was discussed after Anna Freud's paper at the 1952 International Seminar of the World Federation for Mental Health, held in England under the chairmanship of Kenneth Soddy. However, the discussant seems likely to have been Soddy (1955), and not Anna Freud (1955a). In her desire to conceptualize and understand the early infant-parent relationship, Anna Freud contributed to the understanding of the early emergence of object relationships. It was here too that her views differed significantly from Fairbairn's theorizing.

The year following the publication of Fairbairn's influential book (1952), Anna Freud attended the 18th International Psychoanalytic Congress in London.[3] Her paper was entitled "About Losing and Being Lost" (1954e), and in it she compared Sigmund Freud's early ideas on losing and misplacing material objects with the early infant-parent relationship to gain a fuller understanding of the ways in which parents attach emotional significance to a child and vice versa. She drew on Winnicott's work on transitional-object phenomena and on Klein's concept of projective identification to explain certain reactions to loss that center on identification with the lost object. Again, Fairbairn's initiatives were not considered,

From July 26 to 30, 1953. At this congress Anna Freud also chaired a symposium on "Mechanisms of Defence and Their Place in Psychoanalytic Technique" (Report of the 18th I. P. A. Congress 1954).

nor was Bowlby's work on separation and loss, though in the latter case the omission was later remedied (1960a).

We do not understand why Anna Freud so completely ignored the work of Ronald Fairbairn. Such are the caliber and complementariness of their works that a detailed comparison of their differing viewpoints is long overdue. Marjorie Brierley did in fact make a wide-ranging survey of psychoanalytic personality theory that does include Anna Freud and Fairbairn, though she found "bewildering" the contrasting types of theory, on the one hand associated with Fairbairn, Guntrip, and others and those types associated with Anna Freud, Hartmann, and others (1969). However, since the development of the Hampstead Metapsychological Profile, we can demonstrate just how well Fairbairn's and Anna Freud's work fit together. We must confirm at once that the Hampstead model is the fuller and more complete. In this model, object relations theory is a subset of the total profile of the individual as pursued by Anna Freud and her followers.

Beginning with Freud's classical-orthodox structural position and using Klein's emphasis on internalization, inner world, and good and bad object representations, Fairbairn began around 1940 to publish a series of new scientific contributions. In their conceptual range and philosophic-epistemological erudition[4] these clearly reflected Fairbairn's standing as an independent thinker. In six years—during which time he also performed wartime military psychiatric duties—Fairbairn drew attention to schizoid phenomena as being more important than Klein's depressive position in the etiology of psychopathology (1940), presented a revised psychopathology of the psychoses and psychoneuroses (1941), formalized a model of endopsychic structure (1944), and developed a consistent object relations theory of personality based on his psychology of dynamic structure (1946) (see Fairbairn 1952).

---

[4]A well-trained academician, W. Ronald D. Fairbairn worked with G. M. Robertson in Edinburgh and at one time held lectureships in both psychology and psychiatry. Ernest Jones (Fairbairn 1952, *Preface*) considered Fairbairn's geographical isolation to be conducive to his originality.

Fairbairn's importance is his purist psychological model of personality, as opposed to one based on instinct, drive theory, impulse, or similar psychobiological foundation. This purist model can be seen especially in the work of Fairbairn's pupil-analysand Harry Guntrip, who initially trained in the school of thought of John MacMurray and Martin Buber and who developed Fairbairn's ideas regarding individual psychology into the social psychology of human interpersonal interaction (1961). Nevertheless, Fairbairn and others who sought a "truly psychological" and essentially non-biological model of human personality risked forgetting that the human being does indeed have a biological-instinctual maturational base at the foundations of his or her experience and behavior. Using Anna Freud's terminology once more, we should formulate any psychological model or theory from *both* sides of the personality, that is, from the id and the ego.

Modell states that Fairbairn's theoretical model "has not replaced The Ego and The Id. His was an unsuccessful revolution . . . he has few adherents amongst contemporary psychoanalysts" (1975, p. 58). Even so, several prominent analysts have used Fairbairn's object relations theory of personality, including Otto Kernberg and L. J. Friedman in the United States and J. D. Sutherland, Ben Morris, Henry Dicks, J. O. Wisdom, R. E. D. Markillie, and Anthony Storr in Britain.

Fairbairn's principal source of data was reconstructive analytical work with mainly schizoid adults. With the viewpoint and interests of a psychopathologist, Fairbairn was led to emphasize the internalized endopsychic situation of the individual. He attached great importance to the process of ego splitting, which he saw as underlying such phenomena as continued infantile dependence and adult psychopathology. Fairbairn also assumed the existence from birth of a "pristine unitary ego" which then underwent the various forms of splitting (1963).

In his assumption regarding the extremely early presence of an ego Fairbairn particularly differs from Anna Freud and other orthodox analysts, many of whom, like Anna Freud and her group, include direct child observation in their methodological arsenal. In the light of this group's more empirically based and equally rigorous theorizing, it is probably no longer possible to maintain the apparent advantageous purity and unilateral conceptual simplicity of Fairbairn's pristine ego theory. The ego, in keeping with the observed development of its earliest phases, has a definite period of synthesis and emergence from an even earlier, undifferentiated state. (Our attention here is confined to Anna Freud's ideas, which have been supported by Margaret Mahler, Ernst Kris, Rene Spitz, and others.)

Several decades ago, early infant feeding behavior provided a rich source that Anna Freud (1946a) used to integrate existing psychoanalytical views with her own extensive wartime observations. The result was one of the earliest and clearest "developmental lines," highlighting the relationship between feeding behavior and the development of object love. Feeding in the newborn is manifested as an intermittent though urgent bodily need, and the very young infant "periodically establishes connections with the environment which are withdrawn again after the needs have been satisfied and the tension is relieved" (1946a, p. 48). On the basis of observations such as this, repeated many times on many infants, Anna Freud concluded that the newborn child was "self-centered and self-sufficient as a being when he is not in a state of tension" (1946a, p. 47). Table 2 summarizes the development of preobjectal and object relations as described in Anna Freud's 1946 feeding behavior study.

Some may find the term *narcissistic* used in stage 1 ambiguous, preferring instead the term *preobjectal*. This is accepted here as both more precise and more consistent with the later object relations stages. Spitz likewise substituted the term *nondifferentiated* for *undifferentiated* (1959).

We should point out that in this earliest phase of life neither visual acuity, nor any other sensory facility, nor indeed time itself is likely to have permitted the awareness, still less the introjection, by the infant of any object representations or part objects. It is accordingly very difficult to refute Anna Freud's contention that at this stage it is the actual pleasurable experience of feeding itself that the infant libidinally cathects (invests with love feeling), and only later with the growth of awareness does the infant cathect

Table 2. Development of Preobjectal and Object Relations
(A. Freud 1946a)

Stage	Behavioral Aspects	Inferred Dynamics
1	Infant self-centered, periodically self-sufficient	Cathects pleasurable experiences. Narcissistic "love." Undifferentiated id-ego.
2	Becoming more aware	Cathects part objects. Transitional stage of libido attachments.
3	Perceives food provider	Cathects mothering person. Object love (stomach love, egotistic love).
4	Egotistic, but less dependent on need satisfaction	Object love now nonmaterial.
5	Less egotistic	Cathects even nonbeneficial aspects of mothering person. Altrusitic love.

the milk, breast or bottle (part objects), and finally the mothering person. At this early stage in postnatal development, therefore, the appropriate theoretical conceptual vehicle for handling these phenomena would be best centered on the orthodox Freudian libido theory rather than on strict object relations theory.

Object relations theory was seen by many as a challenge to orthodox psychoanalysis and as a revolution, implying that it sought the overthrow of Freud's conceptual edifice. Before the development of the Hampstead Metapsychological Profile as a conceptual unification, Fairbairn's theoretical model might have prompted Anna Freud to reject it. Certainly Fairbairn's argument as described on the dust jacket of his book (1952)—that his research offered a new scheme based on the theory that the libido is not pleasure seeking but object seeking—seemed to refute many of the gains in psychoanalysis so familiar to Anna Freud, and it also leaned toward a style of single-minded theory making, which itself countered Anna Freud's preference for a more total view of the individual's biological and psychological organization.

Anna Freud set forth this total view of mental structure and function in her profile, at the heart of her *Normality and Pathology in Childhood,* to which we shall now return. The whole profile easily encompasses the narrower model based only on object relations. Indeed, as we suggested earlier, in *Normality and Pathology in Childhood,* the sequence or developmental line for object relations is "the prototype for all others," since it is a basic line that "has received attention from analysts from the beginning" (1965a, p. 61). The sequence runs from the complete dependency of the newborn to the adult's emotional self-reliance and mature object relationships, a sequence for which "the successive stages of libido development (oral, anal, phallic) merely form the inborn, maturational base" (1965a, p. 61). A modified scheme of the development of object relations according to Anna Freud (1965a, chap. 3, II) may be seen in Table 3. This table also illustrates some of the advances made in the 20 years after Anna Freud's 1946 paper. The details were only roughly presented, and they had long been common knowledge in analytical circles. Anna Freud also drew attention to the many interferences with such development and the range of pathology that follows such interference. For example, the failure of the mothering person to be a reliable, need-fulfilling figure at stage 2 will lead to a breakdown in individuation (Mahler), anaclitic depression (Spitz), other deprivation (Alpert), precocious ego development (James), or formation of a "false self" (Winnicott). Many other practical lessons and applications also can be drawn from the same developmental sequence (A. Freud 1967a, 1974d, 1976c, 1977c, 1978a).

Several "developmental lines" illustrate the child's progression to bodily independence of the parents, e.g., from suckling to rational eating (1965a, pp. 65–67), from wetting and soiling to bladder and bowel control (pp. 67–69), and from irresponsibility to responsibility in body management (pp. 69–71). In these and other "lines" of development, "every step is known to the analyst" and may be traced "either through working backward by reconstruction from the adult picture, or through working forwards by means of

Table 3. Modified Scheme of the Development of Object Relations
(A. Freud 1965a)

Stage	Behavior	Dynamics
1	Biological unity of infant and mother	Narcissistic internal milieu (Hoffer). Autistic and symbiotic separation-individuation (Mahler).
2	Need fulfillment, urgent but intermittent	Anaclitic; fluctuating cathexis. Part object (Klein).
3	Stable internal image	Object constancy
4	Ambivalent; clinging, dominating, and controlling ego attitudes	Preoedipal, anal-sadistic
5	Possessiveness; jealousy and rivalry of parent of child's own sex; protectiveness; exhibitionism	Completely object centered, phallic-oedipal
6	Lessening of drive urgency; transfer of libido to objects beyond parents	Postoedipal, latency
7	Return to need-fulfilling and ambivalent attitudes	Preadolescence
8	Conflicts over loosening of ties to infantile objects; defenses against pregenital behaviors; interest in opposite sex beyond family	Adolescence

longitudinal analytic exploration and observation of the child"
(1965a, p. 71). Many data are thus set out along sequences "from
egocentricity to companionship" and "from the body to the toy and
from play to work." Moderate disharmony between these developments is not pathological as such and serves to produce the many
variations of normality.

In addition to these developments and their disharmonies, the complexities of childhood are enhanced by regressive factors, and an important section of *Normality and Pathology in Childhood*, entitled "Regression as a Principle in Normal Development," considers this (A. Freud 1965a, chap. 3 [III]).

THE METAPSYCHOLOGICAL PROFILE

Anna Freud's diagnostic profile is a detailed conceptual synthesis and organization and offers for any stage of childhood a cross-sectional insight into overall development and childhood task mastery, as well as indications for deprivations, deficits, and failures. The profile has nine sections:

1. Reason for referral
2. Description of child
3. Family background and personal history
4. Possible significant environmental influences
5. Assessments of development
   A Drive development
      (1) libido (phases, distribution, object)
      (2) aggression (quantity, quality, direction)
   B Ego and superego development
      (1) intactness or defects of apparatus serving perception, motility, and the like
      (2) ego functions of memory, reality testing, synthesis, IQ, and the like
      (3) defense organization
      (4) secondary interference of defense activity with ego achievements
   C Total personality—lines of development and task mastery
6. Genetic assessments (regression and fixation points)
   A behavior
   B fantasy activity
   C symptomatology
7. Dynamic and structural assessments (conflicts)
   A external between id-ego and object world

B   internal between ego-superego and id
C   internal between insufficiently fused or incompatible drives
8.   Assessment of general characteristics
A   child's frustration tolerance
B   child's sublimation potential
C   child's overall attitude toward anxiety
D   progressive developmental forces versus regressive tendencies
9.   Diagnosis (recombination of all previous items into clinically meaningful assessment)

Taken as a whole the profile seems to incorporate virtually all existing psychodynamic models of personality and function. Sigmund Freud's foundation is evident, as are Anna Freud's ideas from *The Ego and the Mechanisms of Defence*. The list of other valuable contributors is already long and includes Hoffer's progression from "milieu interne to psychological object," Hartmann's transition from "need-satisfying object to object constancy," Klein's "part-objects to whole objects," Winnicott's "transitional object phenomena," and elements of the work of Margaret Mahler, Rene Spitz, and many others. Even after exhausting the list of workers whose parallel models and schemes were explicitly considered by Anna Freud and her associates, the profile scheme also absorbs much else in the general field of psychoanalysis and child psychology.

Item 4, "possible significant environmental influences," is of particular interest to us and refutes any contention that child analysis is still merely a "depth psychology." Anna Freud further pursued the issue of environmental factors and their potential interference with development in her paper "Indications and Contraindications for Child Analysis" (1968c), presented at the Third Annual Scientific Meeting of the American Association for Child Psychoanalysis, at Yale University on April 21, 1968.

Many clinical and theoretical applications have been based on item 5, "assessments of development" (Kleeman 1966, Shane 1967, Gould 1970, Kestenberg 1971, Ross 1971, Newman, Dember, and Krug 1973, W. E. Freud 1975, Yorke 1977, Radford 1979). The profile also illustrates the essential difference between "description" and true "diagnosis," as was shown by Anne Hayman of the Hampstead group (1978). Hayman was able to demonstrate three quite different underlying disorders in three children, all of whom presented identical symptoms of school phobia. The uses of the profile spread beyond the needs of overt clinical pathology and came to include population and variational (intersex, age-related, and the like) studies of normality. Educational and developmental psychologists also could compare the Hampstead Profile with, for example, such established measures as the Bayley Motor Scales, the Reynell Developmental Language Scales, and other, largely behavioral-descriptive standard instruments.

Using Anna Freud's convergence of developments and Spitz's neoembryological concept of psychological "organizers" (Spitz, Emde, and Metcalfe 1970), Spitz's group explored the earliest phases of ego formation and structure. They found that any physiological or psychological prototype or component element of the developmental lines would inevitably mesh with various other developmental processes and progressively converge to form what they called an "organizer" of the psyche (Spitz, Emde, and Metcalfe 1970).

These ideas were taken a stage further by the group working at the Child Development Center in New York, who related much of the material on organizers to their own concept of a "central psychic constellation" (Silverman, Rees, and Neubauer 1975). They noted that within the developing psychic apparatus there is a periodic regrouping of central tendencies and characteristics into a new central organization, which incorporates the previous one and supercedes it as a "central, guiding, developmental constellation" (Silverman, Rees, and Neubauer 1975). Their methodological design was a longitudinal study of eight children aged 3 to 6 years. Each child was assessed twice yearly using the Hampstead Profile, and there was an annual follow-up.

The New York group applied their findings and concepts to other theoretical models of development, notably Anna Freud's concept of an "early psychosomatic matrix" arising from the interactions between mother and infant (1971a), her concept of multiple convergence and divergence of "lines of development," Spitz's work on psychic organizers, and Sybille Escalona's work on the evolution of "patterned modes of functioning" (1963). The group concluded that it was by no means a new idea to suggest that certain developmental strivings coalesce periodically into stable dynamic groupings. We should point out, however, that largely through the advances made possible by Anna Freud and Spitz, among others, the concept of the ego and its early emergence is now much more rigorously grounded in a discernable and scientifically respectable psychosomatic matrix of reproducible and measurable correlates. With such an increasingly strong empirical basis, ego theorists should find their work more acceptable to academic psychology. Irving Steingart, for example, aligns his work closely to that of Anna Freud and is known beyond the confines of psychoanalysis for his views on character, the development of a psychic apparatus, the emergence of ego-ideal and superego constellations within the personality, and so on (1969). Similarly, Annemarie Weil's notion of a "basic core" of personality and the individual has attained a new conceptual validity (1970).

All the studies cited above share a general viewpoint that has been basic to psychoanalysis from the beginning, namely, that successive levels of psychological structure and function are based on previous levels. Seymour Lustman (1967) was one of the first to use this concept to pursue a "hierarchical, multistage, suprastructural model" linked with the developmental profile. The value of this model, shared alike by biology, Freud, the Hampstead Clinic, the Yale group, and other groups, is that the academic, clinician, or researcher can see more clearly the individual as an interrelated, complex organization functioning at different dynamic levels and at different ontogenetic phases.

Before leaving the discussion of the Metapsychological Profile, we shall make a final comment on item 9, "Diagnosis." When following the elaborate plan in the earlier sections, the unwary clinician may encounter some obstacles. Thus, the clinician-diagnostician "will have to decide between a number of categorisations" (A. Freud 1965a, p. 125). The following are examples of these obstacles: (1) manifest behavior disturbance versus variation in normality, (2) pathological symptom formation versus transitory by-product of developmental strain, (3) primary deficiencies (organic) versus early deprivations (environmental), and (4) drive regression versus drive regression plus ego and superego regression.

In addition to her diagnostic-developmental studies of the 1960s, Anna Freud's work is notable for other reasons also. Her concern for the infant-mother relationship, much in evidence since the wartime Hampstead Nursery, if not earlier, was refined in the light of the psychoanalytic concepts of stimulus barrier and trauma. She viewed the ego as "the central victim in the traumatic event," postulated protective barriers against both external and internal dangers, and concluded that "the entire defence organisation of the ego is endowed with the characteristics of a protective shield" (1967e, p. 223). Before developing a defense organization, the infant is assailed by both the outside world and his or her own insistent drives, and at this earliest phase of extrauterine existence the mothering person is preeminent as the only protective shield available to the child.

In *Normality and Pathology in Childhood,* Anna Freud referred to the "caretaking mother" who provides or withholds satisfaction and who is thus not only the infant's first need-fulfilling object but also "the first external legislator" (1965a, pp. 142–143). As the young child struggles to develop the ego organization required to mediate among the conflicting demands of drives, internal object representations, and environment, the mother functions as a vital "auxiliary ego" assisting the child in this otherwise formidable task. In an adequate infant-mother relationship it is the mother's judicious selection of fulfillment, frustration, and postponement for the child that serves as "a prototype for the childish ego's own later dealings" (1969e, p. 279). Even time sense, memory, and orientation are enhanced by early exposure to mothering procedures involving familiar routine and regularity. Needless to say, without the auxiliary ego and protective maternal shield, the very young infant would be constantly flooded with tension and excitation and would be incapable of forming adequate stimulus barriers, ego boundaries, and that later psychosocial organization that others recognize and accept as a consistent presence of self or person.

In delivering the opening paper on the theme of "acting out" to the 25th I. P. A. Congress, in Copenhagen, July 23 to 28, 1967, Anna Freud set a new precedent and a fine example of historical-literary finesse in the field. Her introductory remarks noted some concern with the history of psychoanalytic concepts in general and with the opportunities for tracing "the vicissitudes of their individual fates in detail" (1968a, p. 94). These concerns had already become an established part of the Hampstead Clinic, where a variety of research and study groups had begun to trace, document, and comment on the gradual emergence and changing use of key areas of psychoanalytic terminology and theory.[5]

In regard to acting out, Anna Freud considered its use against the background of a theoretical shift in interest to the preoedipal, infant-parent attachments and against what had become known as the "widening scope of application" of psychoanalysis, namely, to areas away from the original field of adult neurosis, with both the diagnostic category and the age range since broadened. She also examined acting out in impulsive patients, in child analysis, and in adolescent analysis. She distinguished among memory, recall, reexperiencing, reenactment in the transference, and other forms of controlled or uncontrolled repetition. Particularly valuable from the child study viewpoint was her emphasis on the normal, acceptable and essentially age-adequate acting-out phenomena of two important developmental phases, prelatency and adolescence.

By 1967 it was apparent that there was potential and actual friction within the international psychoanalytical community over the issue of the independent child analysis courses such as the Hampstead course in London and the similar courses in Cleveland, Ohio, Leyden, Holland, and perhaps elsewhere. (The Cleveland Center for Research in Child Development was discussed in Chapter 5.)

The group in Leyden was organized by the Dutch analyst J. P. Teuns, with regular exchange visits from Hampstead Clinic staff

[5]For instance, libido theory, dream theory, and instinct theory.

members. Joseph Sandler, in particular, had been a visiting professor of psychoanalysis at Leyden University in the mid-1960s. Miss Freud herself had visited Leyden to read a paper (1966c) for the 35th anniversary of the Leyden Child Guidance Clinic.[6] On January 1, 1971, the Leyden Foundation for Child Psychotherapy eventually handed over responsibility for the child analysis training program to the Dutch Psychoanalytic Society.

Following the 1967 I. P. A. Congress, the Dutch Society, always most loyal to the Freuds, attempted to equalize the status of those who trained solely in child analysis, as at the Hampstead and similar centers, and those who trained in adult analysis, as at the regular institutes. At the next I. P. A. Congress, held in Rome in 1969 and not attended by Anna Freud, the Dutch proposal gave rise to much controversy. Members of the British Society in particular—Limentani, Hanna Segal, and Masud Khan—pointed to the large number of analytical child therapists at the Hampstead Child Therapy Clinic whose admission as full members of the British Society might cause an "imbalance" (Report of the 26th I. P. A. Congress 1970). Over the next two years Anna Freud made application for the Hampstead Child Therapy Course and Clinic to be admitted to the International Association as an independent study group. In his remarks concerning this, the president of the I. P. A., Leo Rangell, noted that the group in Hampstead had recently undertaken to include adult training in their program and that they already had more than the required number of fully qualified (i.e., adult trained) analysts needed to secure study group status (Report of the 27th I. P. A. Congress 1972). The I. P. A. Council accordingly accepted the Hampstead Clinic as a new study group of the International Psychoanalytic Association.

In another two years Anna Freud had withdrawn her application for separate study group status, as noted again by Leo Rangell (in her absence) at the 1973 Paris Congress (Report of the 28th I. P. A. Congress 1974). But Rangell stressed that the group in Hampstead had in the meantime been cooperating closely with the British

[6]The association between Leyden and the Freud family is one of the oldest in psychoanalysis.

Society on training matters, with a view to establishing acceptable parallel courses. An agreement on shared training was in fact reached, and a historic statement was signed on May 15, 1972, by W. H. Gillespie on behalf of the British Society and by Anna Freud for the Hampstead Clinic.[7]

The Hampstead Clinic was henceforth to be known as the Hampstead Centre for the Psychoanalytic Study and Treatment of Children, a title in keeping with those of the corresponding centers at Yale University and in Cleveland. The old name promises to endure for some time yet, however, as in the *Bulletin of the Hampstead Clinic*, established in 1978.

Anna Freud's preference for a parallel training scheme in association with the more eclectic British Society was consistent with her previous attitude toward the Kleinian controversy (Chapters 4 and 5), and in both these episodes she was regarded as one who avoided internal divisiveness. I believe that her nonpartisanship in such matters stemmed from a close identification with her father's belief in the value of psychoanalysis as a discipline to be kept as the higher goal of allegiance, above even any personal loyalty to himself and certainly above private incompatibilities and difficulties. Ernest Jones recorded that Freud was "deeply concerned with the transmission of his main function in life, the care of psychoanalysis. . . . We were trustees for that 'child' . . ." (1957, p. 46). It is in this sense, I believe, that we can best view Anna Freud's own attitude to all controversial issues in psychoanalysis.

In the 25 years after World War II Anna Freud had become the foremost custodian of child psychoanalysis. Her professional success was assured by the Hampstead Training Course and the Hampstead Child Therapy Clinic, and her international success continued to be attested by well-received visits abroad, especially to the United States. Finally, her scientific eminence was now confirmed by her many publications, particularly her developmental-diagnostic metapsychological profile of the child.

[7]A number of other centers, all variants of Hampstead (A. Freud 1966e), usually were sympathetic to Anna Freud's lead: the James Putnam Clinic (Boston), the Child Study Center (Yale), the Child Development Center (New York), the Cleveland Center, and others in New York, Los Angeles, and Chicago.

During this extremely productive 25 years, Anna Freud had trained or otherwise encouraged and gathered about her an expanding circle of active students, followers, and colleagues. Some of the more noteworthy included Joseph Sandler, W. Ernst Freud, John Klauber, Clifford Yorke, and Moses Laufer. Others, such as Martin James and Cecily de Monchaux, were associated with her for a time before striking out as independents. Still others returned or moved on to the United States, there to strengthen or begin "little Anna Freud centers." These included Ishak Ramzy in Topeka, Humberto Nagera in Ann Arbor, Erna Furman in Cleveland, Dale Meers in Washington, and Christoph Heinicke in Los Angeles. Inevitably, the greatest concentration of followers remained in London, with the older generation such as Liselotte Frankl, Ilse Hellman, Hedwig Schwarz, Ruth Thomas, and Alice Goldberger now joined by younger colleagues such as Hansi Kennedy, Sara Rosenfeld, Alex Holder, Marjorie Sprince, Anne-Marie Sandler, Rose Edgecumbe, Ann Hurry, Marion Burgner, Audrey Gavshon, Anne Hayman, and others.

In 1966 Anna Freud received her first honorary degree from a British university, the University of Sheffield, the third such in her long career.[8] Her old Viennese colleague, Erwin Stengel, then professor of psychiatry at Sheffield, was instrumental in securing the award. The presentation and address were given by Professor W. Harry G. Armytage of the Division of Education at Sheffield. In 1967 the Establishment in the United Kingdom recognized Anna Freud's work by awarding her the C. B. E.

VIENNA REVISITED

The decade of the 1970s began with Anna Freud, then 74, presenting major scientific and clinical papers on three separate occasions and in three different countries. First was her visit in April 1970 to the Western New England Psychoanalytic Society, where she advanced her previous diagnostic initiatives and again

---

[8]The others were from Clark University and Jefferson Medical College.

declared her opposition to crude overt labeling of manifest symptoms (1970a). Always the true analyst, she sought both a deeper
and a more meaningful account of the personality's inner structure
and dynamics. In her role as a developmental psychologist, moreover, she also sought to relate that already more meaningful
description to the individual's level of development and to notions
of what is acceptable to and normal for differing stages and phases
of growth.

Another American commitment accepted by Anna Freud at this
time stemmed from an invitation extended by Seymour Lustman,
then professor of child study and psychiatry at the Yale University
Child Study Center. As master of Davenport College at Yale,
Lustman asked Anna Freud to accept a post as fellow-in-residence
and to teach with him an undergraduate course on normal and
abnormal development in childhood and adolescence (1973b).
Lustman took as his starting point Anna Freud's discussion of
adolescence in the final chapters of *The Ego and the Mechanisms
of Defence* (1936a). In Lustman's view, this was the classic developmental description of the phenomena involved, and he proposed that he and Anna Freud compare the position held in 1936
with that in 1970. Although there was now much new terminology,
the two psychoanalysts concluded that "the underlying process,
geared to biological epigenetic alterations as it is, remains strik-
ingly similar," and the adolescent difficulties of a fine intellect
faced with biologically driven behavior "have been better described
in Anna Freud's 1936 book than ever since" (Lustman 1973b).

Lustman died shortly thereafter, having only recently joined the
editorial board of the *Psychoanalytic Study of the Child*. In his own
work he had, in 20 years, ranged from the experimental study of
3-day-old neonatal perception and other rudimentary ego functions,
through the precursors of defense mechanisms and other aspects
of psychoanalysis, to studies of cultural deprivations and a general
perspective of humankind. In every sphere he had allied his work
closely with Anna Freud's. In his last, posthumously published
work (1973a), he criticized the experimental psychologies associated with Skinner and Mowrer, in that they encouraged human
engineering or "ratomorphism," and he looked forward to when

the "few existing great universities" would direct the necessary synthesis and extension of our knowledge. Lustman's views reflect those of Theodor Roszak, R. M. Hutchins, and others who see the university as "a center of independent thought" and "a dissenting academy" which declines to do simply what society believes and sees instead that its task is one of understanding and criticism.

Anna Freud's second international visit in 1970 was to Geneva, where the European Psychoanalytic Federation met on June 27–28 for a symposium on "Child Analysis as a Subspeciality of Psychoanalysis." The theme of this symposium was the same as that at the Rome International Psychoanalytic Congress the year before, when the practical and administrative problems had been aired and Anna Freud, though absent, had been made honorary president of the new European federation. Now Anna Freud (1971b) took up the historical and scientific implications, pointed to the advantages and disadvantages of child analysis training with and without full adult training, and named the Dutch Society as the outstanding and solitary example of formal experimentation in this field. In looking to the future, she drew attention to multiple training (child, adolescent, adult) and the need for specialization to follow broadly based initial work.

Later that year the British Psychoanalytic Society hosted in London the Conference of English-Speaking Psychoanalysts from European Countries. Its theme was "Changing Concepts of Infantile Neurosis and Their Effects on Theory and Technique," and Joseph Sandler, Clifford Yorke, and Anna Freud all gave papers (1971a). After reviewing the material of Little Hans and the Wolf Man, Anna Freud considered the current scene largely from the theory point of view. In regard to therapy she confined herself to a single remark concerning the difference between the treatment application in the original area of the neuroses proper and the modern therapeutic ambition that covered the basic faults, failures, defects, and deprivations of the whole person. She noted, "I cannot help feeling that there are significant differences between the two therapeutic tasks and that every discussion of technique will need to take account of these" (1971a, p. 203).

Associated with the events of the London Conference was the

unveiling on October 2, 1970, near Swiss Cottage in North London, of the Oscar Niemon statue of Sigmund Freud. The imposing white marble figure of the patriarchal analyst had largely been the project of D. W. Winnicott, who had been able to complete the task before his own death the following year. Winnicott at one time had been the president of the British Psychoanalytic Society and was a gifted and noted independent. His principal work, *Through Paediatrics to Psychoanalysis,* was cited frequently by Anna Freud (1953a, 1954b, 1955b, 1961a, 1962d, 1963a, 1965a, 1966e, 1967b, 1969a, 1969i, 1973e, 1974d).

The signal event of 1971 in the world of psychoanalysis was the 27th International Psychoanalytic Congress in Vienna from July 25 to 30. The congress's scientific and clinical proceedings coincided with a number of related events of great psychoanalytic significance and interest, which was appropriate for Anna Freud's return to the city of her own earliest life, work, and recognition.

Two years earlier, when invitations for the congress had been sent by the branch societies of Paris, New York, Mexico City, and New Delhi, in addition to Vienna, President P. J. van der Leeuw informed the membership that "concerning Vienna, once we know that the membership wishes to have it there we can state that Miss Freud is willing to attend and participate" (Report of the 26th I. P. A. Congress 1970).

The theme of the Vienna Congress was "Aggression," and Anna Freud closed the scientific proceedings with a major paper. In the subsequent evaluation session a number of participants, including Martin Waugh (New York), Joel Zac (Argentina), Helen Tartakoff (Cambridge, Massachusetts), Luis Feder (Mexico), and Kenneth Calder (U.K.), spoke of the masterful clarity with which Anna Freud had discussed this difficult topic. Even the customary bi-annual "roll of honor" confirmed Anna Freud's now unique position, as Eduardo Weiss, Herman Nunberg, and Heinz Hartmann had recently died. Only the inactive Helene Deutsch, together with Imre Hermann in Budapest, had more years of seniority.

The topic of aggression, particularly in the theory of the "death instincts," has from its inception been one of the more controversial issues to both psychoanalysis and psychology generally. In his 1920 book, *Beyond the Pleasure Principle,* Freud abandoned his tentative conception of ego instincts, which in the case of aggressive behavior had given rise to a frustration model of aggression. As Anna Freud later explained, he then went on to ascribe "instinctual nature and origin to the aggressive manifestations, and thereby gave them in his evaluation equal status with the manifestations of sex" (1949g, p. 66). From Freud's radical reformulation came the widely known theory of the life and death instincts, otherwise known as *eros* and *thanatos.* Although the term *libido* has wide currency as the energy that drives *eros,* Freud never coined a term for the energy of *thanatos.*[9] The controversial term *death instinct* was much criticized by psychologists, particularly in the social science climate of America, and in Britain it was largely restricted to the writings of Klein and certain other biologically oriented theorists such as Joan Riviere and Roger Money-Kyrle.

The applied study of aggressive behavior proved to be much more widely acceptable. In studies of antisocial delinquents, for example, it had formed the life work of Anna Freud's colleague August Aichhorn. Anna Freud's own studies in the field of aggression and aggressive behavior were relevant to early childhood states, instinct transformation, and so forth (1947b, 1949a, 1949f, 1949g), and in later years her interest widened to cover the legal and diagnostic aspects of early failures in socialization (1965a, chap. 5, II).

On her first postwar return to Vienna, in her congress summary (1972a), Anna Freud, for the first time and with startling frankness, publicly addressed the controversial topic of the death instinct. In her concluding remarks it became clear that in regard to a relationship between aggression and the notion of a death drive, she held essentially the same pessimistic view as her father did. She cited a study by Kurt Eissler written to "lend support to Freud's theory of a death drive" (1971, p. 25). Whereas Eissler used material from the physiologist Rudolph Ehrenberg, Anna

[9]In later years others suggested *mortido* (Federn) and *destrudo* (Eduardo Weiss).

Freud used material with which she had been familiar since at least 1915, from the poet Rainer Maria Rilke who "sees the move towards death as one of the main purposes of life" (1972a, p. 173). To Anna Freud there were "two supra-ordinate biological forces with contrary goals," and she saw libido and aggression as each pursuing "their own limited and mundane aims while serving at the same time the vaster biological purposes of life and death" (p. 175). Her final sentence reflects an inversion, however, when she states that on a higher plane "death cannot be attained except via the vicissitudes of life" (p. 175). We, on the contrary, believe that one's life cannot evolve except by paying the price of mortality. This philosophical view is consistent with that of the biologist Julian Huxley.

We do not view death as an aim of life. All theorizing that leads to such an illogical conclusion is itself symptomatic of the plight of the human intellect when faced with the inevitability of death. Our position is categorical: there are no death instincts. Life has only one supraordinate biological goal, its own continuation. All instinctual drives evolved by living organisms are thus life instincts.

For decades child analysis has in fact accepted that "the development of aggression is inseparably bound up with the developmental phases of infantile sexuality . . . without this admixture of aggression, the sexual impulses remain unable to reach any of their aims" (A. Freud, 1949g, p. 67). It must remain one of the paradoxes of modern, observation-centered child analysis that such a clear indication of the positive-striving and life-fulfilling nature of biological aggression should nevertheless permit the indication of the contrary goal of destruction and the notion of a death drive.

Max Schur and his coworkers (Schur and Ritvo 1970), approaching the matter from a psychoanalytical and behaviorist viewpoint, managed to reconcile Freud's mechanism of repetition compulsion with the biologist Schnierla's "approach and withdrawal" theory of animal behavior. Accordingly they also were able to refute any necessity for postulating a death drive.

We make the following general argument: In a universe subject to entropic thermodynamic degradation, life is apparently unique in being able to avoid entropic trends. There are two means by which this may be achieved: (1) by the constant intake and expenditure of energy and materials in complex and largely self-renewing structures, it is possible for the individual to evade temporarily the law of entropy during his or her lifetime, and (2) by the transmission of germ plasm in a process that is potentially inexhaustible, it is possible to evade relatively permanently the thermodynamic degradation of the species. Life thus continues to survive and propagate to the limits of its capacities. Life is inherently positive and self-sustaining, though its emergence required the preformation of methods for evading the otherwise universal and inevitable thermodynamic death and ultimate inorganic stasis.

Sigmund Freud, on the other hand, postulated a group of non-libidinal instinctual forces—the so-called death instincts—that actually propel an individual toward the inanimate inorganic state (S. Freud 1920a, pt. VI). He supported this view with the biological experiments of the day, but he also went further and aligned his theory with chemical and prebiological data. In this he went too far and fell into the error of what other disciplines term *reductionism*, the attempt to reduce biology to chemistry and chemistry to physics. Admittedly, by 1920 the error of unwarranted reductionism had not yet been exposed, and the nonreductionist "organismal" views of biologists such as J. B. S. Haldane, E. S. Russell, Woodger, Bertalanffy, and others were still some years away. No such excuse is available, however, if we today attempt to advocate the death instinct misconception on prebiological grounds.

Thus instinct is a biological concept and is therefore applicable only to biological theorizing, i.e., to whole organisms. Instinct can have no meaning in relation to prebiological and chemical states, and so it follows that no instinct can be accepted as tending to return the living organism to the inanimate state, whether the latter be defined as complex macromolecular or merely as inorganic.

Psychoanalysis may still be correct in postulating the existence of a group of instincts and drive derivatives that tend to return the organism to an ontogenetically earlier state. The earliest state that would then be relevant, however, is when the new individual comes into being. Regardless of whether one takes this as being conception or birth, one corollary would be that there the individual is closest to possessing characteristics of a thermodynamically "open system," with minimal cellular aging, rigidification, and senescence, and with maximal capacity for evading the law of entropic degradation. On this basis, the repetition compulsion and allied forces would seem grounded in a vigorous life instinct. Freud's view of the philosophy of life and death thus seems unduly gloomy, though the ultimate fate of the individual remains the same. Finally, this argument supports therapeutic measures of the "new start" kind (Balint, Winnicott), though naturally the argument is extremely conjectural.

The mere fact that the individual dies need not imply any direct involvement of biological drive forces. It is (after J. Needham and others) the processes of increasing cellular structuralization and rigidity that eventually lead organisms into being closed as opposed to open energy-transfer systems until a point is reached at which the actual evasion of entropic degradation ceases and death and disintegration ensue. Such processes are essentially prebiological, occurring in the component macromolecular fabric of tissues and cells. As such they are subject to laws of a chemical rather than biological order. The biological concept of instinct is thus not applicable to the cellular aging processes that lead eventually to senescence and death, though Eissler (1971) apparently believes the opposite. He accordingly, though misguidedly, gathered many biochemical data to support his gloomy and ill-conceived death instinct notion.

Contrary to Eissler and his unwarranted use of the work of Rudolph Ehrenberg, one could stand with the English neurophysiologist Charles Sherrington, who after long reflection and epochal discoveries noted that the conservation of self is a principle in psychology as real and important as the physicist's principle of the conservation of energy (Sherrington 1951). It would seem to be to the conservation of this self of higher ideals and beliefs that our biological drives, particularly in their sublimations and related transformations, are ultimately linked. In summary, then, there is no logical basis for the notion of a death instinct, though such a belief may well have a kind of efficacy and validity for areas of experience that are beyond logical explanation. Here, however, one would need to maintain a strict demarcation between one's own philosophy of life and the *Weltanschauung* of science.

On June 15, 1971, there was in Vienna another event of great moment in the world of psychoanalysis, the final public opening of the Sigmund Freud Society Museum situated in the old Freud apartment at Berggasse 19. From her London home Anna Freud had donated to the museum much of the original furniture of her father's waiting room, along with books, pictures, and antiques from Freud's collection (Leupold-Lowenthal and Lobner 1975). Two years later a similar occasion opened to the public Anna Freud's former consultation and living room and a special photographic exhibit of "Berggasse 1938: The Engelman Pictures." The International Congress of 1971 included a visit to the Berggasse by the congress members. Within a few years the Sigmund Freud Gesellschaft had introduced a new journal, the *Sigmund Freud House Bulletin*, the inaugural number of which included an introduction by Anna Freud (1975e).

At the close of the 1971 Vienna Congress, Anna Freud was again reelected to the office of joint vice-president of the International Psychoanalytic Association, a position she had filled from 1934 to 1938 and again continuously from 1951 onward. Her coofficers were W. H. Gillespie, P. J. van der Leeuw, Heinz Kohut, Samuel Ritvo, Lebovici, Dahlheim, Valenstein, and Mitscherlich (Report of the 27th I. P. A. Congress 1972). The entire congress had been a success, and for none more so than for Anna Freud. In the following year, no doubt stimulated by her triumphal return to their city, the authorities of the University of Vienna bestowed on her the high award of Honorary M.D. Although Anna Freud still viewed herself as a lay analyst, she had in fact made vast contributions to the realm of psychological medicine and psychopathology, not to mention child psychiatry, all facts that had no doubt not escaped the honorary degrees committee.

On its 20th anniversary in July 1972, the Hampstead Clinic welcomed 292 colleagues from the world of psychoanalysis and allied professions who came to hear the scientific and other papers making up the clinic's special celebratory program. That the occasion gave rise to a scientific, as opposed to a purely social, event was entirely according to "the Clinic's custom" (A. Freud 1975b). Anna Freud gave the opening address, participated in a symposium on training at Hampstead, and gave the closing remarks. She was then 76 years old. The published proceedings of the event[10] also include her paper (1975a) on the nursery school run on analytical lines, which the Hampstead Clinic provides in addition to its diagnostic and treatment services. Other papers or addresses were given by A. J. Solnit of Yale, Joseph Goldstein of Yale, and Kurt Eissler of New York, and from Hampstead, Sara Rosenfeld, Agnes Bene, Hansi Kennedy, Ilse Hellman, Maria Berger, Bianca Gordon, Rose Edgecumbe, Clifford Yorke, Patricia Radford, Stanley Wiseberg, Thomas Freeman, Joseph Sandler, and Dorothy Burlingham.

Central to the Hampstead Clinic's recent work on early childhood observation is the Well-Baby Clinic, directed by the analytical pediatrician Josephine Stross, and the Well-Baby Research Group.[11] In the Well-Baby Clinic, babies are seen weekly lengthening to monthly during the first year of life and bimonthly in the second year of life. Mother and infant are interviewed and seen by the pediatrician and a qualified child therapist, with one student generally being present as part of training. The clinic has half-day sessions three times weekly, but anxious mothers may telephone more frequently. As Stross noted, most child welfare clinics are staffed by doctors and nurses with training only in physical and not mental health, and diagnostic consultations and follow-up at the Hampstead Clinic are more frequent than usual and also more wide-ranging (1977). Stross also pointed out that around the 1930s, eating disturbances had been the principal child problem in Vienna,

---

[10]*Studies in Child Psychoanalysis: Pure and Applied. The Scientific Proceedings of the 20th Anniversary Celebrations of the Hampstead Child-Therapy Course and Clinic.* Monograph no. 5 of the *Monograph Series of the Psychoanalytic Study of the Child.* New Haven and London: Yale University Press, 1975.

[11]The group's members during this period were Anna Freud, Dorothy Burlingham, Liselotte Frankl, Hansi Kennedy, W. Ernst Freud, Irene Freud, Mrs. E. Model, Humberto Nagera, Marjorie Sprince, and Josephine Stross (Stross 1977).

and bed-wetting was the main problem in England. In recent years the availability of disposable baby materials and washing machines is felt to have contributed to the contemporary reluctance to initiate toilet-training at too young an age or too rigidly (1977). The presenting symptoms for child cases in recent decades typically have been much more diffuse and varied than previously.

A key figure and major publishing author of the Hampstead Well-Baby Research Group is W. Ernst Freud, who has argued for analytical training to be organized around intensive longitudinal studies of the first four to six years of the child's life (1975). Through infant observation W. E. Freud meant observation of the infant, the mother, and the infant-mother interactions. By this means students would be readily grounded in what Anna Freud termed the "solid knowledge of child development" (1971b, p. 215). Among other important points noted by W. E. Freud were the presence in the observer of nonobjective interference by personal blind spots or other preoccupations; the prevalence of the error of "adultomorphising" of children's behavior; the potential value of mothers as informants; and the continuing need to correct the widely held view of defenses as signs of abnormality which, "like warts," have to be removed (1975).

Born in Hamburg in 1914 and named Ernst Halberstadt, W. Ernst Freud is Anna Freud's oldest nephew (see Figure 2). After 1920 he spent considerable time living in close family association with Sigmund Freud and appeared on Freud's visa list as "Enkel Ernst Halberstadt" at the time of their departure from Vienna in 1938 (Schur 1972). As an associate member of the British Psychoanalytic Society, the name W. E. Freud first appeared on the members' list for 1954, with full membership coming later. From his close association with the Hampstead Clinic, the obvious family tie, and the strong influence of Anna Freud's work visible in his own publications, one might guess that W. E. Freud indeed did train with Anna Freud, probably in the late forties to early fifties. Like the work of his teacher, W. Ernst Freud's scientific contributions reflect much of the best in latter-day child psychoanalysis and show careful observation and testing wedded to widely acceptable areas of orthodox Freudian psychology. His 1975 paper aligned Anna Freud's own theoretical writings with the ongoing empirical researches of the Hampstead Clinic, illustrating thereby the interactions of theory and observation.

Anna Freud again visited the United States in April 1973 when she gave the 20th Annual Freud Memorial Lecture to the Philadelphia Association for Psychoanalysis. The old *Bulletin of the Philadelphia Association for Psychoanalysis* was reshaped into a new-format journal, the opening issue of which was a special Anna Freud edition. This contained not only her 20th Freud Memorial Lecture (1974d) but also the First Annual Freud Memorial Lecture (1974c), which she had given in Philadelphia 20 years previously but which had not been published at that time.

Anna Freud's address in 1973 was entitled "A Psychoanalytic View of Developmental Psychopathology," with the Hampstead Developmental Profile listed as the key investigative and interpretive instrument for securing the necessary detail and order in the overall picture of the child's integrated personality. The work of Spitz and Mahler was included, as was Klein's concept of the part object as an early developmental position.

From the data of clinical psychopathology on the one hand and of the developmental lines on the other, Anna Freud made a twofold classification of early psychopathology: (1) the infantile neuroses proper (phobic, obsessional, hysterical, and anxiety states), all of which are abnormal conditions caused by "the incidence of trauma, and of conflict between the internal agencies followed by anxiety, defense and compromise formation" (1974d, p. 70); and (2) defects in personality per se (psychosomatic symptomatology, backwardness, atypical and borderline states) which are caused by developmental irregularities and failures. The latter she noted as having received much less attention in the literature, though she acknowledged relevant work by Augusta Alpert and Peter Neubauer in the United States, and Michael Balint in England with his concept of "basic faults."[12] Anna Freud accepted that, clinically, the two types of early psychopathology were intertwined, "a fact which

[12]Pioneering clinical studies on borderline states were made by a number of workers in the Hampstead Clinic group, for example, Marie Singer, Marjorie Sprince, and, in particular, Sara Rosenfeld. See also A. Freud (1969d), a paper first delivered in 1956; and A. Freud (1977b).

accounts for their being treated usually as one" (1974d, p. 71). However, in encouraging her colleagues to try to disentangle the two pathogenic processes, she repeated her view, expressed in "The Infantile Neurosis: Genetic and Dynamic Considerations" (1971a), that there are significant differences between the therapeutic tasks in the two situations. Now, in particular for developmental defects and their therapy, Anna Freud pointed to the need for admixtures in the orthodox analytic technique, as in the form of new positive object attachment, corrective emotional experience, and the like. This recommendation was by no means new, though the increasingly rigorous rationale that Anna Freud now provided for it was.

As early as 1946 Margaret Fries proposed the appropriate administration of "doses of life experiences," basing her proposal on Anna Freud's view in *The Ego and the Mechanisms of Defence* (1936a) that the strength of the ego is determined by the type of life experiences which the child encounters. Fries also noted the fundamental role attributed to kinesthetic sensation in early infant development by the Hampstead War Nursery and pointed to bodily contact of child with the parent surrogate as an important part of adjustment to new situations. One thinks immediately of Ferenczi and others, who had already experimented with "active" therapies, and of recent therapists, such as Harry Guntrip, who was not averse to reaching out and placing a hand on his patient.

In her *Normality and Pathology in Childhood* (1965a), Anna Freud further commented on the notion of "corrective emotional experience," and her implication that it may, in certain types of cases, be more appropriate than traditional analytical methods was taken up at once by Marvin Ack (1966). Similarly, Morton Shane (1967) supported Anna Freud's view that the whole range of therapeutic possibilities should be kept open, including forms of corrective emotional experience and the analyst seen as a new object.

Undoubtedly the most forceful views in this area were those of D. W. Winnicott (1965) with his concepts of therapeutic regression and management. Although Anna Freud's view of therapy had always implicitly allowed for initiatives such as Winnicott's and from 1970 had explicitly called for them or similar ones, this essential complementariness was apparently overlooked by certain members of the Hampstead group. Thus, Kennedy (1971) criticized Winnicott's technique involving regression, reliving, and correcting with a view to reworking the past in a more satisfactory way, and gave as her reason the fact that Anna Freud had often pointed out (in discussions) that classical psychoanalytic technique was devised "not to *undo* experiences" but to help the individual understand and deal with them internally. However, although this argument is valid in the realm of the equally classical psychoneuroses, it is inappropriate in the different realm of the severe developmental retardations and failures, which were Winnicott's foremost concern. Now, thanks to Anna Freud's systematization of the differing types of psychopathology and their attendant and differing therapies, it seems unlikely that there will in the future be any room for error and confusion of this kind.

Anna Freud did not attend the 28th International Psychoanalytic Congress which took place in Paris in 1973. However, the next congress (July 20–25, 1975) was in London, and this she did attend. At this meeting, Anna Freud finally allowed her colleagues in the analytical movement to bestow on her the title of honorary president of the I. P. A. The presence of the new honorary president was far from being merely decorative, however, and she presented the opening discussion paper to a session on "Changes in Psychoanalytic Practice and Experience" (1976a).

In her discussion of the modern and widespread tendency to equate the analyst-patient relationship with that of the mother-child, Anna Freud objected that in fact there were great dissimilarities between the two. The adult patient, for example, cannot require or demand satisfaction of body care as the infant does, and in regard to the demand for constant and exclusive attention from the analyst-mother figure, the adult patient has necessarily to tolerate "frustration of wishes, limitation to set times and the existence of rivals" (1976a, p. 183). Specific criticisms such as these naturally support Anna Freud's more general contention that there is a need for some form of child analysis training, even for those who intend to study and treat only adults, and that specialization should not begin until a broader-based training has been completed.

Reporting on behalf of the Sigmund Freud Archives at the London Congress, Kurt Eissler noted that in the name of her family Anna Freud had donated all the relevant letters in the possession of the family to the Library of Congress in Washington, D.C.

The following year London hosted the meeting of the now international Association for Child Psychoanalysis, with Anna Freud in attendance. Her remarks were spoken with "the privilege of age" and began with the now almost customary flourish of historical breadth and sagacity before turning to deal with the clinical and theoretical aspects of "Fears, Anxieties, and Phobic Phenomena (1977e).

The year 1977 saw a series of important, indeed symbolic, events taking place in the sphere of child psychoanalysis. The Sigmund Freud House Society (Gesellschaft) of Vienna, at 19 Berggasse and directed by Harold Leupold-Lowenthal, organized a Vienna symposium on work at the Hampstead Clinic. The participants included Anna Freud, Ilse Hellman, W. E. Freud, Alex Holder, Hedwig Schwarz, Josephine Stross, and Clifford Yorke. In her prefatory remarks [13] Miss Freud noted the special significance of the event for herself and the other former Viennese. In reviewing the various contributions to the symposium, as well as the earlier work of Hoffer, Bernfeld, Aichhorn, Jackson, and herself, she asserted that "there was hardly anything in the content of [the] presentations for which, though developed further in London, the foundation had not been laid more than forty years ago during work in Vienna" (1977a, p. 12).

Clearly, like her father before her, Anna Freud had for many years successfully hidden from the world at large her close identification with Vienna. Freud himself had spent a lifetime disparaging Vienna, as his biographer Ernest Jones informed us.

---

[13]Dated London, June 1977 and printed in English, German, and Spanish.

Scarcely did he arrive in England in 1938, however, than Freud was writing to Max Eitingon about having "always greatly loved" the prison from which he had been released (Jones 1957, chap. 6). For her part Anna Freud had been away from Vienna for over 30 years, though during the intervening period she did express her deeper views. Thus, when the Vienna Psychoanalytic Society celebrated its 50th anniversary on April 15, 1958, although Anna Freud did not accompany her colleague Willi Hoffer to Vienna, she did send a letter in which she congratulated Alfred Winterstein, the honorary president, who was also celebrating his own 50 years of membership in the society. In her letter she wrote, "I admit to some envy because I myself would have liked to achieve the same, and would have done so had not external events of grave significance interfered with my desire" (Report of the Vienna Psychoanalytic Society 1959, p. 79).

During the 1977 Vienna symposium, attended by members of the Hampstead Clinic staff, the Freud Memorial at Bellevue in the Vienna suburbs was unveiled. This was to mark the 121st anniversary of Sigmund Freud's birthday, and a photographic insert was placed in the *Sigmund Freud House Bulletin* (1977). The memorial plaque was placed on a pedestal along which Anna Freud stood, and on it is inscribed Freud's rhetorical question written many years earlier to this friend Wilhelm Fliess (S. Freud 1950, letter dated June 12, 1900). In the letter Freud revealed when and where he had reached his interpretation of the now famous "Dream of Irma's Injection," which largely gave rise to his celebrated statement that "a dream is the fulfillment of a wish" (1900). He wrote to his friend Fliess, "Do you suppose that someday a marble tablet will be placed on the house, inscribed with these words: 'In this house, on July 24th 1895 the secret of dreams was revealed to Dr. Sigmund Freud'. At the moment there seems little prospect of it."   .

The event took place in the year of Anna Freud's birth, and the tablet fulfilling her father's hidden wish was unveiled in her 81st year. Although the memorial now stands in an open space surrounded by trees, Ernest Jones once remarked that the place used to be a restaurant, and Freud once took him to sit at the very table on the northeast corner of the terrace where "the great event" of insight had taken place (1953, p. 354).

With the account of this symbolic event, one might think that the study of Anna Freud's professional life would draw to a close. But Miss Freud, until her death in 1982, simply did not know the meaning of retirement and continued to lead both her clinic and no small part of the world of psychoanalytic child psychology. In 1978 she and her associates launched a new quarterly publication, *Bulletin of the Hampstead Clinic*. Published in London, with Anna Freud as consultant editor, the *Bulletin* was designed solely for contributions from the Hampstead Clinic group and represented the latest and most specialized logical development of Anna Freud's editorial labors spanning almost half a century.

The 30th International Psychoanalytic Congress took place in Jerusalem, the first time that the meeting had gone outside Europe during its 70 years of existence. Though not attending in person, Anna Freud nonetheless contributed an inaugural lecture for the Sigmund Freud Chair of the Hebrew University in Jerusalem. This was read simultaneously, on October 19, 1977, in Jerusalem by Arthur Valenstein and in London by Anna Freud (1978e). A number of her associates from Hampstead journeyed to Israel for the congress, among them Hansi Kennedy, Maria Berger, Alex Holder, and Elspeth Earle.

On November 11, 1978, Anna Freud introduced the Anna Freud–Hampstead Center Symposium held by the Michigan Psychoanalytic Society. Her theme was "The Role of Insight in Psychoanalysis and Psychotherapy" (1979a), which she admitted was never her special subject. In regard to children, for example, she had grouped their characteristic lack of insight with their other immature traits. Now she enlisted her great insight and experience to illustrate the complexities of the child's reaction to a number of anxiety-provoking situations, including accepting the need for therapy and correction.

The work of the Hampstead Clinic has continued to flourish and diversify and beginning in September 1978 included a new, one-year course in the nonclinical applications of child psychoanalysis for experienced workers in allied professions. On May 17, 1978, at

Columbia University in New York, Anna Freud was awarded the degree of doctor of science, *honoris causa*. She was then 82 years old. In his official citation President William J. McGill proclaimed that "from your observations have come an extraordinary series of scientific contributions" (*Bulletin of the Hampstead Clinic* 1978, opposite p. 114). It would scarcely be possible to find a more fitting epithet for Anna Freud, who raised the status of child analysis from a clinical and therapeutic branch of psychoanalysis to a rigorous psychoanalytic and developmental child psychology.

Sigmund Freud died at Maresfield Gardens in 1939. Forty-five years later at the age of 86, on October 9, 1982, her father's daughter, Anna Freud, died in the family home.

APPENDIX

CHRONOLOGICAL LIST OF THE PUBLICATIONS
OF ANNA FREUD, 1922–1982

The material presented here has been compiled according to
Tyson's and Strachey's "Chronological Hand-List of Freud's
Works."[1] As such it is the most complete available list on the
subject.

In this list, the titles are given according to first publication, and
works published in the same year are differentiated by letter.
Whenever available the reference source is *The Writings of Anna
Freud*,[2] which contains full bibliographical data, not repeated here,
on all their entries. Titles not included in *The Writings of Anna
Freud* are given a full entry.

The titles up to around 1952 were compared with entries in *The
Index of Psychoanalytic Writings*,[3] and those up to 1962 were also
compared with the list in the *Menninger Bulletin's "Anna Freud
Number."*[4] For later titles the writer is indebted to the assistance
of Miss Gertrud Dann, librarian of the Hampstead Clinic in
London, who for many years has maintained her own card index of
Anna Freud's works.

For the period between 1922 and 1952 the Grinstein Index
shows 54 titles for Anna Freud, and our list has 64. Between 1922
and 1962 the Menninger Bulletin lists 75 titles, and our study lists
95, the addition being mostly edited reports and previously un-
listed abstracts. In total, our list contains over 200 titles, plus a

---

[1]Tyson, A. and Strachey, J. (1956). A chronological hand-list of Freud's works.
International Journal of Psychoanalysis 37:19–33.

[2]*The Writings of Anna Freud*, 8 vols. (1982a). New York: International
Universities Press. London: Hogarth Press. Munich: Kindler Verlag (10 vols).

[3]Grinstein, A. (1956). *The Index of Psychoanalytic Writings*. New York:
International Universities Press.

[4]*Bulletin of the Menninger Clinic* (1963) 27(3):154–157.

supplement of some of the remaining unpublished lectures and papers.

Chronology is particularly difficult in the case of Anna Freud's writings, owing to their author's not infrequent policy of delaying publication until long after the initial (verbal) presentation of the material. In such instances both the year of actual first publication and a retrospective date for the earlier first presentation are given.

(1922a).   Schlagephantasie und Tagtraum. (Beating fantasies and daydreams). *Writings* I:137–157.

(1923a).   Ein hysterisches Symptom bei einen zweieinvierteljahrigen Knaben. (A hysterical symptom in a child of two years and three months). *Writings* I:158–161.

(1927a).   Einführung in die Technik der Kinderanalyse. (Four lectures on child analysis). *Writings* I:3–69.

(1928a).   Zur theorie der Kinderanalyse. (The theory of child analysis). *Writings* I:162–175. See also 1946d, pt. II.

(1928b).   Report of the Tenth International Psychoanalytic Congress. *International Journal of Psychoanalysis* 9:132–159.

(1928c).   Die Einleitung der Kinderanalyse. (Preparation for child analysis). *Almanach der Psychoanalyse*, pp. 187–198. See also 1927a, lect. 1.

(1929a).   Die Beziehung zwischen Psychoanalyse und Pädagogik. (The relation between psychoanalysis and education). See also 1930a, lect. 4.

(1929b).   Ein Gegenstuck zur Tierphobie der Kinder. (A counterpart to the animal phobias of children). *Internationale Zeitschrift für Psychoanalyse* 15:518. See also 1936a, chap. 6.

(1929c).   Report of the Eleventh International Psychoanalytic Congress. *International Journal of Psychoanalysis* 10:489–526.

(1930a).   Einführung in die Psychoanalyse für Pädagogen. (Four lectures on psychoanalysis for teachers and parents). *Writings* I:73–133.

(1931a).   Psychoanalysis of the child. In *A Handbook of Child Psychology*, ed. C. Murchison, pp. 555–567. Worcester: Clark University Press. (Psychoanalyse des Kindes. *Zeitschrift für Psychoanalytische Pädagogik [1932]* 6:5–20).

(1932a).   Erzieher und Neurose. *Zeitschrift für Psychoanalytische Pädagogik* 6:393–402.

(1933a).   Report of the Twelfth International Psychoanalytic Congress. *International Journal of Psychoanalysis* 14:138–180.

(1934a). Die Erziehung des Kleinkindes vom psychoanalytischen Standpunkt aus. (Psychoanalysis and the upbringing of the young child). *Writings* I:176–188.

(1934b). Report of the Central Executive Committee of the International Psychoanalytic Association. *Internationale Zeitschrift für Psychoanalyse* 20:125–126.

(1935a). Ich und Es in der Pubertät. (The ego and the id at puberty). *Writings* II:chap. 11. See also 1936a.

(1935b). Introduction. (Child Analysis Number). *Psychoanalytic Quarterly* 4:1–2.

(1936a). Das Ich und die Abwehrmechanismen. (The Ego and the Mechanisms of Defence). *Writings* II. See also 1966h.

(1937a). Ich-Einschränkung. (Restriction of the ego). *Writings* II: chap. 8. See also 1936a.

(1937b). Triebangst in der Pubertät. (Instinctual anxiety during puberty). *Writings* II:chap. 12. See also 1936a.

(1942a). Young children in wartime: a year's work in a residential war nursery. *Writings* III:142–211 (with Dorothy Burlingham).

(1942b). What children say about war and death. *New Era in Home and School* 23:185–189 (December) (with Dorothy Burlingham).

(1942c). Tony. *New Era in Home and School.* Vol. 23 (June). See also *Writings* III:240–246.

(1944a). Infants without families: the case for and against residential nurseries. *Writings* III:543–664 (with Dorothy Burlingham).

(1944b). Sex in childhood. *Health Education Journal* 2:2–6.

(1944c). Difficulties of sex enlightenment. *Health Education Journal* 2:81–85.

(1945a). Indications for child analysis. *Writings* IV:3–38. See also 1946d, pt. III.

(1946a). The psychoanalytic study of infantile feeding disturbances. *Writings* IV:39–59.

(1946b). Freedom from want in early education. *Writings* IV:425–441.

(1946c). Problèmes d'adaptation posés par l'éducation des enfants qui ont souffert de la guerre. *Psyché-Paris* 1:181–188.

(1946d). *The Psychoanalytic Treatment of Children* (new preface). London: Imago. See also 1927a, 1928a, 1945a.

(1946e). Bulletin of the International Psychoanalytic Association. *International Journal of Psychoanalysis* 27.

(1947a). The establishment of feeding habits. *Writings* IV:442–457.

(1947b). Emotional and instinctual development. *Writings* IV:458–488.

(1948a). Sublimation as a factor in upbringing. *Health Educational Journal* 6:25–29.

(1948b). Foreword to H. Sachs, *Masks of Love and Life: The Philosophical Basis of Psychoanalysis*. London: Peter Owen.

(1948c). Bulletin of the International Psychoanalytic Association. *International Journal of Psychoanalysis* 29:260.

(1949a). Certain types and stages of social maladjustment. *Writings* IV:75–94.

(1949b). Some clinical remarks concerning the treatment of cases of male homosexuality (Summary). *International Journal of Psychoanalysis* 30:195.

(1949c). Foreword to E. Buxbaum, Your child makes sense. *Writings* IV:610–613.

(1949d). Nursery school education: its uses and dangers. *Writings* IV:545–559.

(1949e). Über bestimmte Schweirigkeiten zwischen Eltern und Kindern in der Vorpubertät. (On certain difficulties in the preadolescent's relations with his parents). *Writings* IV:95–106.

(1949f). Aggression in relation to emotional development: normal and pathological. *Writings* IV:489–497.

(1949g). Notes on aggression. *Writings* IV:60–74.

(1949h). Report of the Sixteenth International Psychoanalytic Congress. *International Journal of Psychoanalysis* 30:178–190.

(1950a). The significance of the evolution of psychoanalytic child psychology. *Writings* IV:614–624.

(1950b). Probleme der Lehranalyse. (The problem of training analysis). *Writings* IV:407–421 (first presented in 1938).

(1951a). The contribution of psychoanalysis to genetic psychology. *Writings* IV:107–142.

(1951b). Observations on child development. *Writings* IV:143–162. Abstracts of the 1950 Anna Freud Lectures in America. *Bulletin of the American Psychoanalytic Association* (1950) 7:117–131.

(1951c). Some clinical remarks concerning the treatment of cases of male homosexuality (abstract).

(1951d). Psychoanalysis and the everyday problems of childhood (abstract).

(1951e). Child psychiatry (abstract).

(1951f). Infantile disturbances of feeding and sleeping (abstract).

(1951g). The role of sickness and hospitalisation in the life of a child (abstract).

(1951h). Variations of psychoanalytic technique (abstract).

(1951i). Present problems of child analysis (abstract).

(1951j). An experiment in group upbringing. *Writings* IV:163–229 (with Sophie Dann).

(1951k). August Aichhorn: 27th July 1878–17th October 1949. *Writings* IV:625–638.

(1952a). The role of bodily illness in the mental life of children. *Writings* IV:260–279.

(1952b). The role of the teacher: answering teacher's questions. *Writings* IV:560–568.

(1952c). Visiting children—the child. *Writings* IV:639–641.

(1952d). A connection between the states of negativism and of emotional surrender (*Hörigkeit*). *International Journal of Psychoanalysis* 33:265 (abstract).

(1952e). The mutual influences in the development of ego and id: introduction to discussion. *Writings* IV:230–244.

(1953a). Film review of James Robertson, *A Two-Year-Old Goes to Hospital*. *Writings* IV:280–292.

(1953b). Introduction to A. Balint, The psychoanalysis of the nursery. *Writings* IV:642–644.

(1953c). Some remarks on infant observation. *Writings* IV:569–585.

(1953d). Instinctual drives and their bearing on human behaviour. *Writings* IV:498–527 (first presented in 1948).

(1954a). Psychoanalysis and education. *Writings* IV:317–326.

(1954b). Problems of infantile neurosis: contribution to discussion. *Writings* IV:327–355.

(1954c). The widening scope of indications for psychoanalysis: discussion. *Writings* IV:356–376.

(1954d). Problems of technique in adult analysis. *Writings* IV:377–406.

(1954e). About losing and being lost. *International Journal of Psychoanalysis* 35:283 (abstract). See also 1967b.

(1955a). Social experiences of young children: particularly in times of social disturbance. In *Mental Health and Infant Development: Proceedings of the International Seminar of the World Federation for Mental Health*, vol. 1, ed. K. Soddy. London: Routledge.

(1955b). The concept of the rejecting mother. *Writings* IV:586–602.

(1956a). Comments on Joyce Robertson, A mother's observations on

the tonsillectomy of her four-year-old daughter. *Writings* IV:
293-301.

(1957a). Introduction to G. Casuso, Anxiety related to the "discovery" of
the penis: an observation. *Writings* V:473-475.

(1957b). Introduction to A. M. Sandler, E. Daunton, and A. Schnurmann,
Inconsistency in the mother as a factor in character
development: a comparative study of three cases. *Writings*
V:476-478.

(1957c). Die Kinderneurose. In *Das Psychoanalytische Volksbuch*,
ed. P. Federn and H. Meng. Berne and Stuttgart: Hans Huber
Verlag.

(1957d). Foreword to M. Milner, On not being able to paint. *Writings*
V:488-492.

(1958a). Child observation and prediction of development: a memorial
lecture in honor of Ernst Kris. *Writings* V:102-135.

(1958b). Adolescence. *Writings* V:136-166.

(1958c). Preface to T. Freeman, J. L. Cameron, and A. McGhie, Chronic
schizophrenia. *Writings* V:493-495.

(1958d). Clinical studies in psychoanalysis: research project of the
Hampstead Child-Therapy Clinic. *Proceedings of the Royal
Society of Medicine* 51:938-942.

(1959a). The concept of normality. Mimeograph copy. Library of the
San Francisco Theological Seminary, San Anselmo, California.

(1960a). Discussion of John Bowlby, Grief and mourning in infancy and
early childhood. *Writings* V:173-186.

(1960b). Entrance into nursery school: the psychological prerequisites.
Writings V:315-335.

(1960c). Introduction to K. Levy, Simultaneous analysis of a mother
and her adolescent daughter: the mother's contribution to the
loosening of the infantile object tie. *Writings* V:479-482.

(1960d). Foreword to M. Ruben, Parent guidance in the nursery school.
Writings V:496-498.

(1960e). The child guidance clinic as a centre of prophylaxis and
enlightenment. *Writings* V:281-300.

(1961a). Answering paediatrician's questions. *Writings* V:379-406.

(1962a). The emotional and social development of young children.
Writings V:336-351.

(1962b). Clinical problems of young children. *Writings* V:352-368.

(1962c). Assessment of childhood disturbances. *Psychoanalytic Study of
the Child* 17:149-158. See also 1965a, chap. 4.

(1962d). The theory of the parent-infant relationship: contribution to the discussion. *Writings* V:187–193.

(1963a). The concept of developmental lines. *Psychoanalytic Study of the Child* 18:245. See also 1965a, chap. 3(II).

(1963b). Regression as a principle in mental development. *Bulletin of the Menninger Clinic* 27:126–139. See also 1965a, chap. 3(III).

(1963c). The role of regression in mental development. *Writings* V:407–418.

(1963d). Preface to H. Meng and E. Freud, eds., *Psychoanalysis and Faith. The Letters of Sigmund Freud and Oskar Pfister.* London: Hogarth Press.

(1963e). Observations on the Topeka Psychoanalytic Institute. *Bulletin of the Menninger Clinic* 27:148–149.

(1964a). Defence mechanisms. *Encyclopaedia Britannica.* Chicago and London.

(1965a). Normality and pathology in childhood: assessments of development. *Writings* VI. See also 1962c, 1963a, 1963b.

(1965b). Diagnostic skills and their growth in psychoanalysis. *International Journal of Psychoanalysis* 46:31–38.

(1965c). Preface to J. Bolland and J. Sandler, The Hampstead Psychoanalytic Index. *Writings* V:483–485.

(1965d). Foreword to J. Lampl-de Groot, The development of the mind. *Writings* V:502–503.

(1965e). Foreword and Conclusion to T. Bergmann, Children in the hospital. *Writings* V:419–435.

(1965f). Preface to R. Spitz, *The First Year of Life: A Psychoanalytic Study of Normal and Deviant Development of Object Relations.* New York: International Universities Press.

(1965g). Heinz Hartmann: a tribute. *Writings* V:499–501.

(1965h). Metapsychological assessment of the adult personality: the adult profile. *Writings* V:60–75 (with Humberto Nagera and W. Ernst Freud).

(1965i). Some recent developments in child analysis. *Psychotherapy and Psychosomatics* 13:36–46.

(1965j). Three contributions to a seminar on family law. *Writings* V:436–459.

(1966a). Links between Hartmann's ego psychology and the child analyst's thinking. *Writings* V:204–220.

(1966b). Obsessional neurosis: a summary of psychoanalytic views. *Writings* V:242–261.

(1966c).   Interactions between nursery school and child guidance clinic.
           Writings V:369–378.

(1966d).   Foreword to H. Nagera, Early childhood disturbances, the
           infantile neurosis, and the adulthood disturbances. *Writings*
           V:486–487.

(1966e).   A short history of child analysis. *Writings* VII:48–58.

(1966f).   Some thoughts about the place of psychoanalytic theory in the
           training of psychiatrists. *Writings* VII:59–72.

(1966g).   Foreword to *Sex and the College Student*. (Group for the
           Advancement of Psychiatry). New York: Atheneum Press.

(1966h).   New Foreword to *The Ego and the Mechanisms of Defence*.
           Writings II.

(1967a).   Eine Diskussion mit Rene Spitz. (A discussion with Rene
           Spitz). *Writings* VII:22–38.

(1967b).   About losing and being lost. *Writings* IV:302–316. See also
           1954e.

(1967c).   Residential-versus-foster care. *Writings* VII:223–239.

(1967d).   Doctoral award address. *Writings* V:507–516 (first presented
           in 1964).

(1967e).   Comments on psychic trauma. *Writings* V:221–241 (first
           presented in 1964).

(1967f).   Foreword to H. Nagera, *Vincent Van Gogh: A Psychoanalytic
           Study*. London: Allen and Unwin.

(1968a).   Acting out. *Writings* VII:94–109.

(1968b).   Contributions to panel discussion. *International Journal of
           Psychoanalysis* 49:506–512.

(1968c).   Indications and contraindications for child analysis. *Writings*
           VII:110–123.

(1968d).   Willi Hoffer, MD, PhD. *Psychoanalytic Study of the Child*
           23:7–9; *International Journal of Psychoanalysis* (1969) 50:
           265–266.

(1968e).   The sleeping difficulties of the young child: an outline.
           Writings IV:605–609 (first presented in 1947).

(1968f).   Expert knowledge for the average mother. *Writings* IV:
           528–544 (first presented in 1949).

(1968g).   Studies in passivity. *Writings* IV:245–259. See also 1949b,
           1951c, 1952d.

(1968h).   *Indications for Child Analysis and Other Papers, 1945–1956.
           The Writings of Anna Freud*, vol. IV. New York: International
           Universities Press; London: Hogarth Press.

(1969a). Difficulties in the path of psychoanalysis: a confrontation of past with present viewpoints. *Writings* VII:124–156.

(1969b). Foreword to *Hampstead Clinic Psychoanalytic Library Series*. *Writings* VII:263–267.

(1969c). Introduction to H. Nunberg, *Memoirs, Recollections, Ideas, Reflections*. New York: Psychoanalytic Research and Development Fund.

(1969d). The assessment of borderline cases. *Writings* V:301–314 (first presented in 1956).

(1969e). Psychoanalytic knowledge applied to the rearing of children. *Writings* V:265–280 (first presented in 1956).

(1969f). The Hampstead child therapy course and clinic. *Writings* V:3–8 (first presented in 1957).

(1969g). The contribution of direct child observation to psychoanalysis. *Writings* V:95–101 (first presented in 1957).

(1969h). Research projects of the Hampstead Child Therapy Clinic. *Writings* V:9–25 (first presented in 1957–1960).

(1969i). Separation anxiety. *Writings* V:167–173 (first presented in 1958).

(1969j). Assessment of pathology in childhood, I–III. *Writings* V:26–59 (first presented in 1962–1966).

(1969k). An appreciation of Herman Nunberg. *Writings* V:194–203 (first presented in 1964).

(1969l). Psychoanalytic knowledge and its application to children's services. *Writings* V:460–469 (first presented in 1964).

(1969m). Psychoanalysis and family law. *Writings* V:76–78 (first presented in 1964).

(1969n). Services for underprivileged children. *Writings* V:79–83 (first presented in 1966).

(1969p). Adolescence as a developmental disturbance. *Writings* VII:39–47.

(1969q). Film review of James and Joyce Robertson, *John, Seventeen Months—Nine Days in a Residential Nursery*. *Writings* VII:240–246.

(1969r). Obituary for James Strachey. *Writings* VII:277–279.

(1969s). A 75th birthday tribute to Heinz Hartmann. *International Journal of Psychoanalysis* 50:721.

(1969t). Remarks on the 50th birthday of the International Journal of Psychoanalysis. *International Journal of Psychoanalysis* 50:473.

(1969u). *Research at the Hampstead Child Therapy Clinic and Other*

    Papers, 1956–1965. The Writings of Anna Freud, Vol. V.
    New York: International Universities Press; London: Hogarth
    Press.

(1970a). The symptomatology of childhood: a preliminary attempt at
    classification. *Writings* VII:157–188.

(1970b). Foreword to B. Gordon, A psychoanalytic contribution to
    paediatrics. *Writings* VII:268–271.

(1970c). Foreword to Zehn jahre Berliner Psychoanalytische Institut.
    Berlin Psychoanalytic Institute (privately printed).

(1971a). The infantile neurosis: genetic and dynamic considerations.
    Writings VII:189–203.

(1971b). Child analysis as a subspeciality of psychoanalysis. *Writings*
    VII: 204–219.

(1971c). Foreword to J. C. Hill, *Teaching and the Unconscious Mind.*
    New York: International Universities Press.

(1971d). Foreword to M. Gardiner, ed., The wolf-man by the wolf-man.
    Writings VII:272–276.

(1971e). The seventieth birthday: a letter to Max Schur. In *The*
    Unconscious Today: Essays in Honor of Max Schur, ed.
    M. Kanzer. New York: International Universities Press.

(1971f). Problems of termination in child analysis. *Writings* VII:3–21
    (first presented in 1957).

(1971g). The ideal psychoanalytic institute: a utopia. *Writings* VII:
    73–93.

(1971h). Painter-v-Bannister: postscript by a psychoanalyst. *Writings*
    VII:247–255.

(1971i). Address to the Yale Law School. *Writings* VII:256–260 (first
    presented in 1968).

(1971j). *Problems of Psychoanalytic Training, Diagnosis and the*
    Technique of Therapy 1966–1970. *The Writings of Anna*
    Freud, Vol. VII. New York: International Universities Press;
    London: Hogarth Press.

(1972a). Comments on aggression. *Writings* VIII:151–175.

(1972b). Muriel Gardiner. *Bulletin of the Philadelphia Association for*
    Psychoanalysis 22:103. See also 1980f.

(1972c). The child as a person in his own right. *Psychoanalytic Study of*
    the Child 27:621–625.

(1973a). *Infants Without Families. Reports of the Hampstead*
    Nurseries, 1939–1945. The Writings of Anna Freud, Vol. III.

New York: International Universities Press; London: Hogarth Press.

(1973b). Foreword to *Anna Freud* (1973a).

(1973c). Foreword to H. Beck, *Don't Push Me, I'm No Computer.* New York: McGraw-Hill.

(1973d). Foreword to S. Bernfeld, *Sisyphus or the Limits of Education.* Berkeley and Los Angeles: University of California Press.

(1973e). *Beyond the Best Interests of the Child.* New York: Macmillan-Free Press (with Joseph Goldstein and Albert Solnit).

(1974a). Foreword to E. Furman, *A Child's Parent Dies: Studies in Childhood Bereavement.* New Haven and London: Yale University Press.

(1974b). On Hilda Abraham's biography of Karl Abraham. *International Review of Psychoanalysis* 1:15.

(1974c). Diagnosis and assessment of childhood disturbances. *Writings* VIII:34–56 (first presented in 1954).

(1974d). A psychoanalytic view of developmental psychopathology. *Writings* VIII:57–74.

(1974e). *Introduction to Psychoanalysis. Lectures for Child Analysts and Teachers, 1922–1935. The Writings of Anna Freud,* Vol. I. New York: International Universities Press; London: Hogarth Press.

(1974f). Bibliography (child analysis pioneers). *Writings* I:189–194.

(1974g). Preface to *Standard Edition of the Complete Psychological Works of Sigmund Freud,* Vol. 24. London: Hogarth Press.

(1975a). The nursery school of the Hampstead Child Therapy Clinic. In *Studies in Child Psychoanalysis: Pure and Applied. The Scientific Proceedings of the Twentieth Anniversary Celebrations of the Hampstead Child-Therapy Course and Clinic.* Monograph no. 5, *Psychoanalytic Study of the Child.* New Haven: Yale University Press.

(1975b). Foreword to *Studies in Child Psychoanalysis: Pure and Applied* (1975a).

(1975c). Foreword to M. Berger and H. Kennedy, Pseudobackwardness in children: maternal attitudes as an aetiological factor. *Psychoanalytic Study of the Child* 30:279–282.

(1975d). Foreword to L. Newman, ed., *Selected Papers of Ernst Kris.* New Haven: Yale University Press.

(1975e). Introduction: Sigmund Freud Society. *Sigmund Freud House Bulletin* 1:2.

(1975f).   On the interactions between pediatrics and child psychology. *Writings* VIII:285–296.

(1975g).   Foreword to H. Nagera, *Female Sexuality and the Oedipus Complex.* New York: Jason Aronson.

(1975h).   Children possessed. Anna Freud looks at a central concern of the children's bill: the psychological needs of adopted children. *Writings* VIII:300–306.

(1975i).   Remarks on receiving the C. Anderson Aldrich Award. *American Academy of Pediatrics* 56:332–334.

(1976a).   Changes in psychoanalytic practice and experience. *Writings* VIII:176–185.

(1976b).   Foreword to H. Nagera, *Obsessional Neuroses: Developmental Psychopathology.* New York: Jason Aronson.

(1976c).   Psychopathology seen against a background of normal development. *Writings* VIII:82–95.

(1976d).   Foreword to A. D. Hofmann, R. D. Becker, and P. H. Gabriel, *The Hospitalised Adolescent: A Guide to Managing the Ill and Injured Youth.* New York: Free Press.

(1976e).   August Aichhorn. *Writings* VIII:344–345. See also 1951k.

(1977a).   Preface to the Vienna symposium on work at the Hampstead Clinic. *Sigmund Freud House Bulletin* 1:12–13.

(1977b).   Foreword to S. Rosenfeld, *Beyond the Infantile Neurosis.* London: Hampstead Clinic, Sara Rosenfeld Research Fund.

(1977c).   Foreword to A. J. Solnit, R. S. Eissler, A. Freud, M. Kris, and P. B. Neubauer, eds., *Psychoanalytic Assessment: The Diagnostic Profile.* New Haven and London: Yale University Press.

(1977d).   Foreword to P. Wilson, The referral of nursery school children for treatment. *Psychoanalytic Study of the Child* 32:479–481.

(1977e).   Fears, anxieties and phobic phenomena. *Writings* VIII: 193–200.

(1977f).   Concerning the relationship with children. *Writings* VIII: 297–299.

(1977g).   Foreword to R. Kramer, *Maria Montessori.* Munich: Kindler Verlag.

(1978a).   The principal task of child analysis. *Writings* VIII:96–109.

(1978b).   On the Hampstead Bulletin. *Bulletin of the Hampstead Clinic* 1:5.

(1978c). Edith B. Jackson: in memoriam. *Journal of the American Academy of Child Psychiatry* 17:730-731.

(1978d). Ansprache zur Denkmalsenthullung am 6 Mai 1977. (Address on the occasion of the unveiling of the Freud statue). *Writings* VIII:331-333.

(1978e). Inaugural lecture for the Sigmund Freud Chair at the Hebrew University, Jerusalem. *Writings* VIII:334-343.

(1978f). Die Bedeutung der Kinderanalyse. (The significance of child analysis). *Sigmund Freud House Bulletin* 2:8-12.

(1978g). Introduction to *Israel Annals of Psychiatry and Related Disciplines*, Vol. 16.

(1978h). Mathilde Hollitscher-Freud 1887-1978. *Sigmund Freud House Bulletin* 2.

(1978i). Foreword to E. J. Anthony, *The Child in His Family*. New York: Wiley.

(1979a). The role of insight in psychoanalysis and psychotherapy: introduction. *Writings* VIII:201-105. See also 1981h.

(1979b). Personal memories of Ernest Jones. *Writings* VIII:346-353.

(1979c). Obituary for Agi Bene-Moses. *Bulletin of the Hampstead Clinic* 2:163.

(1979d). Foreword to A. J. Solnit, R. S. Eissler, A. Freud, M. Kris, and P. B. Neubauer, eds., The development of blind children. *Psychoanalytic Study of the Child* 34:3-4.

(1980a). In memoriam: Dorothy Burlingham. *Bulletin of the Hampstead Clinic* 3:75-77.

(1980b). *The Technique of Child Psychoanalysis: Discussions with Anna Freud*. London: Hogarth Press and the Institute of Psychoanalysis.

(1980c). Child analysis as the study of mental growth (normal and abnormal). *Writings* VIII:119-136.

(1980d). Discussions in the *Hampstead Index* on *The Ego and the Mechanisms of Defence* I: *The ego as the seat of observation*. *Bulletin of the Hampstead Clinic* 3 (with Joseph Sandler).

(1980e). Foreword to S. Freud, Analysis of a phobia in a five-year-old boy. *Writings* VIII:277-282.

(1980f). Foreword to M. Gardiner, Lest we forget. *Writings* III: 354-357.

(1981a). Discussions in the *Hampstead Index* on *The Ego and the Mechanisms of Defense* II: *The application of analytic technique to the study of the psychic institutions. Bulletin of the Hampstead Clinic* 4.

(1981b). Discussions in the *Hampstead Index* on *The Ego and the Mechanisms of Defence* III: *The ego's defensive operations considered as an object of analysis. Bulletin of the Hampstead Clinic* 4.

(1981c). Discussions in the *Hampstead Index* on *The Ego and the Mechanisms of Defence* IV: *The mechanisms of defence*, pt. 1. *Bulletin of the Hampstead Clinic* 4.

(1981d). Answers to students' questions. *Bulletin of the Hampstead Clinic* 4.

(1981e). Obituary for G. G. Bunzl. *Bulletin of the Hampstead Clinic* 4.

(1981f). Foreword to M. Brierley, ed., *W. Hoffer. Early Development and Education of the Child.* London: Hogarth Press; New York: Jason Aronson.

(1981g). A psychoanalytic view of sexual abuse by parents. In M. P. Beezley and H. C. Kempe, eds., *Sexually Abused Children and Their Families.* Oxford: Pergamon.

(1981h). Insight: its presence and absence as a factor in normal development. *Writings* VIII:137–148.

(1981i). Foreword to M. Bonaparte, Topsy. *Writings* VIII:358–361.

(1982a). *Psychoanalytic Psychology of Normal Development. The Writings of Anna Freud*, 1970–1980, Vol. VIII. London: Hogarth Press and the Institute of Psychoanalysis; New York: International Universities Press. See also 1968h, 1969u, 1971j, 1973a, 1974e, 1936a, 1965a.

(1982b). Introduction. *Writings* VIII:3–7.

(1982c). The widening scope of psychoanalytic child psychology, normal and abnormal. *Writings* VIII:8–33.

(1982d). Beyond the infantile neurosis. *Writings* VIII:75–81.

(1982e). Mental health and illness in terms of internal harmony and disharmony. *Writings* VIII:110–118.

(1982f). Remarks on problems of psychoanalytic training. *Writings* VIII:186–192 (first presented in 1976).

(1982g). A study guide to Freud's writings. *Writings* VIII:209–276.

(1982h). Dynamic psychology and education. *Writings* VIII:307–314 (first presented in 1976).

(1982i). The nursery school from the psychoanalytic point of view. *Writings* VIII:315–330.

SUPPLEMENT OF UNPUBLISHED PAPERS
(WHEN KNOWN)

(1928). Child analysis: review of the symposium on child analysis. *International Journal of Psychoanalysis,* 1927. Presentation to the Vienna Psychoanalytic Society, January 25, 1928.

(1928). Report of a discussion held in Berlin on the psychoanalytical training of teachers. Presented to Vienna Psychoanalytic Society, May 16, 1928 (with S. Bernfeld).

(1929). Paedagogy. Public lecture at opening of Frankfurt Psychoanalytic Institute.

(1936). An address in celebration of May 6, 1936, Vienna Psychoanalytic Society.

(1936). Phenomena of disintegration in the waking thoughts of children. Read before Vienna Psychoanalytic Society, December 16, 1936.

(1936). A contribution to the analysis of teachers. Presented to Vienna Psychoanalytic Society, June 17, 1936.

(1937). A review of psychoanalytic paedagogy. Paper to the Second Four-Countries-Conference, Budapest, May 15–17, 1937.

(1959). The nature of the therapeutic process. Paper to Los Angeles Psychoanalytic Society, March 30, 1959.

(1959). The problem of research in psychoanalysis. Paper to San Francisco Psychoanalytic Society, April 8, 1959.

(1959). Edward Bibring Memorial Meeting Lecture. Presented to Boston Psychoanalytic Society, April 14, 1959.

(1962). Infantile dependency as a factor in psychoanalytic theory and practice. Second Sloan Lecture, Topeka, Kansas, September 25, 1962.

(1966). The interaction between body and mind in the child's physical illness. Lecture to Amsterdam University and Guy's Hospital Medical School.

(1973). Tribute to Sara Rosenfeld. Read at the memorial meeting, Hampstead Child Therapy Clinic, London, October 3, 1973 (mimeo copy).

REFERENCES

Abraham, H. C., and Freud, E. L., eds. (1965). *A Psychoanalytic Dialogue: The Letters of Sigmund Freud and Karl Abraham, 1907–1926.* New York: Basic Books.

Abstracts of Anna Freud's 1950 United States Lectures. (1951). *Bulletin of the American Psychoanalytic Association* 7:117–130.

Ack, M. (1966). Julie: the treatment of a case of developmental retardation. *Psychoanalytic Study of the Child* 21:127–149.

Aichhorn, A. (1935). *Wayward Youth.* New York: Viking.

Alexander, F., Eisenstein, S., and Grotjahn, M. (1966). *Psychoanalytic Pioneers.* New York: Basic Books.

Alpert, A., and Krown, S. (1953). Treatment of a child with severe ego restriction in a therapeutic nursery. *Psychoanalytic Study of the Child* 8:333–354.

Alpert, A., Neubauer, P., and Weil, A. P. (1956). Unusual variations in drive endowment. *Psychoanalytic Study of the Child* 11:125–163.

Anna Freud Number (1963). *Bulletin of the Menninger Clinic* 27.

Anna Freud Number (1974). *Journal of the Philadelphia Association for Psychoanalysis* 1.

Announcement. (1964). *International Journal of Psychoanalysis* 45:625.

Armytage, W. H. G. (1975). Psychoanalysis and teacher education: part I. *British Journal of Teacher Education* 1:227–236.

——— (1975). Psychoanalysis and teacher education: part II. *British Journal of Teacher Education* 1:317–334.

——— (1976). Psychoanalysis and teacher education: part III. British Journal of Teacher Education 2:95 111.

Balint, M. (1949a). Early developmental states of the ego: primary object love. *International Journal of Psychoanalysis* 30:265–273.

——— (1949b). Introduction to psychoanalysis and education. *International Journal of Psychoanalysis* 30:220.

——— (1957). Individual differences of behaviour in early infancy. In Balint M., *Problems of Human Pleasure and Behavior.* New York: Liveright.

——— (1962). Contribution to discussion: the theory of the infant-parent relationship. *International Journal of Psychoanalysis* 43:246–257.

Barchilon, J. (1964). Development of artistic stylization: a two-year evolution in the drawings of a normal child. *Psychoanalytic Study of the Child* 19:256.

Bender, L. (1952). *Child Psychiatric Techniques*. Springfield: Charles C Thomas.

Bergen, M. E. (1958). *Psychoanalytic Study of the Child* 13:407.

Bergmann, Th. (1965). *Children in the Hospital*. New York: International Universities Press.

Bernfeld, S. (1922). *Kinderheim Baumgarten*. Berlin: Jewish Press.

Besser, R. (1976). Leben und Werk von Anna Freud. M.D. Thesis, Johannes Gutenberg University, Mainz.

Bettelheim, B. (1943). Individual and mass behaviour in extreme situations. *Journal of Abnormal and Social Psychology* 38:417.

—— (1969). The education of emotionally and culturally deprived children. In *From Learning for Love to Love of Learning: Essays on Psychoanalysis and Education*, eds. R. Ekstein and R. L. Motto. New York: Brunner/Mazel.

Bibring, G. L., Dwyer, T. F., Huntingdon, D. S., and Valenstein, A. F. (1961). A study of the psychological processes in pregnancy and of the earliest mother-child relationship, pts. I and II. *Psychoanalytic Study of the Child* 16:9–72.

Bick, E. (1962). Symposium on child analysis: I, child analysis today. *International Journal of Psychoanalysis* 43:328–332.

Biermann, G. (1973). Vorwort. In A. Freud, *Einführung in die Technik der Kinderanalyse*. Munich: Kindler Verlag.

Binet, A., and Henri, V. (1895–1896). La psychologie individuelle. *L'Année Psychologique* 2:411–465.

Boll, T. (1962). May Sinclair and the medico-psychological clinic of London. *Proceedings of the American Philosophical Society* 106:310–326.

Bolland, J., and Sandler, J. (1965). *The Hampstead Psychoanalytic Index*. Monograph no. 1, *Psychoanalytic Study of the Child*. New York: International Universities Press.

Bonaparte, M. (1946). A l'Unesco presentation d'Anna Freud. *Psyché-Paris* 1:180.

Bowlby, J. (1946). *Forty-Four Juvenile Delinquents: Their Characters and Home Life*. London: Bailliere Tindall and Cox.

—— (1951). *Maternal Care and Mental Health*. New York: UNESCO-WHO.

Breuer, J., and Freud, S. (1895). Studies on hysteria. *Standard Edition* 2:1–309.

Brierley, M. (1951). Trends In Psychoanalysis. London: Hogarth Press and Institute of Psychoanalysis.

——— (1969). Hardy perennials and psychoanalysis. *International Journal of Psychoanalysis* 50:447–452.

British Psychoanalytical Society (1967). The 1943 "controversial" discussions. *Scientific Bulletin of the British Psychoanalytic Society and Institute of Psychoanalysis,* no. 10.

Brody, S. (1974). Contributions to child analysis. *Psychoanalytic Study of the Child* 29:13–20.

Brome, V. (1967). *Freud and His Early Circle: The Struggles of Psycho-Analysis.* London: Heinemann.

Brown, J. A. C. (1961). *Freud and the Post-Freudians.* Harmondsworth: Pelican.

Buber, M. (1937). *I And Thou.* New York: Scribner.

Buckle, D., and Levovici, S. (1960). *Child Guidance Centres.* Geneva: WHO.

Bulletin Report of the I. P. A. (1929). *International Journal of Psychoanalysis* 10.

——— (1938). *International Journal of Psychoanalysis* 19.

——— (1939). *International Journal of Psychoanalysis* 20.

——— (1945). *International Journal of Psychoanalysis* 26.

——— (1948). *International Journal of Psychoanalysis* 29.

——— (1954). Members List. *International Journal of Psychoanalysis* 35.

——— (1972). *International Journal of Psychoanalysis* 53.

Bulletin Reports of the British Psychoanalytic Society 1950–55. (1954). *International Journal of Psychoanalysis* 35.

Burlingham, D., and Freud, A. (1942). *Young Children in Wartime: A Year's Work in a Residential Nursery.* London: Allen and Unwin.

Burt, C. (1922). The dreams and daydreams of a delinquent girl, pts. I–IV. *Journal of Experimental Paedagogy and Training College Record,* vol. 6.

Buxbaum, E. (1969). Three great psychoanalytic educators. In *From Learning for Love to Love of Learning: Essays on Psychoanalysis and Education,* eds. R. Ekstein and R. L. Motto, pp. 32–35. New York: Brunner/Mazel.

Child Analysis Number. (1935). *Psychoanalytic Quarterly* 4.

Clouzet, M. (1974). *Sigmund Freud: A New Appraisal.* Westport, Conn.: Greenwood.

Cleveland Center for Research in Child Development. (1976). *Tenth Anniversary Report,* Cleveland, Ohio.

Colonna, A. (1968). *Psychoanalytic Study of the Child* 23:391.

Dicks, H. V. (1950). In search of our proper ethic. *British Journal of Medical Psychology* 23:1.

Dyer, R. (1974). Scoring procedures, external criteria and the effects of some variables on divergent thinking tests. M. Phil. Thesis, University of Leeds.

―― (1980). Anna Freud and Education: Studies in the History, Philosophy, Science and Applications of Child Psychoanalysis. Ph.D. Dissertation, University of Sheffield.

Eidelberg, L. (1968). *Encyclopedia of Psychoanalysis.* New York: Free Press.

Eissler, K. R. (1971). Death drive, ambivalence and narcissism. *Psychoanalytic Study of the Child* 26:25–78.

Eissler, R. S., Freud, A., Kris, M., and Solnit, A. J. (1975). Thirty years later. *Psychoanalytic Study of the Child* 30:xi–xiv.

Ekstein, R., and Motto, R. L. (1969). Psychoanalysis and education—an historical account. In *From Learning for Love to Love of Learning: Essays on Psychoanalysis and Education,* eds. R. Ekstein and R. L. Motto, pp. 3–27. New York: Brunner/Mazel.

Erikson, E. H. (1945). Childhood and tradition in two American Indian tribes: a comparative abstract with conclusions. *Psychoanalytic Study of the Child* 1:319–350.

―― (1946). Ego development and historical change: clinical notes. *Psychoanalytic Study of the Child* 2:359–396.

―― (1950). *Childhood and Society.* Rev. ed. New York: Norton, 1964.

―― (1968). *Identity: Youth and Crisis.* New York: Norton.

―― (1956). The problem of ego identity. *Journal of the American Psychoanalytic Association* 4:56–121.

Escalona, S. (1963). Patterns of infantile experience and the developmental process. *Psychoanalytic Study of the Child* 18: 197–244.

Extraordinary Meeting on Training Proposals. Report of the British Psychoanalytic Society. (1946). *International Journal of Psychoanalysis* 27:82.

Fairbairn, W. R. D. (1936). The effect of a king's death upon patients undergoing analysis. *International Journal of Psychoanalysis* 17.

——— (1952). *Psychoanalytic Studies of the Personality*. Boston: Routledge & Kegan Paul, 1966.

——— (1963). Synopsis of an object relations theory of personality. *International Journal of Psychoanalysis* 44:224–225.

Federn, P. (1952). *Ego Psychology and the Psychoses*. New York: Basic Books.

Fenichel, O. (1932). Outline of clinical psychoanalysis. *Psychoanalytic Quarterly* 1:121–165.

——— (1938). Review of Anna Freud. *International Journal of Psychoanalysis* 19:116–136.

Ferenczi, S. (1908). Psychoanalysis and education. *International Journal of Psychoanalysis* (1949) 30:220–224.

Flagg, G. W. (1966). Felix Deutsch. In *Psychoanalytic Pioneers*, eds. S. Alexander, S. Eisenstein, and M. Grotjahn. New York: Basic Books.

Flugel, J. C. (1945). *Man, Morals and Society*. New York: International Universities Press, 1970.

French, T. M. (1938). Defense and synthesis in the function of the ego. *Psychoanalytic Quarterly* 7:537–553.

Freud, E. L., ed. (1960). *Letters of Sigmund Freud, 1873–1939*. New York: Basic Books.

———, et al. (1978). *Sigmund Freud: His Life in Pictures and Words*. New York: Harcourt, Brace Jovanovich. Trans. by Christiane Trollope.

Freud, M. (1957). *Glory Reflected: Sigmund Freud—Man and Father*. London: Angus and Robertson.

Freud, S. (1894). The neuro-psychoses of defence. *Standard Edition* 3:43–61.

——— (1900). The interpretation of dreams. *Standard Edition* 4/5:1–361.

——— (1905). Three essays on the theory of sexuality. *Standard Edition* 7:123–243.

——— (1907). The sexual enlightenment of children. *Standard Edition* 9:129–140.

——— (1908a). Creative writers and daydreaming. *Standard Edition* 9:141–156.

——— (1908b). On the sexual theories of children. *Standard Edition* 9:205–226.

——— (1909). Analysis of a phobia in a five-year-old boy. *Standard Edition* 10:1–152.

——— (1910). Contributions to a discussion on suicide. *Standard Edition* 11:231–232.

—— (1910). Five lectures on psychoanalysis. *Standard Edition* 11:3–58.

—— (1912a). Contributions to a discussion on masturbation. *Standard Edition* 12:239–254.

—— (1912b). Totem and taboo. *Standard Edition* 13:1–164.

—— (1913a). The claims of psychoanalysis to scientific interest. *Standard Edition* 13:165–192.

—— (1913b). Introduction to O. Pfister's *Psychoanalytic Method*. *Standard Edition* 12:327–332.

—— (1913c). The theme of the three caskets. *Standard Edition* 12:289–302.

—— (1913d). Two lies told by children. *Standard Edition* 12:303–310.

—— (1914a). On the history of the psychoanalytic movement. *Standard Edition* 14:3–66.

—— (1914b). On narcissism: an introduction. *Standard Edition* 14:73–104.

—— (1914c). Some reflections on schoolboy psychology. *Standard Edition* 13:241.

—— (1916). Introductory lectures on psychoanalysis. *Standard Edition* 15/16:1–477.

—— (1919a). A child is being beaten: a contribution to the study of the origin of sexual perversions. *Standard Edition* 17:175–204.

—— (1919b). Lines of advance in psychoanalytic therapy. *Standard Edition* 17:157–168.

—— (1919c). Victor Tausk. *Standard Edition* 17:273.

—— (1920a). Beyond the pleasure principle. *Standard Edition* 18:3–66.

—— (1920b). Supplements to the theory of dreams. *Standard Edition* 18:4.

—— (1921a). Group psychology and the analysis of the ego. *Standard Edition* 18:67–145.

—— (1921b). Introduction to J. Varendonck, *The Psychology of Daydreams*. *Standard Edition* 18:271.

—— (1923). The ego and the id. *Standard Edition* 19:1–68.

—— (1925). *Gesammelte Schriften*. Vienna and Leipzig: I. P. Verlag.

—— (1926). Inhibitions, symptoms and anxiety. *Standard Edition* 20:77–178.

—— (1927a). The future of an illusion. *Standard Edition* 21:1–58.

—— (1927b). Humour. *Standard Edition* 21:160–166.

—— (1933). New introductory lectures on psychoanalysis. *Standard Edition* 22:1–184.

—— (1939). Moses and monotheism. *Standard Edition* 23:1–140.

—— (1950). The origins of psychoanalysis. *Standard Edition* 1:177–388.

Freud, W. E. (1971). The baby profile: part II. *Psychoanalytic Study of the Child* 26:172–194.

—— (1975). Infant observation: its relevance to psychoanalytic training. *Psychoanalytic Study of the Child* 30:75–94.

Friedlander, K. (1947a). *The Psychoanalytic Approach to Juvenile Delinquency: Theory, Case Studies, Treatment.* New York: International Universities Press, 1960.

—— (1947b). Review of Anna Freud. *New Era in Home and School* 28:20.

Fries, M. E. (1946). The child's ego development and the training of adults in his environment. *Psychoanalytic Study of the Child* 2: 85–112.

Geleerd, E. R. (1962). Symposium on child analysis: contribution to discussion. *International Journal of Psychoanalysis* 43:338–341.

—— (1963). Evaluation of Melanie Klein's *Narrative of a Child Analysis. International Journal of Psychoanalysis* 44:493–506.

Gilbert, M. (1981). *Auschwitz and the Allies.* London: G. Rainbird.

Gitelson, M. (1962). The curative factors in psychoanalysis: I, the first phase of psychoanalysis. *International Journal of Psychoanalysis* 43:194–205.

Glover, E. (1930). Grades of ego differentiation. *International Journal of Psychoanalysis* 11:1–11.

—— (1942). Notes on the psychological effects of war conditions on the civilian population: III, the blitz, 1940-41. *International Journal of Psychoanalysis* 23:17–37.

—— (1945). Examination of the Klein system of child psychology. *Psychoanalytic Study of the Child* 1:75–118.

—— (1966). Psychoanalysis in England. In *Psychoanalytic Pioneers,* eds. F. Alexander, S. Eisenstein, and M. Grotjahn. New York: Basic Books.

Goodenough, F. L., and Tyler, L. E. (1959). *Developmental Psychology.* 3rd ed. New York: Appleton-Century-Crofts.

Gould, R. L. (1970). Preventative psychiatry and the field theory of reality. *Journal of the American Psychoanalytic Association* 18:440–461.

Green, G. H. (1922). *Psychoanalysis in the Classroom.* London: University of London Press.

Greenson, R. R. (1971).The "real relationship" between the patient and the psychoanalyst. In *The Unconscious Today: Essays in Honour of Max Schur*, ed. M. Kanzer. New York: International Universities Press.

————— (1972). The voice of the intellect is a soft one: review of *The Writings of Anna Freud*, Vol. IV, 1945–56. *International Journal of Psychoanalysis* 53:403–417.

Grossman, C. M., and Grossman, S. (1965). *The Wild Analyst: The Life and Work of Georg Groddeck*. London: Barrie and Rockliff.

Guntrip, H. J. S. (1961). *Personality Structure and Human Interaction*. New York: International Universities Press, 1964.

Guttman, S. (1969). Obituary: Robert Waelder. *International Journal of Psychoanalysis* 50:269–273.

Harries, M. (1952). Sublimation in a group of four-year-old boys. *Psychoanalytic Study of the Child* 7:230–240.

Hartmann, H. (1939). *Ego Psychology and the Problem of Adaptation*. New York: International Universities Press, 1958.

Hayman, A. (1972). *Psychoanalytic Study of the Child* 27:476.

————— (1978). The diagnostic profile: II, some clinical and research aspects of the developmental profile. *Bulletin of the Hampstead Clinic* 1:75–85.

Heimann, P. (1968). The evaluation of applicants for psychoanalytic training. *International Journal of Psychoanalysis* 49:527–539.

—————, and Valenstein, A. (1972). The psychoanalytic concept of aggression: an integrated summary. *International Journal of Psychoanalysis* 53:31–35.

Hellman, I. (1962). Symposium on child analysis: reply to discussion. *International Journal of Psychoanalysis* 43:342–343.

Hendrick, I. (1938). Review of Anna Freud. *Psychoanalytic Review* 25:476–497.

Hitschmann, E. (1932). A ten years report of the Vienna Psychoanalytic Clinic. *International Journal of Psychoanalysis* 13:245–255.

Hoffer, W. (1945). Psychoanalytic education. *Psychoanalytic Study of the Child* 1:293–307.

————— (1946). Diaries of adolescent schizophrenics (hebephrenics). *Psychoanalytic Study of the Child* 2:293–312.

————— (1965). *Siegfried Bernfeld and Jerubbal. Tenth Yearbook*. London: Leo Baeck Institute.

―――― (1968). Notes on the theory of defence. *Psychoanalytic Study of the Child* 23:178–188.

Holder, A. (1975). *Psychoanalytic Study of the Child* 30:197.

―――― (1977). Contribution to Vienna symposium on work in the Hampstead Clinic. *Sigmund Freud House Bulletin* 1.

Hug-Hellmuth, H. (1913). Aus dem Seelenleben des Kindes (A study of the mental life of the child). In *Papers on Applied Psychology* no. 15, ed. S. Freud. Vienna: Deuticke.

―――― (1920). Collective review: child psychology and education. *International Journal of Psychoanalysis* 1:316–323.

―――― (1921). On the technique of child analysis. Trans. R. Gabler and B. Low. *International Journal of Psychoanalysis* 2:287–305.

Ilan, E. (1963). The problem of motivation in the educator's vocational choice. *Psychoanalytic Study of the Child* 18:266–285.

I. P. A. Announcement. (1955). *International Journal of Psychoanalysis* 36.

Isaacs, S. (1933). *Social Development in Young Children: A Study of Beginnings*. Atlantic Highlands, N.J.: Humanities, 1965.

Jackson, E. B. (1955). Child development patterns in the United States. In *Mental Health and Infant Development: Proceedings of the International Seminar, World Federation for Mental Health*. Vol. 1, ed. K. Soddy. London: Routledge.

Jacobs, L. (1949). Dr. Kate Friedlander. *New Era in Home and School* 30:101–103.

Jacobson, E. (1971). Obituary: Annie Reich. *International Journal of Psychoanalysis* 52:334–336.

Jones, E. (1918). Anal-erotic character traits. *Journal of Abnormal Psychology* 13:261–284. Trans. by A. Freud, Über analerotische Charakterzuge. *Internationale Zeitschrift für Psychoanalyse* (1919) 5:69–92.

―――― (1921). Preface to S. Freud, *Introductory Lectures on Psychoanalysis*. London: Allen & Unwin, 1922, pp. 5–6.

―――― (1922). Some problems of adolescence. *British Journal of Psychology* 13:31–47. Trans. Einige Probleme der jugendlichen Alters. *Imago* (1923) 9:145–168.

―――― (1938). Review of Anna Freud. *International Journal of Psychoanalysis* 19:115–116.

―――― (1953). *The Life and Work of Sigmund Freud*. Vol. 1. New York: Basic Books.

———— (1955). *The Life and Work of Sigmund Freud.* Vol. 2. London: Hogarth Press.

———— (1957). *The Life and Work of Sigmund Freud.* Vol. 3. New York: Basic Books.

———— (1959). *Free Associations: Memoirs of a Psychoanalyst.* New York: Basic Books.

Kanzer, M., ed. (1971). *The Unconscious Today: Essays in Honour of Max Schur.* New York: International Universities Press.

————, and Blum, H. P. (1967). *Psychoanalytic Techniques: A Handbook for the Practicing Psychoanalyst.* New York: Basic Books.

Kaplan, D. (1968). Since Freud. *Harper's,* August, pp. 55–60.

Kaplan, L. J. (1971). The work of Anna Freud. *Psychiatry and Social Science Review* 5:22–29.

Katan, A. (1961). Some thoughts about the role of verbalisation in early childhood. *Psychoanalytic Study of the Child* 16:184–188.

Katan, M. (1964). Fetishism, splitting of the ego and denial. *International Journal of Psychoanalysis* 45:237–245.

Kennedy, H. E. (1971). Problems in reconstruction in child analysis. *Psychoanalytic Study of the Child* 26:386–402.

———— (1978). The Hampstead centre for the psychoanalytic study and treatment of children. *Bulletin of the Hampstead Clinic* 1:7–10.

———— (1980). Dorothy Burlingham 1891–1979. *Psychoanalytic Quarterly* 59:508–511.

Kestenberg, J. S. (1971). A developmental approach to disturbances of sex-specific identity. *International Journal of Psychoanalysis* 52:99–102.

Kleeman, J. A. (1966). Genital self-discovery during a boy's second year: a follow-up. *Psychoanalytic Study of the Child* 21:358–392.

Klein, E. (1949). Psychoanalytic aspects of school problems. *Psychoanalytic Study of the Child* 3/4:369–390.

Klein, M. (1932). *The Psychoanalysis of Children.* New York: Delacorte, 1975. Trans. 1949 by Alix Strachey.

———— (1948). *Contributions to Psychoanalysis* 1921–1945. London: Hogarth Press and Institute of Psychoanalysis.

———— (1952). Discussant: the mutual influences in the development of ego and id. *Psychoanalytic Study of the Child* 7:51.

Kris, E. (1938). Review of Anna Freud. *International Journal of Psychoanalysis* 19:136–146.

—— (1948). Child analysis. In *Psychoanalysis Today,* ed. S. Lorand, pp. 50–63. London: Allen and Unwin.

—— (1951). Ego psychology and interpretation in psychoanalytic therapy. In *Selected Papers of Ernst Kris.* New Haven: Yale University Press, 1975.

—— (1953). Psychoanalysis and the study of creative imagination. In *Selected Papers of Ernst Kris.* New Haven: Yale University Press, 1975.

—— (1975). *Selected Papers of Ernst Kris.* New Haven: Yale University Press.

Lampl-de Groot, J. (1928). The evolution of the oedipus complex in women. *International Journal of Psychoanalysis* 9:332.

Lantos, B. (1966). Kate Friedlander. In *Psychoanalytic Pioneers*, eds. F. Alexander, S. Eisenstein, and M. Grotjahn. New York: Basic Books.

Leupold-Lowenthal, H., and Lobner, H. (1975). Sigmund Freud House Catalogue. (Sigmund Freud Gesellschaft). Vienna: Locker and Wogenstein.

Levine, I. (1925). *The Unconscious: An Introduction to Freudian Psychology.* Vienna and Leipzig. Deuticke.

Lobner, H. (1975). From our archives: some additional remarks on Freud's library. *Sigmund Freud House Bulletin* 1:18–29.

Long, C. (1917). Psychoanalysis in relation to the child. *Journal of Experimental Paedagogy & Training College Record* 4:57–70.

Lorand, S. (1969). Reflections on the development of psychoanalysis in New York from 1925. *International Journal of Psychoanalysis* 50:589–595.

Low, B. (1922). Review. *International Journal of Psychoanalysis* 3:236.

—— (1923). Review. *International Journal of Psychoanalysis* 4:205–206.

—— (1929). A note on the influence of psychoanalysis upon English education in the last 18 years. *International Journal of Psychoanalysis* 10:314–320.

Lustman, S. L. (1963). Some issues in contemporary psychoanalytic research. *Psychoanalytic Study of the Child* 18:51–74.

—— (1967). The scientific leadership of Anna Freud. *Journal of the American Psychoanalytic Association* 15:810–827.

—— (1973a). A perspective on the study of mankind. *Psychoanalytic Study of the Child* 27:18–54.

—— (1973b). Yale's year of confrontation: a view from the master's house. *Psychoanalytic Study of the Child* 27:57–73.

Mackinnon, D., and Dukes, W. F. (1962). Repression. In *Psychology in the Making: Histories of Selected Research Problems,* ed. L. Postman. New York: Knopf.

Mahl, G. F. (1969). *Psychological Conflict and Defense.* New York: Harcourt Brace Jovanovich.

McGuire, W., ed. (1974). *The Freud-Jung Letters: The Correspondence Between Sigmund Freud and C. G. Jung.* Princeton: Princeton University Press. Trans. by Ralph Manheim and R. F. Hall.

Meehl, P. H. (1954). *Clinical versus Statistical Prediction.* Minneapolis: University of Minnesota Press.

Meng, H. (1939). Psychoanalytische Erziehung und Kinderanalyse. In *Das Psychoanalytische Volksbuch,* eds. H. Meng and P. Federn, 3rd edition, pp. 175–192. Berne: Hans Huber.

———, and Freud, E. L., eds. (1963). *Psychoanalysis and Faith. The Letters of Sigmund Freud and Oskar Pfister.* New York: Basic Books. Trans. by Eric Mosbacher.

Middlemore, M. P. (1941). *The Nursing Couple.* London: Hamilton.

Miller, D. R., and Swanson, G. E. (1960). *Inner Conflict and Defense.* New York: Schocken, 1966.

Modell, A. H. (1975). The ego and the id: fifty years later. *International Journal of Psychoanalysis* 56:57–68.

Morris, B. S. (1966). The contribution of psychology to the study of education. In *The Study of Education,* ed. J. W. Tibble. Atlantic Highlands, N.J.: Humanities.

Munroe, R. (1957). *Schools of Psychoanalytic Thought.* London: Hutchinson.

Murphy, G. (1947). *Personality: A Biosocial Approach to Origins and Structure.* New York: Harper and Row.

Nagera, H. (1963). The developmental profile: Notes on some practical considerations regarding its use. *Psychoanalytic Study of the Child* 18:511–540.

——— (1966). Sleep and its disturbances approached developmentally. *Psychoanalytic Study of the Child* 21:393–447.

Neubauer, P. B. (1967). Trauma and psychopathology. In *Psychic Trauma,* ed. S. S. Furst. New York: Basic Books.

Newman, L. M. (1975). Vorwort. *Das Ich und die Abwehrmechanismen (Neuausgabe).* Munich: Kindler Verlag.

Newman, C. J., Dember, C. F., and Krug, D. (1973). He can but he won't: a psychodynamic study of so-called "gifted underachievers." *Psychoanalytic Study of the Child* 28:83–129.

Novick, J., and Kelly, K. (1970). *Psychoanalytic Study of the Child* 25:69.

Nunberg, H. (1931). The synthetic function of the ego. *International Journal of Psychoanalysis* 12.

—— (1932). *Allgemeine Neurosenlehre auf Psychoanalytischer Grundlage*. Berne: Hans Huber Verlag. Trans. *Principles of Psychoanalysis, Their Application to the Neuroses*. New York: International Universities Press, 1955.

—— (1969). Memoirs, Recollections, Ideas, Reflections. New York: Psychoanalytic Research and Development Fund.

——, and Federn, P., eds. (1962). *Minutes of the Vienna Psychoanalytical Society*. Vol. 1. New York: International Universities Press.

——, and Federn, P., eds. (1975). *Minutes of the Vienna Psychoanalytic Society*. Vol. 4. New York: International Universities Press.

Paneth, M. (1946). Notes on painting and drawing with children from concentration camps. *New Era in Home and School* 27:179–182.

Peters, R. S. (1965). Emotion, passivity and the place of Freud's theory in psychology. In *Scientific Psychology: Principles and Approaches*, eds. B. B. Wohnan and E. Nagel. New York: Basic Books.

Peters, U. H. (1979). *Anna Freud, ein Leben für das Kind*. Munich: Kindler Verlag.

Pfeiffer, S. (1930). A form of defence. *International Journal of Psychoanalysis* 11:492–496.

Pfieffer, E., ed. (1972). *Sigmund Freud and Lou Andreas-Salomé: Letters*. London: Hogarth Press and Institute of Psychoanalysis.

Piaget, J. (1951). *Play, Dreams and Imitation in Childhood*. New York: Norton, 1962.

Pumpian-Mindlin, E. (1966). Anna Freud and Erik Erikson: Contributions to the theory and practice of psychoanalysis and psychotherapy. In *Psychoanalytic Pioneers*, eds. F. Alexander, S. Eisenstein, and M. Grotjahn, pp. 519–525. New York: Basic Books.

Radford, P. (1973). *Psychoanalytic Study of the Child* 28:225.

—— (1979). The diagnostic profile: VII, an oedipal boy (Jonathan). *Bulletin of the Hampstead Clinic* 2:177–208.

Rangell, L. (1963). The scope of intrapsychic conflict. *Psychoanalytic Study of the Child* 18:75–102.

—— (1975). Psychoanalysis and the process of change: an essay on the past, present and future. *International Journal of Psychoanalysis* 56:87–98.

Reich, W. (1935). *Character Analysis.* New York: Noonday Press.
—— (1967). *Reich Speaks of Freud,* eds. M. Higgins and C. M. Raphael. New York: Farrar, Straus & Giroux.

Reik, T. (1941). Aggression from anxiety. *International Journal of Psychoanalysis* 22:7–16.

Report of the Ninth I. P. A. Congress. (1926). *International Journal of Psychoanalysis* 7.

Report of the Tenth I. P. A. Congress. (1928). *International Journal of Psychoanalysis* 9.

Report of the 13th I. P. A. Congress. (1935). *International Journal of Psychoanalysis* 16.

Report of the 14th I. P. A. Congress. (1937). *International Journal of Psychoanalysis* 18.

Report of the 15th I. P. A. Congress. (1939). *International Journal of Psychoanalysis* 20.

Report of the 18th I. P. A. Congress. (1954). *International Journal of Psychoanalysis* 35.

Report of the 19th I. P. A. Congress. (1956). *International Journal of Psychoanalysis* 37.

Report of the 26th I. P. A. Congress. (1970). *International Journal of Psychoanalysis* 51.

Report of the 27th I. P. A. Congress. (1972). *International Journal of Psychoanalysis* 53.

Report of the 28th I. P. A. Congress. (1974). *International Journal of Psychoanalysis* 55.

Report of the 29th I. P. A. Congress. (1976). *International Journal of Psychoanalysis* 57.

Report of the Berlin Psychoanalytic Society. (1929). *International Journal of Psychoanalysis* 10.

Report of the British Psychoanalytic Society. (1939). *International Journal of Psychoanalysis* 20.

—— (1940). *International Journal of Psychoanalysis* 21.
—— (1941). *International Journal of Psychoanalysis* 22.
—— (1942). *International Journal of Psychoanalysis* 23.
—— (1944). *International Journal of Psychoanalysis* 25.
—— (1946). *International Journal of Psychoanalysis* 27.
—— (1974). *International Journal of Psychoanalysis* 55.

Report of the Dutch Psychoanalytical Society. (1947). *International Journal of Psychoanalysis* 28.

Report of the Frankfurt Psychoanalytic Institute. (1930). *International Journal of Psychoanalysis* 11.

Report of the London Institute of Psychoanalysis (1948). *International Journal of Psychoanalysis* 29.

Report of the Russian Psychoanalytic Society. (1924). *International Journal of Psychoanalysis* 5.

Report of the Vienna Psychoanalytic Society. (1920). *International Journal of Psychoanalysis* 1.

—— (1922). *International Journal of Psychoanalysis* 5.

—— (1926). *International Journal of Psychoanalysis* 7.

—— (1928). *International Journal of Psychoanalysis* 9.

—— (1929). *International Journal of Psychoanalysis* 10.

—— (1930). *International Journal of Psychoanalysis* 11.

—— (1931). *International Journal of Psychoanalysis* 12.

—— (1932). *International Journal of Psychoanalysis* 13.

—— (1933). *International Journal of Psychoanalysis* 14.

—— (1934). *International Journal of Psychoanalysis* 15.

—— (1935). *International Journal of Psychoanalysis* 16.

—— (1937). *International Journal of Psychoanalysis* 18.

—— (1938). *International Journal of Psychoanalysis* 19.

—— (1959). *International Journal of Psychoanalysis* 40.

Ritvo, S., and Ritvo, L. B. (1966). Ernst Kris. In *Psychoanalytic Pioneers,* eds. F. Alexander, S. Eisenstein, and M. Grotjahn. New York: Basic Books.

Roazen, P. (1969). *Brother Animal: The Story of Freud and Tausk.* New York: Knopf.

—— (1975). *Freud and His Followers.* New York: Knopf.

Roheim, G. (1932). Psychoanalysis of primitive cultural types. *International Journal of Psychoanalysis* 13:2–224.

Rosenfeld, S. K., and Sprince, M. (1965). *Psychoanalytic Study of the Child* 20:495.

Ross, H. (1963). Report of a six-weeks visit with Anna Freud at the Hampstead Clinic. Panel contribution to psychoanalytic contributions to the nosology of childhood psychic disorders. American Psychoanalytic Association Meeting, New York. *Journal of the American Psychoanalytic Association* 11:595–604.

—— (1971). Anna Freud's diagnostic profile. In *Currents in Psychoanalysis,* ed. I. Marcus. New York: International Universities Press.

Rycroft, C. (1968a). *Anxiety and Neurosis*. London: Allen Lane.

—— (1968b). *Critical Dictionary of Psychoanalysis*. Totowa, N.J.: Littlefield, 1973.

Sachs, D. M. (1961). Abstract. *Bulletin of the Philadelphia Association for Psychoanalysis* 11:80–87.

Sandler, J. (1960). *Psychoanalytic Study of the Child* 15:128.

—— (1962). Research in psychoanalysis: the Hampstead Index as an instrument of psychoanalytic research. *International Journal of Psychoanalysis* 43:287–291.

——, Holder, A., Kawenoka, M., Kennedy, H., and Neurath, L. (1969). Notes on some theoretical and clinical aspects of transference. *International Journal of Psychoanalysis* 50:633–645.

——, and Joffe, W. G. (1965). Notes on childhood depression. *International Journal of Psychoanalysis* 46:88–96.

——, and Joffe, W. G. (1969). Towards a basic psychoanalytic model. *International Journal of Psychoanalysis* 50:79–90.

——, Kennedy, H., and Tyson, R. L. (1975). Discussions on transference: the treatment situation and technique in child psychoanalysis. *Psychoanalytic Study of the Child* 30:409–441.

——, and Nagera, H. (1963). Some aspects of the metapsychology of phantasy. *Psychoanalytic Study of the Child* 18:159–194.

——, and Novick, J. (1969). Some recent developments in child psychoanalysis at the Hampstead Clinic. In *Modern Perspectives in International Child Psychiatry*, ed. J. G. Howells. New York: Brunner/Mazel.

Schafer, R. (1968). The mechanisms of defense. *International Journal of Psychoanalysis* 49:49–62.

Schmideberg, M. (1935). Review of Anna Freud. *International Journal of Psychoanalysis* 16:105.

Schmidt, V. (1924). *Psychoanalytische Erziehung im Sowjetrussland*. Vienna: I. P. Verlag.

Schur, M. (1972). *Freud: Living and Dying*. New York: International Universities Press.

——, and Ritvo, L. B. (1970). A principle of evolutionary biology for psychoanalysis: Schnierla's evolutionary and biphasic processes underlying approach and withdrawal and Freud's unpleasure and pleasure principles. *Journal of the American Psychoanalytic Association* 18:422–439.

Schwarz, H. (1974). Comments. Report of the 28th I.P.A. Congress. *International Journal of Psychoanalysis* 55.

Shane, M. (1967). Encopresis in a latency boy: an arrest along a developmental line. *Psychoanalytic Study of the Child* 22:296–314.

Sharpe, E. F. (1946). Review of Anna Freud. *International Journal of Psychoanalysis* 27:156–158.

Sheehan-Dare, H. (1945). Review of Anna Freud. *International Journal of Psychoanalysis* 26:78–79.

Sherrington, C. S. (1951). *Man on His Nature.* 2nd ed. New York: Cambridge University Press.

Shevrin, H., and Toussieng, P. W. (1965). Vicissitudes of the need for tactile stimulation in instinctual development. *Psychoanalytic Study of the Child* 20:310–339.

Silverman, M. A., Rees, K., and Neubauer, P. B. (1975). On a central psychic constellation. *Psychoanalytic Study of the Child* 30:127–157.

Slap, J. W. (1974). Panel report: *The Ego and the Mechanisms of Defence. Journal of the Philadelphia Association for Psychoanalysis* 1:36–42.

Soddy, K., ed. (1955). *Mental Health and Infant Development*, vol. 1. London: Routledge.

Sperling, O. (1954). An imaginary companion representing a pre-stage of the superego. *Psychoanalytic Study of the Child* 9:252–258.

Sperling, S. J. (1958). On denial and the essential nature of defence. *International Journal of Psychoanalysis* 39:25–38.

Spitz, R. A. (1959). *A Genetic Field Theory of Ego Formation: Its Implications for Pathology.* New York: International Universities Press.

———, Emde, R. A., and Metcalfe, D. R. (1970). Further prototypes of ego formation: a working paper from a research project on early development. *Psychoanalytic Study of the Child* 25:417–441.

Sprince, M. P. (1971). *Psychoanalytic Study of the Child* 26:453.

Steingart, I. (1969). On self, character and the development of a psychic apparatus. *Psychoanalytic Study of the Child* 24:271–303.

Sterba, R. (1953). Clinical and therapeutic aspects of character resistance. *Psychoanalytic Quarterly* 22:1–20.

Stone, L. (1975). Some problems and potentialities of present-day psychoanalysis. *Psychoanalytic Quarterly* 44:331–370.

Strachey, J. (1969). The nature of the therapeutic action of psychoanalysis. *International Journal of Psychoanalysis* 50:275–292.

Strawson, G. (1981). Freud et après. *Sunday Observer Review,* September 27.

Stross, J. (1977). Function and praxis of the Well-Baby Clinic. *Sigmund Freud House Bulletin* 1.

Suppes, P., and Warren, H. (1975). On the generation and classification of defence mechanisms. *International Journal of Psychoanalysis* 56:405–414.

Sutherland, J. D. (1972). Obituary: Michael Balint. *International Journal of Psychoanalysis* 52.

Suttie, I. D. (1963). *The Origins of Love and Hate*. London: Peregrine Books.

Symposium on Child Analysis. (1927). *International Journal of Psychoanalysis* 8:370–377 (J. Riviere); 8:377–380 (M. N. Searl); 8:380–384 (E. F. Sharpe); 8:385–387 (E. Glover); 8:387–391 (E. Jones).

Tartakoff, H. (1970). Obituary: Elizabeth Geleerd Loewenstein. *International Journal of Psychoanalysis* 51:71–73.

Tausend, H. (1959). Abstract. *Bulletin of the Philadelphia Association of Psychoanalysis* 9:111–112.

Thoma, H. (1969). Some remarks on psychoanalysis in Germany, past and present. *International Journal of Psychoanalysis* 50:683–692.

Thomas, R. (1966). *Psychoanalytic Study of the Child* 21:527.

Ticho, E. A., and Ticho, G. R. (1972). Freud and the Viennese. *International Journal of Psychoanalysis* 53:301–306.

Toman, W. (1972). Defence. In *Encyclopedia of Psychology*, Vols. 1–3, ed. H. J. Eysenck. New York: Continuum, 1979.

Valenstein, A. F. (1962). The psychoanalytic situation: affects, emotional reliving, and insight in the psychoanalytic process. *International Journal of Psychoanalysis* 43:315–324.

——— (1973). On attachment to painful feelings and the negative therapeutic reaction. *Psychoanalytic Study of the Child* 28:365–392.

Van Dam, H., Heinicke, C., and Shane, M. (1975). On termination in child analysis. *Psychoanalytic Study of the Child* 30:443–474.

Van Der Leeuw, P. J. (1971). On the development of the concept of defence. *International Journal of Psychoanalysis* 52:51–58.

Varendonck, J. (1921). *The Psychology of Daydreams*. New York: Macmillan. Trans. A. Freud, Über das vorbewusste phantasierende Deuten (I. P. Verlag: Vienna and Leipzig, 1922.)

Vienna Symposium on Work at the Hampstead Clinic. (1977). *Sigmund Freud House Bulletin* 1.

Wallerstein, R. S. (1976). Summary of the 6th pre-congress conference on training. *International Journal of Psychoanalysis* 57:198–199.

Weil, A. P. (1970). The basic core. *Psychoanalytic Study of the Child* 25:442–460.

Weiss, E. (1966). Paul Federn. In *Psychoanalytic Pioneers*, eds. F. Alexander, S. Eisenstein, and M. Grotjahn. New York: Basic Books.

———— (1970). *Sigmund Freud as a Consultant: Recollections of a Pioneer in Psychoanalysis*. New York: International Medical Books.

Winnicott, D. W. (1963). Dependence in infant-care, in child-care and in the psychoanalytic setting. *International Journal of Psychoanalysis* 44:339.

———— (1962). A personal view of the Kleinian contribution. In Winnicott, D. W., *Maturational Processes and the Facilitating Environment*. New York: International Universities Press.

Wolf, K. (1945). Evacuation of children in wartime: a survey of the literature with bibliography. *Psychoanalytic Study of the Child* 1:389–404.

Wolff, S. (1976). Review of studies in child psychoanalysis, pure and applied. *British Journal of Psychiatry* 128:412.

Wyss, D. (1961). *Depth Psychology: A Critical History*. London: Allen and Unwin, 1966.

Yorke, C. (1971). Some suggestions for a critique of Kleinian psychology. *Psychoanalytic Study of the Child* 26:129–155.

———— (1977). The role of the developmental point of view in research and therapy at the Hampstead Clinic. *Sigmund Freud House Bulletin* 1.

Zetzel, E. R. (1965). The theory of therapy in relation to a developmental model of the psychic apparatus. *International Journal of Psychoanalysis* 46:39–52.

———— (1966). Additional notes upon a case of obsessional neurosis: Freud 1909. *International Journal of Psychoanalysis* 47:123–129.

———— (1969). 96, Gloucester Place: some personal recollections. *International Journal of Psychoanalysis* 50:717–719.

———— (1971). The relationship of defence to affect and its tolerance. In *The Unconscious Today: Essays in Honour of Max Schur,* ed. M. Kanzer. New York: International Universities Press.

Zulliger, H. (1966). Oskar Pfister. In *Psychoanalytic Pioneers*, eds. F. Alexander, S. Eisenstein, and M. Grotjahn. New York: Basic Books.

INDEX

Abbate, G., 215
Abnormal development. *See*
    Development, abnormal
Abraham, H. C., 8, 31*n*, 61, 285
Abraham, K., 8, 12, 16–17, 20, 31,
    31*n*, 32, 38, 62, 68, 92, 228
Ack, M., 263, 285
Acting out, 111, 248
Action research, 206–207, 212
Active-passive, 204–205
Active therapy, 11, 37, 39
Adaptation, 105, 119, 120–125,
    183–184, 197
Adler, A., 12, 15*n*
Adolescence, 49, 54, 119, 127, 143,
    183, 219, 221, 228, 242, 248,
    252
Adoption. *See* Children's rights
Aesthetics, 38, 49
Age-adequate behaviors, 125, 175,
    248, 252
Aggression, 111, 125, 155–156, 180,
    181, 184–186, 209, 212, 234,
    243, 254–256
Agoraphobia, 157
Aichhorn, A., x–xi, xiv, 10, 29, 59,
    65, 66, 67, 71, 82, 88, 92, 100,
    110, 127, 128–129, 133,
    186*n*, 187, 189, 203, 216,
    255, 265, 285
Alexander, F., 61, 66, 80, 211, 285
Allport, G. W., 175, 233
Alpert, A., 116, 125, 241, 262, 285
Altruism, 112
Ambivalence, 90, 160, 186, 215
American Association of Child
    Psychoanalysis. *See also*
    Association for Child
    Psychoanalysis

Foster Parents Plan, Inc., 148,
    149, 180
Psychoanalytic Association, 8,
    187, 203, 210, 229
Amsterdam, 184, 221
Anaclitic relation, 214–215,
    215–216
Anal phase, 5, 30, 63, 176
Andreas-Salomé, L., xi, 16, 24, 29,
    33, 37, 39–43, 49–50, 54,
    56–57, 78, 85, 87, 98–99,
    103, 113
Angel, A. *See* Katan, A.
Animal phobias, 17, 98
Anna Freud Centers, 183, 189, 251
Antigone, 103, 103*n*, 145
Anxiety, 17, 66, 99, 105–106,
    110–111, 125, 201, 212, 217,
    223, 265, 267
    five types of, 156–158
Applications. *See* Psychoanalysis
Arden House symposium, 215–216
Arlow, J., 97
Armytage, W. H. G., xvii, 16, 25*n*,
    146, 163, 206*n*, 251, 285
Artificial families, 167
Asceticism, 112
Assessment, 233–235, 244–245. *See
    also* Diagnosis; Hampstead
    Metapsychological Profile
Association for Child Psycho-
    analysis, 192*n*, 265
    of Child Psychotherapists (U.K.),
    192
Austen Riggs Foundation, 119, 208
Authority, in analysis, 90
Autoerotism, 167
    aggression, 210
Auxiliary ego, 153, 199, 247